The Eastside Kid

Passion of a Gamer

The John F. DeCosta Story

Trafford
PUBLISHING

Order this book online at www.trafford.com
or email orders@trafford.com

Most Trafford titles are also available at major online book retailers.

Editor: Jessika Vitelli

Printed in the United States of America.

ISBN: 978-1-4269-5470-2 (sc)
ISBN: 978-1-4269-5469-6 (hc)
ISBN: 978-1-4269-5468-9 (e)

Library of Congress Control Number: 2011900864

Trafford rev. 06/30/2011

www.trafford.com

North America & International
toll-free: 1 888 232 4444 (USA & Canada)
phone: 250 383 6864 ♦ fax: 812 355 4082

The East Side Kid: Reviews

Ruth Perman
Lodi, California
3 Nov 2008

Dear John,

Did I ever tell you that I have started to read your book! I sure hope so, because I am enjoying it to the fullest as it's so interesting. I love the way you had worded it as it's so easy to read. Do not apologize for the print as for me I can easily read it. Maybe, because you had a connection with my Son-Lanny... Your life has been so interesting and easy to understand. With all you have been through, you toughed it out and your love for life, what else can I say; I am so happy you sent it to me! My niece from Washington State was visiting us as she read some of the book aloud to us pertaining to our Son Lanny and she thought it was so well written even the emotional areas concerning our family.

Hugs,
Ruth Perman

Gian Pietro Boschiroli
Derovere- Cremora, Italy
5 May 2009

John, I just finished reading your book. The book you wrote and kindly sent to me as a gift. We'll I read it with calm, first because I don't keep good knowledge of your language and because I wanted to enjoy step by step about what you wrote. Your way to write is very clear, I think one can define it "Queen English" So I haven't had any problem to understand it. I am not a literature's critical; however I enjoyed the manner in which you narrated your life's story. What Chapter Did I Prefer? Ginger and other...My first job, California Dreaming, Terrorism training and guardian Angel. John, now It looks and feel like I know you from many times... Thanks for a great gift you gave me. I think you should have success with your autobiographical book. Further more, I am sure many

Readers will enjoy reading it. I wish you the best and thanks again.

YF Gian Pietro Boshiroli

John A Alexander
Over thirty Baseball
Umpire
24 May 2009

Great Read! You were able to take me back to my boyhood days growing up and playing baseball in Medford, Mass. The picture on the cover totally describes an era long ago. The bike those uniforms and the expression on a young mans face says it all. Boy was those uniforms a bit warm and itchy on a hot summer day? I have passed the book onto my brothers so they too can relive those great years. I am sure they will enjoy it as much as I have, Thanks again.

John A. Alexander

David Kaufman
Mountain View, Arkansas
12 February 2009

Dear John.
Thank you so much for sharing, by your writing, what is inside of you. While most of the book was about baseball, the principles...hard work, perseverance and dedication...apply.

To everything that is worth pursuing, whether it is a sport, career or any undertaking. Also, you want to play with fair rules and appreciation for others (that played well and put the time and effort to do so) can heartily agree with. Your book is very insightful and enjoyable.

Appreciatively,
David Kaufman

———————————————————

Herb (Herby) Jones
Brockton 'Eastside"
Arlington, Texas

John, after finally finishing your book, I am so full of envy. A young boy from my side of the tracks determined to achieve his pursuit of happiness, no matter what and 50 years later still gong as strong as ever. This book told of a never ending passion and determination that most of us could only dream of. Great Job John and I will surely pass the word about your great book. Herb (Herby) Jones (mentioned in chapter 2)...From Brockton, "Eastside" now re-siding in Arlington, Texas.

———————————————————

Herb (Herby) Jones
Robert Carlos Ortiz...Age 11
Brooklyn, New York

I had fun reading your book John and I did a book report on it and got an "A". My Dad and John are good friends and play in the same league and once played on the same team. I liked reading about the way John liked to play baseball and the stories of him going fishing. I like baseball and fishing too. The pictures in the book were cool. Maybe when I grow up I can write a book too about baseball in Brooklyn and Staten Island.

Robbie Ortiz

Paul Harrington,
Boston MSBL Manager

John I received your book as a birthday gift and enjoyed it so much. My wife is reading it now as she also like's your book. Good luck with the off season and hope you can pitch for our over 48 team next season.

Paul Harrington

Paul Colombo
Lakeville, Ma

"What a great story" of inspiration and perseverance. It brought me back to the time of innocence and wide eyed wonder for our national pastime. It's a great gift to have lived it for so long. Your passion and patriotism has come through loud and clear. Thank you for all of the memories".

Paul Colombo

Joe Hallett
Sergeant Major US, Army Retired
82nd Airborne

I did finish reading and my wife is reading your book now. I enjoyed it very much as it brought back memories of my early days in Stoughton, Ma but also spending time in Brockton. I did not know John DeCosta before I read the book and I am proud to be your friend.

Joe Hallett

Brian Cole
Pepperell, Ma

John, definitely do a second book. Just consider the notes of the past baseball year, one of the most interesting seasons as your team outlasted all others. You beat all of the top teams as you will receive MVP award this year. Truly, an inspiring story, definitely do it John as your books will sell themselves, as they are definitely interesting. You have inspired me for a long time as well as your accomplishments. I am happy for you.

Brian Cole

Patricia Owens
Andover, ma

Thank you for sharing your wonderful book-it's an amazing tale. I found myself smiling & frequently tearing up-you touched on all of the things that make us love baseball. Even with the temperatures below freezing could envision a warm day watching my beloved game. I think you should consider contacting a publisher. I think you have got a great story, thank you again.

Pat Owens   (one who's infected with the baseball bug)

Robert Butler
Police Officer 27 years (retired)
East Bridgewater, Ma

I got your book, read it that day I received it and thought it was excellent.... I want to read it again, a little slower, so I can absorb it better. But with the holidays etc; your writing style was excellent, perhaps you should be angry with your teachers as well as your coaches for not recognizing your writing abilities. I'm really impressed with your memory. That day so many years ago, at Mill Pond, has always been etched in my mind. I am retired from the Police Department after 27 years. I also spent a year in Viet Nam. It was delightful to hear from you and as I said I will re-read your book, slowly this time, and try to absorb some of the old memories. You did an excellent job and I congratulate you!!

Bob

James Costa
Author, Soldier, entrepreneur, Paratrooper and baseball friend;

John it is heart warming reading your book. I am nearly done with it and my wife Ingrid wishes to read it as well. I am also interested in the different contents within the book. My family thought when I wrote my book-I should have mentioned many things similar to your thoughts. I'm sure; many will love your story as we have.

Regards,
Jim Costa

Colonel William J. Davis USA, Retired

Dear John,
Thank you so very much for the wonderful gift of sharing your inspiring life story in the book, The Eastside Kid, Passion of a

found my way back to the ball field. Mom and Dad would always put up the vegetables in jars for the winter months. I especially remember the hard work invested in making jelly or jam. The wax would be at the top as a preservative. We had enough for several winters but Dad would give away so much that each summer, again we would all restore the stock. Mom and Dad also made wool braided rugs and therefore you would find these rugs all over our home.

Dad enjoyed fishing as a hobby and on his off-time be brought home barrels full of haddock, cod, flounder, smelt, and fresh water trout. We only had a small refrigerator and small freezer so; again there was much to give away to the neighborhood.

Mom read books and kept up with current events. I can still remember her reading the newspaper on our back steps with Ginger our dog lying next to her with the lilac blossoms in the background and lilac aroma and spring bees flying about. I was coming home from either cutting lawns or playing baseball, as I greeted Mom and Ginger in the search of a cold drink. Sometimes, I would come home and find my Mom playing the ukulele, a small banjo. I took lessons on that instrument but Mom taught herself. She would laugh with embarrassment as I caught her; she loved to learn something new always.

Dad served in World War 11, worked in the CC camps and logging camps and was a boxer for a time. He especially liked the Friday night fights. The only sport he ventured in other than boxing was football. He and mom also loved to dance and they often won dance contest, as they enjoyed that so much. I can still remember them dancing away to the Lawrence Welk show on Saturday nights or listening to the Ink Spots or Glenn Miller.

My brother Douglas, the eldest enjoyed his love for basketball as he enjoyed his stardom at his high school as well as Boston College. He later became a school teacher and basketball coach and retired over 30 some odd years later. My other brother Stephen enjoyed a career in mechanics and electronics. His favorite hobbies were hunting, fishing, trapping and running sled dogs. My sister Joanne could swing a bat pretty good but had a prosperous career with a large corporation and retired. She had also been a very patriotic citizen with high respect for veterans and pursues her religious beliefs and enjoys her grandchildren. Both my brothers were also veterans as I and both brothers and my sister have college degrees, as well. I had some college at Northeastern University but we all elevated our expectations more than we expected.

Mom was our leader and led us to become achievers. Our abilities strength and work ethic have set a standard we are only too proud to enjoy. Mom had taken in elderly nursing type of patients to live in our home and be cared for to earn extra money. This was the way Mom had paid for our home. She worked very hard doing this for us, as at the time we hadn't really recognized how hard this really was. When Dad got sick with his heart problems, Mom found a job with the government at Boston Army Base and quickly rose to higher achievements. She not only typed 120 words per minute but copied in short hand 140 words per minute which is a lost talent by the standards of today. She self taught her self numerous things such as musical instruments and with her reading abilities challenged herself whenever opportunity had risen.

My Military background as a paratrooper and my numerous military experiences, I will share with you, the reader. In addition, my love for animals, bird's technical trades have absorbed much of my personal time and will be noted. I first stopped playing baseball at the age of 13 but left the game on a successful and promising talent. I was forced to quit due to a wrist tumor formed by throwing curveballs with little corrective instruction at a young age. My passion and love for the game of baseball formed an inner spirit that clawed at my heart for thirty five years, as late in life I found baseball once again. I attacked it with a vengeance as I am full throttle, green light; take no prisoners playing baseball again. I will share my story from 1957 through 2008. The story starts on the eastside of Brockton, Massachusetts. I lived at 22 Massasoit Avenue as my baseball started from the back yard to many sand lots nearby and this all leads to my present baseball experience.

There are battles with disabilities with my heart, broken bones, comebacks and an inside view of how deeply baseball beats in my heart. If you dare, follow the seams of the baseball and watch the ball bounce from bat to glove and experience baseball through my eyes and listen to my heartbeat. My passion is alive and well as I am always ready for another game.

John F DeCosta

Gamer. Little did I know of your life and love for baseball when we served together in A Company, 3rd Battalion, 5th Special Forces Group (Airborne) back at Fort Bragg. Even though we grew up in different places, with you in Brockton, and me in Philadelphia, we are so similar in many ways: of the Catholic faith, children of the fifties, work ethics instilled by members of the greatest generation, and infused with love of baseball that continues to this day.

Little League flannel uniforms, PF Flyers worn leather gloves, pre-game rituals, swinging cracked Louisville Sluggers against taped-covered balls; The Eastside Kid brought it all back as if it just happened yesterday. With true authenticity you have captured the essence and simplicity of one who has lived and breathed baseball throughout your remarkable life's journey.

The great baseball writer Roger Agnell once said; "Since baseball time is measured only in outs, all you have to do is succeed utterly. Keep hitting, keep the rally alive, and you have defeated time you remain forever young." "Knowing the Gamer" that you are, I am certain that this rally will continue for many more years to come. God Bless You and Yours.

Bill Davis
Colonel, Special Forces (Ret)

Tina Burchill
Towsend, MD
1 Jan 2009

Got the opportunity, to read your book. I must say it was exceptional. I love the fact you always remembered to bring back something special for your lovely wife Beth as well as remember all your great friends by mentioning them in your book. You are so fortunate to have such good friends. The fact you continue to keep in touch is very important. Your love for baseball has continued to give you the strength to overcome many obstacles in your life. It is wonderful you followed your dream. I started reading your book and could not put it down. I read it in a couple of hours and thoroughly enjoyed it. Thank you for sharing your life with the world. Best wished and good health to you and your family for the upcoming year,

Your friend Tina

Leslie Grant
Poughkeepsie, New York

Dear John,

I finished your book today and I really enjoyed reading about your life. Sounds like you had wonderful parents who you respected and have been an inspiration to you. You definitely seem to value qualities of that enduring...too bad those things are not stressed today. I admire your enthusiasm and optimism... not to mention, your persistence in face of obstacles. I agree with you on so many levels. Playing sports such as baseball does require loyalty and teamwork as well as the passion of the game. In the end, I am happy you were able to retrieve your plaque...It meant so much to you. I am glad you found friends through the years that have shared your vales and laughter... I am sorry to read of the loss of them. You have experienced life, the good and the bad, but retain who you are as a person with good values. Not too many people can do that. I enjoyed reading about your love for animals. They definitely show more loyalty than some people... too bad that many people abuse them. You spoke of your guardian angel... You certainly have, you have left on others that matters... what you can teach and inspire others. Good reading... left me smiling feeling optimistic and hopeful.

Sincere Lesley

Robert Guarino;

22 March 2010

I read your book with obvious interest since I was also born and raised on the Eastside of Brockton, a bit earlier than you, but in much the same circumstances. I had forgotten how truly special it was to have been a Brockton native and part of the Eastside experience. The Eastside Kid brought back many great memories-Brockton, the Littler League scene, the people connected with Eastside Improvement Association, the baseball coaches and players.

Although I was just a young Stone hill College student in 1959, I thoroughly enjoyed the Little League Coaching experience. Looking at the pictures in the text and reading your book brought back so many memories, John. Thank you for the pleasant reminiscence. Thank you for the memories of 50 years past. Wishing you and yours the best of everything in your future, I remain your friend.

Sincerely,

Bob Guarino

Barnstable, Mass 02630

BROCKTON TODAY

BY OUR READERS

Sports was a way of life for East Side kids

On Mondays, The Enterprise invites readers to share their thoughts, views and remembrances on the people, places and events of Brockton. To do so, submit up to three typewritten pages to "By Our Readers," c/o The Enterprise, P.O. Box 1450, Brockton 02303; fax it to 508-586-6506; or e-mail it to newsroom@enterprisenews.com. Be sure to add a paragraph of autobiographical information at the end.

By John F. DeCosta
SPECIAL TO THE ENTERPRISE

To many, the stories of the '50s are unimportant, exaggerated, with old dreams. There are, of course, many people like myself who have lived and enjoyed these experiences firsthand and cherish these memories. From my point of view, I can share with you as I recall baseball on the '50s scene in Brockton's East Side.

We were very proud of being East Side kids. Other parts of the city were more affluent than the East Side, especially the West Side. The city in those days was filled with blue collar workers and factories, but as I remember, family values were very strong.

The city had always provided sports at no cost. The opportunity was there to participate. There were Olympic size pools in all parts of the city as well.

I can share with you how an average day would be for me, at say age 10, 11, and 12 years old, at about 1957 through 1959. I would cut lawns for a $1 in the neighborhood and a few chores at our home. Then of course baseball, after making a round of hot chocolate at Pats Good Food.

There would be a game, wiffle ball, just for a quick warm-up with Al Manoli, Chet Perry, Tom Smith and the Carbonara family.

Later we'd go up the street to Brockton Hospital and get into a hardball game with the usual black-taped baseballs, wood bats restored with tape, old beat-up gloves and some great ballplayers like Dana Blanchard, the Gonzalez family, Pixy Garner, Richie Parino, Bruce Young and Fred Barnard.

In the afternoon, I may have gone over to Crescent Street and played some more wiffle ball with Butch Crealese, Leroy Baker, Steve Stack and all, in preparation for a game that night.

I played in the Downey Little League for two years then moved over to the East Side Improvement for my 12-year-old, or major league, playing.

Our East Side kids were very talented. East Junior High, for example, always produced city champs or state champs in basketball, football and baseball. We didn't have much, but we shared team esprit de corps, a lot of guts and had the will to win. Many talented kids in those days came from across the street — The Hill Street Boys.

The Morrison, Reed and Shanks families, to name a few. Members of the Map family just up the street were all very talented basketball players who starred in so many victories.

The other part of our East Side, near O'Donnell's Playground, we had other contributing legends.

There was of course Steve Sarantopoulos, Mr. Basketball; and Ro......ette (baseball). I still remember his home runs.

The first older guy I remember as a kid was Herby Jones. He was an original Babe Ruth in those days, much older than I, but one to emulate. I didn't do so bad myself at East Side Improvement Association.

The old Bay Street in those days had many large families, and again contributed many talents at our schools and playgrounds. During the summer months we could participate in park leagues as well. That program allowed us to go see the Red Sox and Ted Williams for a $1. That was a treat.

Photographer Stanley Bauman was always on the scene in those days; all over the city sharing in many families' special moments.

I must add that at the East Side Improvement Association is quite an experience. A few years back I was visiting Brockton and reminiscing. I drove down to the East Side Improvement Association where many of my most memorable special moments began. So many years later, I see Mr. Trum opening a gate.

He recognized me right away and I was amazed on how much expansion had taken place. He offered a tour, so I went inside and what a treat. They had pictures of teams, plaques and baseball history from 1957 to present. I had seen my contribution on a plaque from 1959. That sure made my day.

They had record hops (dances) there, a memorable teenage experience.

The local churches had basketball church leagues and sports very much dominated kids' lives in those days. Homegrown fun was always a specialty. There were no computers, videos or cell phones. Neighbors helped each other when someone was out of work or sick. There were no prejudices. We were all sports oriented and learned strong work ethics at an early age.

There were many who wanted to be an East Side Kid. I think there was a rule: You had to live there for a while to be accepted.

At any rate we always stuck together, played hard together and could count on one another. I wish I could have had many of them with me in the paratroopers.

I am very proud of my family, my roots and for this opportunity to share with you.

John F. DeCosta is a retired U.S. Army paratrooper and after years as a contractor, is now maintenance director at an assisted living complex called Cadbury Commons in Cambridge. After recovering from five heart attacks, baseball has been his rehab and way of life. He is thankful for the support of his wife.

Acknowledgements

With Special Love
And Appreciation to My Parents
Concessa Gloria (Rodrigues) DeCosta (My Mom)
And John Frederick DeCosta Sr. (My Dad)

I thank my Mom and Dad with all of my heart for being the best parents anyone could possibly be gifted with. I lost you both when I was in my very early twenties, and though many years have passed, it still feels like a moment ago. You have laid the foundation of morals, work ethics and integrity, as your loss to me has been tremendous. I owe you so much that there are no words to describe. My special warm feelings of respect and love have molded my character, with which I know you would be pleased. At this point in my life, I feel you would be proud of my work ethics, positive accomplishments in my later years especially. I miss you both and love you deeply, as I feel you are truly my guardian angels. Thank you for giving me life.

I love you Mom and Dad
Your Son, John

My Very Special Love to My Wife
My Bride Always
Elizabeth Ann DeCosta

My wife Elizabeth has been a strong element of inspiration for me to gain confidence to write. She and I are partners, lovers, and best friends. She has enlightened me on culture, reading, and made this difference for me to excel in my career field as well as a husband. With her love and support I have been able to pursue, compete and secure numerous accomplishments thus far. I am indeed indebted to her for further looking out for my best interest with my medical and heart issues. It's been a battle in life's challenges as we have been each others rock. Thank you Baby.

I Love You, John

Additional and Special Thanks to my Baseball Friends, Opponents,
And Friends Associated With Me During My life.

My special thanks and respect go to my opponents, baseball friends. I appreciate the challenges you have set before me, and your support has extended my courage to bring my baseball game to the next higher level. The fire in my belly, the sweat, and the emotional journey from each game was shared with teamwork. I was able to pursue a strong competitive edge in competitions, wing it through injuries and find the warrior within myself in your presence. Thank you for your sharing baseball in my life. The next time we meet on that special ball field, we will once again share victory together.

Thank you,
Your Friend Always,
John "The Eastside Kid"

About the Author

I am John F. DeCosta, and I was born in Brockton, Massachusetts on the fifth of December, 1946, at 4:50 a.m. I went to St. Colman's Parish, as I was raised a Catholic, and played a lot of baseball on Brockton's eastside ballparks and playgrounds.

I have numerous interests, such as baseball, baseball and more baseball! Other interests are basketball, my deep love for animals and birds as well. When possible I love watching movies, dramas and some reality shows, and I keep myself quite busy with building projects, carpentry projects, traveling and meeting new friends.

I have developed an interest in reading and writing as a relaxing type of therapy. Being a workaholic and obsessed with baseball, I have found that writing soothes my soul. My more enjoyable biographical reads are those of Sadaharu Oh, the Japanese Babe Ruth of Baseball, Ty Cobb, Lou Gehrig, Mickey Mantle, Joe DiMaggio and Derek Jeter. Other athletes I have enjoyed watching are Doug Flutie, Bobby Orr, Larry Bird, and Cal Ripken. If I had the choice or an opportunity to meet one of them, I would be honored to meet Sadaharu Oh.

The values I have earned from the military are precious, especially since I was a paratrooper. I had numerous accomplishments in the military, but due to my heart condition, I was led to retirement earlier than planned.

My strong family culture, work ethic, integrity, and morals have established my energetic attitude towards attacking goals. My desire and courage were established at home from my parents. I do not seek riches nor am I jealous of anyone. If I want something I shall go after it.

I am truly satisfied with my passion and desire that has become such an enjoyable piece of my puzzled life. My hopes of sharing my personal passion of baseball, my experiences and my desires are only a footprint for leaving a legacy, in hopes that I may inspire someone else. This would be a great gift to me.

The Eastside kid,
John F. DeCosta

Readers, to share your opinion and especially a review of my book, The Eastside Kid: please send review or thoughts to, theeastsidekid@comcast.net Thank you

Preface

The Eastside Kid is a baseball story about a young boy John F. DeCosta growing up in the fifties on the eastside of Brockton, Massachusetts. This is a fun baseball beginning to a wonderful era in my life. This story has become my autobiography, depicting my experiences and passion for baseball. There is also a variety of other experiences described in detail along the way-changes of venue, the trials of fighting heart disease, discovering confidence and the dedication to the sport I love-baseball.

One day, I wrote a baseball story from my memories of sandlot baseball, as well as growing up on the east side of Brockton. I wrote this story thinking I was sending it to an acquaintance who worked at the city newspaper. I mailed this story and forgot about it. Then, weeks later, I started receiving calls from friends and relatives about this story being published in the newspaper. I did not take this seriously at the time until I received a copy of the actual printed story from a newspaper clipping. The caption was: "Sports Was a Way of Life for Eastside Kids."

This was my official starting point in writing, and maybe a good omen too. I thought maybe I could expand on this story and see what happened. My creativity soon took over and other opportunities have since presented themselves. I have written The Buck O'Brien Story, and Berge Avadanian D-day Hero's Story and more than eighty plus other stories. Writing has become therapeutic and enjoyable for me. I have further been inspired by Jim Costa, another Korean War Veteran who wrote Diamonds in The Rough. Jim was a wonderful paratrooper and he became a wonderful baseball friend as well.

I honor my Mom and Dad (John Senior and Concessa G. Rodriques DeCosta), as they are both deceased, but they will always be very close to my heart. My wife Elizabeth Ann DeCosta has inspired me with enormous emotional support in pursuing baseball late in my life, despite my disabilities. Elizabeth's influence on my reading and writing skills has driven me down this road. I am sure my Mom would have enjoyed her presence in my life.

Mom passed away in 1969 at the age of fifty three from cancer and Dad passed away in 1972 at the age of fifty five due to a heart condition. Since they have been gone our family, like so many others, drifted apart. The faster lifestyles and life changes created much distance between what little is left of our family. But in recent years an attempt to edge closer has been positive. Mom and Dad are missed terribly and their loss has been overwhelming and devastating for me. They are missed and loved by all of us.

My family was an average blue- collar, hard working family with high moral fiber and character. My Mom was most definitely the best super-mom anyone could ask for. Her support and guidance and understanding were so special. She was not afraid to tackle any challenge and I as well as my siblings inherited her work ethic. My Mom was Portuguese; Dad was French, Irish, and German.

I have two brothers, Stephen and Douglas and one sister, Joanne. They are much older than me, so growing up I was pretty much by myself. We were brought up Catholic and we attended Saint Colman's Parish nearby. My brother Doug and I were altar boys for a while-the thing to do at the time. Our family was quite religious; we always said grace before a meal and after supper we would say the rosary as a family together.

My Mom was such a great cook. She constantly baked home-made bread and shared it with the neighborhood. When someone was sick or out of work she would cook something special for them too. I often got the job of delivering it. The neighborhood was reasonably close, not like you see today. There was much respect from passer-by's as gentleman tipped their hats, families walked together and people in uniform, like mailman, police or fireman were held in high regard.

Mom and Dad had this enormous vegetable garden in our yard. Besides cutting the lawn I did my time weeding the garden. If I was in a hurry to play baseball I would cover the weeds with dirt, grab my glove and bat and I was gone. I usually got caught but I found corrective actions later and always found my way back to the ball field. Mom and Dad would always put up the vegetables in jars for the winter months. I especially remember the hard work invested in making jelly or jam. The wax would be at the top as a preservative. We had enough for several winters but Dad would give away so much that each summer, again we would all restore the stock. Mom and Dad also made wool braided rugs and therefore you would find these rugs all over our home.

Dad enjoyed fishing as a hobby and on his off-time be brought home barrels full of haddock, cod, flounder, smelt, and fresh water trout. We only had a small refrigerator and small freezer so; again there was much to give away to the neighborhood.

Mom read books and kept up with current events. I can still remember her reading the newspaper on our back steps with Ginger our dog lying next to her with the lilac blossoms in the background and lilac aroma and spring bees flying about. I was coming home from either cutting lawns or playing baseball, as I greeted Mom and Ginger in the search of a cold drink. Sometimes, I would come home and find my Mom playing the ukulele, a small banjo. I took lessons on that instrument but Mom taught herself. She would laugh with embarrassment as I caught her; she loved to learn something new always.

Dad served in World War 11, worked in the CC camps and logging camps and was a boxer for a time. He especially liked the Friday night fights. The only sport he ventured in other than boxing was football. He and mom also loved to dance and they often won dance contest, as they enjoyed that so much. I can still remember them dancing away to the Lawrence Welk show on Saturday nights or listening to the Ink Spots or Glenn Miller.

My brother Douglas, the eldest enjoyed his love for basketball as he enjoyed his stardom at his high school as well as Boston College. He later became a school teacher and basketball coach and retired over 30 some odd years later. My other brother Stephen enjoyed a career in mechanics and electronics. His favorite hobbies were hunting, fishing, trapping and running sled dogs. My sister Joanne could swing a bat pretty good but had a prosperous career with a large corporation and retired. She had also been a very patriotic citizen with high respect for veterans and pursues her religious beliefs and enjoys her grandchildren. Both my brothers were also veterans as I and both brothers and my sister have college degrees, as well. I had some college at Northeastern University but we all elevated our expectations more than we expected.

Mom was our leader and led us to become achievers. Our abilities strength and work ethic have set a standard we are only too proud to enjoy. Mom had taken in elderly nursing type of patients to live in our home and be cared for to earn extra money. This was the way Mom had paid for our home. She worked very hard doing this for us, as at the time we hadn't really recognized how hard this really was. When Dad got sick with his heart problems, Mom found a job with the government at Boston Army Base and quickly rose to higher achievements. She not only typed 120 words per minute but copied in short hand 140 words per minute which is a lost talent by the standards of today. She self taught her self numerous things such as musical instruments and with her reading abilities challenged herself whenever opportunity had risen.

My Military background as a paratrooper and my numerous military experiences, I will share with you, the reader. In addition, my love for animals, bird's technical trades have absorbed much of my personal time and will be noted. I first stopped playing baseball at the age of 13 but left the game on a successful and promising talent. I was forced to quit due to a wrist tumor formed by throwing curveballs with little corrective instruction at a young age. My passion and love for the game of baseball formed an inner spirit that clawed at my heart for thirty five years, as late in life I found baseball once again. I attacked it with a vengeance as I am full throttle, green light; take no prisoners playing baseball again. I will share my story from 1957 through 2008. The story starts on the eastside of Brockton, Massachusetts. I lived at 22 Massasoit Avenue as my baseball started from the back yard to many sand lots nearby and this all leads to my present baseball experience.

There are battles with disabilities with my heart, broken bones, comebacks and an inside view of how deeply baseball beats in my heart. If you dare, follow the seams of the baseball and watch the ball bounce from bat to glove and experience baseball through my eyes and listen to my heartbeat. My passion is alive and well as I am always ready for another game.

John F DeCosta

Chapters

Chapter One

———————

Sandlot Baseball

The field was worn with battered base paths, signs of a mound and where bases should have been, and an imaginary spot for home plate. There were kids running around on this spring sunny day as the sounds of a wood bat echoed. You could hear the excitement of chatter, fists into gloves (one size fits all), the dirty ripped clothes, no special gear…and they had so much in common. They came from all over the neighborhood and none cared at all about riches, fancy new things, or what nationality they were. All they cared about was playing baseball.

Yes, the atmosphere was similar at most playgrounds, sand lots, or little league fields. The normal routine each day would be like this: one youngster would grab his baseball stuff and after breakfast go to a nearby baseball friend's home. Instead of knocking on the door they would call out loud the friend's name a few times, and suddenly he would come out, ready with his glove and bat, and off to another's home. Eventually, they would make it to the sandlot. The balls were usually taped with electrician's tape. The old wooden bats were used so much that in many cases they had splits and cracks, so nails and screws were used to repair them. Then the black electrical tape was applied and they were ready to be swung again.

It really didn't matter whether there were four friends or eight friends you got together. They would use a bat to choose up sides and then positions were taken and the pitch was thrown to start the game. Choosing up was a special ceremony. You would toss a bat vertically to a friend. He would catch the bat near the barrel. The second player would put his hand on top of the first player's hand around the barrel and then the first kid would again grasp the next higher position until one of them reached the top of the handle, then the other would slap the top as he won. This would give the winner first pick on choosing baseball teams. It was a very unique process, and I haven't seen that again in all these years. There was another method also used, called bucking up. The two people, usually the popular or best players, would flash either one finger or two. There were many different rules to playing that game. We won't go there.

This was simple baseball with horrible equipment. If you had a bicycle that was great, but many did not, so there was a lot of walking, with sometimes long distances to and from the ball fields. Many would simulate the professional players during that period, like Ted Williams or Mickey Mantle. That was fun – to imagine late in the game you were one of them and you called your shot.

The hours would pass like minutes. There would be a game in the morning, a break for lunch and maybe go to the city pool, then meet later for throwing the ball, another quick game, or even stick ball. Then after supper, you would go to your game. If there was no game, then wiffle ball was on somewhere, or you could practice throwing to a friend, perfecting your curve balls in preparation for the next game. Baseball was everywhere, it seemed, and most friends felt the same way about it.

During the ages of seven to nine years, this was very normal activity. There was a farm system at the time and the ball seemed to come in so fast, but that was our learning era. There were mixed uniforms but you received a good new hat. You felt like you finally belonged to something and of course the rivalries had just begun between classmates. The school rivalries were serious but at the same time it helped each player build their skills and baseball relationships. The bonds extended to this day. In the 1950s we played with all races. We sometimes referred to others as the "colored" kids because we hadn't known any different. But there were never, ever any racial undertones at any time that I can remember. The time was baseball and the other kid was your opponent or the next batter or the short stop – never anything derogatory. There was mutual respect all the time. When there was a problem, the two would throw a few punches, shake hands and you were friends for life.

Usually there were certain sand lots where the kids would keep track of their home runs, whether it was hardball or wiffle ball. There was absolutely no way to verify how genuine each person was, but it was fun to spout off bragging rights.

To further share happenings of myself as well as siblings and friends, with more to come. Some things you generally would not see in today's lifestyle but back then very normal. My Brother Stephen found a camera somewhere. We thought it was expensive. When ever there was something you didn't have, you automatically assumed it was expensive.

We'll after showing this camera to our family for his great find, he then walked a mile to the police department and turned it in. Never to hear if they found an owner or not! I too wondered what happened to that camera.

It just so happened that during the same time period, I had a sleeping problem. That is, I walked in my sleep. I would go out the second floor window, cross over the roof, down a vine to the ground and walk where ever. One time we had a new cesspool dug out which was about 12' deep and I walked and fell into the hole in the night time. I guess that woke me up as well as the household. Then not to long after, I went my same escape route and they were digging up the street to lay new pipes and once again I fell into the ditch. I think I was only about 8 years old then.

On a happier note my very first real friend was Chester Perry. He lived up the street a ways and we did everything together. We'll his Mom apparently felt brave enough to be a Den Mother for our Cub Scouts. Yes, we had the little uniforms with the little hat and pin and off course our Cub Scout book and our meetings, were just a time to wrestle and play it seemed. I don't think it lasted very long. It was a neat thing to belong to something but for me, never as cool as baseball.

One special time I will always remember is this; one day when Chester was over at my home my mom fixed us lunch as we set up boxes and a make shift table outside our homes window as my mom made us bacon lettuce and tomato sandwiches and lemonade or milk forget what the drink was now! It was so special at the time.

Chester had 3 other brothers as he was the oldest so we would always ditch his brothers. His house had a lot of neat sheds, garage and property but we liked the summer house the best. His dad had a huge GP medium army tent as we went camping a few times and got soaked during the night because of a severe rain storm but we kids were resilient at the time and forgot about being soaked by time the morning sun appeared. Chet as I called him did not play sports very often because he lacked the skills but went along to partake in whiffle ball and sandlot baseball. We managed to stay close friends all through the years but after he returned home after a tour of duty in Viet Nam he went fishing and drowned in the ocean with one of his cousins.

This was definitely the age of playing lots of baseball, basketball whiffle ball, or stick ball and just looking for any interest to latch on to. It seemed that friends' would be so busy and you wanted to be like them as well. So, building club houses and working with carpentry really interested me. Then one of my school mates, that I chummed around with talked about his hobby of raising pigeons! I thought wow; let me have a look see at this. His name was Dennis. I went to Dennis's home after school and I was blown away with interest in this hobby! He had his coop and he was handy as I was and built his own coop!

He let the birds out and they were beautiful pigeons and nothing as you see on the street. They flew together in a group and after twenty minutes, they landed and soon went back inside. Dennis brought me to see this older man, Martin Slazes not very far from his location and watch his birds fly and soon after, I came to know about 25 kids in my junior high school that shared in the same hobby. I began to be a regular visitor at Martins home and enjoyed watching his birds fly and soon I had picked up the pigeon lingo and felt like I fit right in. Martin's birds flew very high and rolled constantly as his birds were definitely "athletes in the sky".

I was much pleased on what I learned and saw but still I wanted to see how the Homing Pigeons operated as they were known for long races of 100 miles etc. So a nearby neighbor and friend of the family Ed Tamulevich had racing pigeons and started me out with a bunch of young birds. I built a coop inside the garage and started letting them out. My Mom went to see her Dad in North Easton, so I tagged along and brought the birds with us and before we went home which was 5 miles away I let the birds out and they sure beat us home, which was so neat but the problem I had was, "How do they get in? I learned to build an entry trap so I did but later built my own coop by myself.

This was the best idea yet my own coop! I learned how to band them and raise the pigeons myself. My teachers in school thought this was silly I am sure but I have enjoyed this hobby for many years now. While I was in junior high school as the school was in sight of my home I would fly the birds in the morning and naturally my home room was in the same line of sight so from my class room I could look out the window and see my birds fly. That was so cool!

Chapter Two

_____

Organized Baseball

Baseball was life and all I knew was baseball. When I was ten years old, I was advanced for my age, as I look back, and I was the starting short stop on my twelve-year-old team. I didn't think much of it then; I was just happy I was playing on a regular basis. I was gifted, advanced quickly and just loved to play.

My teammates were tough gritty kids from the eastside. It seemed that someone would show up with a black eye or scrapes from a fight way too often. I had a school acquaintance that lived near the ball field. His name was Leroy. Leroy played on another team and was not only young but powerful. He hit unbelievable home runs and would laugh at the opponents while running the bases. There were twins on my team, Bobby and Dickey. They were tough and very good ballplayers and they did not like Leroy at all. I remember him hitting a home run and yakking all around the bases, nearly getting into a fight with them during the game. When the game was over the twins would be in their station wagon with their parents and younger brothers and all of them would go berserk yelling and swearing at Leroy. On the ball field they were so mad they would throw their gloves and hats at the ground and Leroy would just laugh and hit more home runs. The three of them carried on their hostilities and rivalry through their high school years. Leroy became very big and muscular by then, so it was no contest anymore.

I intimidated the older kids but they also scared me to death.

They would say things like, "I'll kill you if you don't hit the ball."

I was afraid of the fast pitching and would usually look for a walk. I was the lead off hitter and, one particular game, I got hit in the head. I had one of the old-style wrap-around red helmets with an open top and fortunately I was just dazed. They asked if I was ok, asked where I lived, my name and a bunch of silly questions, to see if I was ok. When I went to first base, the small crowd cheered, and that was confusing because I just got hit. I thought to myself, *What's so great about getting hit?*

The next game against this same pitcher, they were yelling at me, "swing the bat!" I then swung as hard as I could and hit one off the centerfield fence and got a double. That was as good as a home run and I sealed the confidence in myself as well as my team that carried on for many more games.

This was Downey Little League on the east side of Brockton. I played there as well as the summer park leagues and whatever camps, pickup games or any baseball I could encounter. The park league and playground league would sanction a trip to Fenway Park to see the Boston Red Sox. This trip would cost one dollar, and you had to bring your own bag lunch and soda. It was a great day, as I saw the bullpen pitcher, Bill Monbouquette, and I saw Ted Williams play, as well as Mickey Mantle, my idol. I remember thinking at the time, *I wish I had his job--playing baseball everyday at the big park.*

I never heard talk about money, to play any sport. I liked the idea of playing for no money. I thought to myself, *what's the big deal? I can throw hard too and I have a curve ball.* So amazing, my thought process at the time—looking at something I knew nothing about but thinking it would be so easy.

I remember getting off the bus all excited with my bag lunch, and viewing the steel beams of Fenway Park, as this was such a huge structure to me. Before entering the large concourse under the bleachers, I noticed a man with a unique music box on wheels with many designs and decorative colors. On a leash attached to his music box was this little monkey in a suit and hat. The man would wind the music box with this gold handle and the music played some carnival song, or sometimes "Take Me Out to the Ball Game." He was selling peanuts and the monkey would hand you the small bag of nuts and retrieve a quarter from you. Better not cheat the monkey--he had a threatening look on his face and was impatient. I don't believe the idea continues these days, but you never know. Our seats were in right field and the stadium was so big to us. That was such a nice experience.

When baseball continued, the city of Brockton was divided into four sections. That's where the real rivalries had started in my early years. The kids watched the sports pages and paid attention to the stars of the other little leagues and saw who was on top, who was the home run king and so on. My team was "Knapp Aerotreds," a sponsored shoe factory supporting the little league team I was on. Yes, I even had a real uniform with the number twelve stitched onto it. My team, Knapp, had a dinner at a conference room at the factory. There was a complete dinner, and for desert, we had small cup cakes with a plastic baseball player on top for each of us. This was 1957 and I still have that plastic player today. This was a keepsake and a special reminder of my baseball roots.

Later there was a real banquet held at St. Colman's church basement, and this was for the whole league. There were about two hundred ballplayers there. They only gave out trophies to each player on the champion team. Then there were special awards: Most Valuable Player; Most Runs Batted In; Most Home Runs; Highest Batting Average; and Sportsmanship Award. I said to myself right then and there, *I want to work hard and receive an award someday.* That's just what I set out to achieve.

The very next season I was a different player, as I became a pitcher besides playing short stop. I set up plywood with a car tire attached to it and a strike zone. I measured forty-six feet for little league distance and I made a pitching rubber and practiced every day. My accuracy improved tremendously and my arm was very strong. I became quite confident, and grew into a strong leader and player. My mom bought me a catcher's mitt for my eleventh birthday and I sure put that to good use, which also increased my workload behind the plate.

The word on the street and ballparks was about this new little league being formed, also on the eastside of Brockton. This little league was called Eastside Improvement Association. The word passed around was about more talent, all the popular kids, splash parties at the big pools, camps, playing traveling games, and overall a fun time. I went to the tryouts and I was a top pick. I was approached during the tryouts by the president of the league, George, or "Scoop", and the vice president, Richard. They got very serious as they made it absolutely clear to me I would not be able to get a jacket like the other twelve-year-olds, and I especially would not be able to win a trophy or any award. I stated immediately, *I just want to play baseball, that's all.*

I got picked by a coach named Danny Dors for his Merchants team. I was again short stop and my arm was so strong and deadly that I wanted to pitch but had no one to catch me. Danny was awesome. He would drive up to the practice with his 1957 red Chevy convertible and his very awesome and pretty girlfriend. His history was quickly a legend on the eastside in most sports and he was just Mr. Cool. We practiced a lot and very hard and some were talented and some looked like the characters in the film *The Bad News Bears*.

Very quickly I became the team leader. I don't know why but I assumed this position, as they seemed to listen to and believe in me. I had an unbelievable year. I would hit three for three, or four for four, and play great defense, yet our team was still in trouble. I needed to pitch and Danny realized that as well.

One day at practice he said to me, "Throw the ball to me as hard as you can." This was done to prove that someone could catch me. He caught me with his bare hands. Soon after my friend Bobby learned to catch me and I went on to have numerous double figure strikeout games.

I pitched forty-nine innings with ninety-two strikeouts. My hitting was also incredible, as I hit over four hundred and fifty, eighteen runs batted in, three home runs, most hits – thirty in an eighteen-game time frame, and I was the leader of the league in all categories. Our all-star team got knocked out on the first game, but I did not pitch. The all-star team's manager had someone else pitch. We did, however, play at the Veterans Hospital, and the Ted Williams Camp. I looked around but saw no Ted Williams at all. This was in Lakeville, Massachusetts. The games at the Veterans Hospital were interesting. There was a bigger crowd there than at our league. They would cheer and we would go to their pool after and enjoy hot dogs and soda after the game. Little did I know I would become, later in life, a veteran and a paratrooper.

We all seemed to have heart. All were gamers and there just wasn't enough baseball. Whenever you had a chance to play, you played hard. Every game was like the World Series. Red dirt, pine tar, sweat, tears, emotion – all those fun baseball experiences…and all to be disturbed by becoming a teenager soon.

I was glad my catching days were over, as I found excitement in pitching and enjoyed being a pitcher with confidence. I had a very strong arm, I was accurate, I threw hard for my size and age, and I was in control. I got a lot of strikeouts and boy, did that feel great. I would just gesture to the batter with my thumb up, *gotcha!* When I struck out any batter, and especially more advanced hitters, that felt even better.

My mom worried that I threw too much and should take it easy. But she continued to support me by collecting news clippings from the newspaper for my scrap book, as I myself didn't pay a lot of attention to all that, but it felt great to see those clippings later. I saved my special baseballs and home run balls but lost them through the years.

Soon, my glory year would be over and I would be left with only distant memories. The end of season came and then in late August there was a league banquet held at the association hall. We had a sit-down dinner with guest speakers, like the mayor and prominent sports people, and it was a really big deal. When dinner was over, there were awards presented to the championship team, and then only to specific achievements such as Most Home Runs, Best Pitcher, Most Runs, Most Batters In, Highest Batting Average and Sportsmanship.

My manager, Danny, was right next to me, and also in the crowd at another table were my mom and dad. During the presentation, my name would be mentioned at the top of each award but someone else would receive it.

Danny said, "You played great, John. Which award would you like to get?"

"Most Valuable Player," I said immediately. "But I can't get it because they told me at the beginning that I can't get an award."

Then it got quiet and the president of the league went to the microphone and talked about how I wanted to play ball so badly and didn't care about the awards, yet I had achieved the highest in every category. So the league had voted and agreed to give me, John DeCosta, the Most Valuable Player award, *The Joseph Arms Trophy*. I was asked to stand and everyone clapped and all I could do was cry my eyes out. I could not stop!

The teammates next to me asked, "Why are you are crying?"

"Because I am so happy," I'd sobbed. My plaque remained on that wall in the banquet hall for many years.

I loved the game so much that I thought cutting lawns, or doing a lot of other chores, would make me stronger and hit the ball further. If I were stronger, I could throw the ball harder as well. I used to cut about fifteen lawns a week in the neighborhood. I felt quite pleased with myself, earning my own money.

Disappointment was on the horizon. This disappointment came at the very same time I needed to think about Pony league, junior high baseball, and any baseball future. My wrist was ailing me badly. I found that I had a tumor in my right wrist. Yes, my throwing arm. When I went to the hospital for wrist surgery, I was in a semi private room. That was fine but I shared this room with a semi-professional football player, a star quarterback, and he had some sort of knee injury. He seemed like a cool guy but he would have ten people in the room, drinking beer, and making loud chatter. They finally threw them out but I was in a lot of pain and uncomfortable the whole time. There were multiple tumors in my wrist and recovery took forever, it seemed.

I had a bad time with the coaches, since they didn't know of my problem. But they weren't helpful to me at the time either. With no sports person to speak to, and being emotionally torn, I dropped out of baseball. I lost the baseball season, and even though basketball was coming up, I played with a sore wrist and I was weak all season with that too. I eventually chose to work and not play sports at all. That proved to be a bad mistake that I look back on to this day.

So I turned in my uniforms, gave no explanation and never looked back at baseball. A cloud of disappointment then absorbed my soul for many years and I did not discuss it with anyone. My achievements were spoken about and I received a lot of encouragement from teachers and coaches, but no one had really known what was up with me. I am sorry I didn't speak with someone.

I knew baseball was over for me but I held some pure baseball thoughts deep in my heart, although I was afraid to express to anyone my desires and disappointments. I then entered a period of being a frustrated teenager, and I took out my frustrations whenever the opportunity arose. At the close of the basketball season, it was Letter Day, so wearing a tie in school was acceptable. I strolled into my Civics class and this guy named Dave was in my way and made a rude comment. When I told him to shut up he grabbed my tie.

I looked around and said, "Get away." He didn't let go, so I proceeded to punch him about eight times, splitting his eye open as well as his mouth. There was blood all over the place and I was sent to the office. They sent me home from school, so I missed the assembly and the awards ceremony. Unfortunately, there was more of the same to come.

I became the head hunter on the basketball team towards our rivals and competition. I could shoot great like a pro, but had trouble dribbling the ball. My biggest problem in sports was the crowd. I got so nervous I could not function at all. Coaches and teachers would say, "Chew gum, dream, sing songs—whatever it takes and you'll be ok."

The crowd would watch before the game, and during half time, as I would put on a show. I would always have my back to the crowd and when the game started I would totally fall apart. You will be happy to know that nowadays, I love a crowd and I especially look forward to a crowd, but in those days, forget it.

I remember trying to come back after missing an important baseball season, and I discovered I had no confidence, with no coaching at all. I went to a pitcher's tryout and the coach said, "Throw a fast ball. Throw a curve ball. Now throw a change-up."

I said to myself, *what is a change-up?* I had no idea what he was talking about. After a grueling disappointment of a somewhat of a comeback, I accepted the fact that it was over and not to look back at all. I had no control over my damaged wrist and, psychologically, I was spent.

The time was supposed to be great for me. I had been the top pick, but my wrist was never the same. The combination of my depression concerning my capabilities, my emotional changes as I was growing up, and the terrible coaches I had, all led to a loss of self-confidence and my entire drive for baseball. There was no one to really console me at the time. I felt it was easier to just walk away and work, make money to purchase school clothes, and move on. That's just what I did. It's very sad as I look back and realize – the cards were just not in my favor.

The eastside was considered special in many ways. The loyalty and teamwork that the poor kids discovered in sports was what helped its popularity spread throughout the city. The eastside kids dominated nearly every sport all through the city schools. State championships were standard in basketball and baseball, as well as football. The kids from other sections of the city were intimidated by the eastside and were actually afraid to travel through it.

Prior to this I had gone earlier years to see older kids play little league. They looked so big and really gifted as I would look on and dream, and wonder if I could ever play that well. I would bring my glove everywhere I went. I would practice throwing different pitches and if only I could get the opportunity – wow. I remember the old legend, Herby Jones.

I first saw Herby Jones when I was 9 years old. I played baseball in the little league farm system and now I was ready to break into the little league program of 10 thru 12 year olds baseball. Herby would hit long homeruns nearly every game. The long line drive homeruns that you were in awe of. He did this from both sides of the plate and so many people came just to see him play baseball. You see he was an incredible pitcher as well. I think he had a few no hitters' as well!

I finally got to meet Herby Jones exactly 53 years later through classmates and face book and we maintained a friendship as it's a true and strong genuine friendship now and forever. He was and s such a super person and friend. Who on earth would ever think that we would become real friends after so many years have passed. We'll Herby and I had met at a baseball field we both knew so well. O'Donnell's playground in Brockton, Mass. We met on a weekday as I brought baseball bats a few buckets of balls and got there a bit early as I was so excited. He finally came and we shook hands and hugged and because our city had changed so much I mentioned, maybe we should go to a better park that I knew so we did. We went to Edgar's playground as the city did that field over nicely. We gathered my bats and balls and went onto the field, stretch, and warmed up slowly as I enjoyed the baseball catch. Then we both pitched a bucket of balls to each other and we did not disappoint each other.

We sat for a while and enjoyed the beautiful fall day with a gorgeous sunshine and talked baseball how things were and occasionally about the current baseball players in MLB that we both liked. We then picked up and went to a breakfast restaurant and talked again and finally said good by as he was waiting to go to a reunion that weekend. He came from Arlington, Texas and he wanted to enjoy his visit at home and I am sure he did. This time this was a real treasured experience for both of us.

He was a home run hitter from the eastside, like a local Babe Ruth. His balls would be line drives fifty feet over the fence. There was another great player, Ronnie, who was also a big-time hitter. I knew Ronnie but Herby I didn't know. I just wondered if I would ever be that kind of player that others would look up to some day in the future.

There are so many clear memories of my childhood and baseball; I remember the bats in those days had autographs of Mickey Mantle, Lou Gehrig, Jimmy Fox, Yogi Berra and so on. I remember as clear as a bell one hot August night on our family porch. It was about eight p.m. and the Red Sox were on the TV. The clouds had moved in quickly, the game was close, and Jackie Jensen was at the plate with bases loaded. Just moments before the heavy rains and intense lightning, Jackie hit a grand slam home run...and then the game was called. I never forgot that. I also recall Jimmy Pearsall climbing fences and running the bases backwards.

This was the era of so many varieties of pastimes and fads. For example, hula hoops. I never could get the hang of those! And the 45 records which had one song on each side, or the 78 records, which had about six songs on each side. The transistor radios became quite popular too. Everyone wanted one but no one could ever hear anything clearly from them. Then there were yo-yos. Everyone had one at one point, but that fad didn't seem to last long. Another fad with the teenagers in that era was hanging dice from the rear-view mirrors of their cars, or wrapping fuzz around the steering wheel, or hanging a rabbit's foot somewhere in the interior, or even putting skirts on the back of their car! Spinners on their wheels were also a big hit.

The corner stores always had penny candy, so that was a treat. When you had extra money, the drug stores also had bars in those days, where you could sit and enjoy a Lime Ricky or a vanilla float with ice cream on the bottom, or a frappe, which is the New England term for a milk shake. You could look out the window and watch the older teens driving by in their Corvettes and T-Birds.

The popular clothing style was plaid Bermuda shorts for the older folks. The school kids would wear barracuda jackets, felt belts, button-down collars, penny loafers and chino pants. When they got bored they wore their jackets inside out. Most always the teenagers were quite neat in their dress, as I look back. The school dress-code in the fifties and sixties required a tie with every shirt, no jeans and neatness. If you forgot a tie, one was provided. You sure didn't forget your tie! I found the string tie to be more tolerant.

Elvis Presley, The Beatles, The Beach Boys and The Platters—they were very popular. There were many more, of course, but these are some of the bigger bands I remember.

Life was so simple and real pleasant to reminisce about. The neighborhoods were close but not too close. Most people wouldn't lock their doors, for most areas were reasonably safe. There were many conveniences that are long-gone and unheard of these days. We actually had the following available at our home: the milk delivered by a milk company in a milk truck, the bread and baked goods delivered, ice and coal delivered, cleaners, trash pick-up and a garbage man...all sorts of personal needs that we now consider errands to deal with.

There was a housing project nearby called Hill Street .This was a project full of a variety of kids, and it was the cool hangout for some time. The kids there had a rock band so when they were not playing basketball they were singing songs from the fifties. I think they even recorded a few songs as well. This same band is still together today, after all these years, which is quite remarkable, I must say.

When I was ten years old or so, I took ukulele lessons. My mom had privately taught herself how to play the ukulele, and she had figured that if I didn't excel and enjoy the instrument, then she would learn and enjoy for herself. She was always hungry to learn. I would come home from school and find her practicing and having a wonderful time playing. That was so nice to see. I also tried singing, and even went to a recital and sang one of the Everly Brothers' songs. I sang a few times and then realized, *maybe it's best to stick to baseball.*

My Mom and sister Joanne had planted a small tree, an Oak tree that My Mom had purchased at a local nursery as they planted it ever so careful to fill a space on the front of the property to grow strong and develop strong roots. The many times I have driven down to the eastside to see our old family home the tree has grown so very tall and strong roots as we were told and also filled the space and became quite beautiful as well.

Our childhood home appeared to be small in stature but growing up it felt like a huge home on top of the hill but now houses around on all sides it looks so small and unloved. The tree is now about 25" high and the home is run by a day care and all of the family history has become a new family's history and you ask, where did all of the time go?

Chapter Three

Ginger and Other Canines in My Life

Having dogs in my life has been a strong emotional high. They are always happy to see you, they recognize when you are sad, and they are ever so patient. They always seem to understand and react to your emotions in a positive way. I have had several dogs and all of them have stories. I will try to share some highlights of those experiences with you. My stories, I'm sure, are similar to yours, just with different names and circumstances, but similar in content.

Ginger was the first real dog of my own. Our family had another dog named Jill when I was too young to remember much about her. So my relationship with Ginger had no past, only our history together. She was very fluffy, and golden in color. I can't remember how we got her. She was no special breed but very special to our family. Many would see her tagging after me and nicknamed her Tumbleweed. She sure could run, and everyone knew who she was and where she lived. She followed me everywhere – baseball, swimming, fishing, and even to school. She was the most loving and loyal dog anyone could ask for.

We would go fishing a lot and Ginger would tail behind, sometimes traveling four miles or more. We would arrive early to Mill Pond, so no one else would be there yet, and on occasion we would go to Big Meadows. Wherever we went, I would immediately look for a good fishing spot, and Ginger would trace the edge of the pond in search of frogs and other creatures. When she finally checked on me, I was afraid to look because she would be covered with mud.

I would most likely end up on a big rock on the edge of the pond and share my lunch with Ginger. She would get excited when I caught a fish but usually I would throw it back into the pond, for I was not about to eat any fish. We often picked up and moved to a spot next to the waterfall, not far from the entrance. That was my favorite spot. Within a few moments I usually caught a bass. That was all the excitement I needed for the day. Ginger was fairly dried by then and ready to go home.

I used to go there with another friend named Paul, along with my dad, and catch hornpout. They were fun to catch but not fun to take off the line because of their horns! And there sure were a lot of them, therefore, a lot of fishing fun. On another occasion I went to that same spot with my friend Bobby Butler. Bobby and I played a lot of baseball together and went fishing as much as possible. I was fishing with this red devil lure with a triple hook, and after casting ten to fifteen times, I felt a tug, a very heavy tug. As I reeled it in I could not believe my eyes. I caught two bass on this triple hook! Bobby saw it as well. That spot beside the waterfall gave me many treasured memories.

Bobby Butler and I played on separate teams in little league. He was the opposing pitcher and I hit a long drive for my first home run ever, and I remember Bobby's smile as I crossed first base. He had such a warm happy smile for me and I can still remember my home run trot. That was definitely the best experience.

There were many fishing trips, and a lot of baseball to come. Ginger had puppies one time but none of the five had lived. There were days when I would come home from school and see Ginger on the steps with my mom. Mom would be reading the newspaper and Ginger would charge after me to greet me. I can still remember the lilacs in the backyard and a happy time in my life. Ginger was special and gave me many years of love and I think, as I look back, I was too immature to have appreciated her properly.

There were many years without a dog due to a disrupted home life after my first enlistment in the army. I did not have a normal secure home life until I was close to forty years old and with Beth, my wife. We, Beth and I, were in the army and stationed at Fort Riley, Kansas. Yes, the Big Red One, Infantry. That was an experience in itself.

Well, Beth had always wanted to have an old English sheep dog. That was her dream, so we went to a pet store (yes, that was a mistake) and they found us one. We had to wait a few days for him to arrive from the breeder (I mean "puppy mill"). Meanwhile, I had not had a dog in a lot of years so Beth thought, *how about a black lab.* So we jumped on that and got him while we were waiting for the sheepdog to arrive. We named the black lab Celtic. He got big, out of control and when Willie, our new sheepdog, came, the fights began. They were endlessly fighting. I ran both dogs with a parachute cord, and they dragged me for miles. I got in shape for the army with those dogs!

At this time, I couldn't decide whether to return to Special Forces duty, which I had done previously, or try Delta Force. I passed the test for Delta Force, but I then changed my mind and soon received orders for Special Forces duty at Fort Lewis, Washington. When it was time to leave, I took Celtic with me in a sports car. That was probably not a wise decision, as he almost killed me numerous times on my trip out there. He was big, afraid of trucks on the highway, and got scared and jumped on me while I was driving.

I got settled but had a problem with Celtic. I had to put him on a farm until Beth and I got housing. Meanwhile, as I was adjusting to the new location, I made a parachute jump and soon after, had a heart attack, my first one, at age forty. When I got out of the hospital, our pre-rented home in Lacy, Washington became available. I picked Celtic up from the farm and got the house ready for Beth's arrival, along with her daughter Shelly. When they came, Celtic had gotten too possessive and showed his teeth and wanted to eat Beth. He turned vicious. Luckily we found a man who had a female lab on a farm, and he wanted Celtic. When he came over to pick up the dog, he left his car door open, and Celtic ran right into his car. We never saw him again. We figured he either had a happy life on the farm or someone shot him. Of course we hoped for the former.

We were now reunited with Beth, Shelly, and Willie. That was great, but Beth had found an Old English sheepdog breeder in Washington and wanted another Old English sheepdog. Although her papers guaranteed her authentic breeding, Sarah, the sheepdog we wanted, had failed the entire test physically so we were lucky to break loose of the breeder's contract.

Thankfully, Willie and Sarah got along well, and were always getting into trouble together. They were constantly tipping over the trash cans, barking or ransacking the house. I built a dog area with a tower and if I was shooting baskets and Willie was locked up, he would go berserk. On one occasion, he leaped off the tower and smashed through the neighbors' tool shed; I had to replace their roof. He sure loved his basketball!

I was riding with Willie one day and as we went around a corner, Willie fell out of the car! Fortunately he was not hurt, just a little shook up. He was more careful after that. We also walked a lot, and as we walked through our neighborhood, out of the blue a little Scottish terrier ran at us ever so quickly and bit Willie's leg. Then the little dog took off. Will's leg was bleeding and the fangs had gone completely through his foot. After some stitches he healed up fine, but he hated little dogs after that.

I completed my cardiac rehabilitation after my heart attack and then I became a runner. Willie trained me every day, as he loved to run. We started at a mile or so and then it was five or six miles every day. We even ran on Christmas morning, Willie trotting beside me with bells and bows on his collar. Willie had started out to be Beth's dog but he and I established a strong bond with each other. He saved my life. We did everything together. He loved basketball the most. If I took a shot he would try to rebound it and slam the ball to the ground and wait for me to shoot it up again.

We ran miles and miles together. We took the trails and climbed the mountains. He was great, but soon I would have to go back east to school in Vermont (wallpapering). I had just retired from the military, and after the school in Vermont, I would get settled in Massachusetts and wait for Beth to be discharged and come home from Fort Lewis, Washington. My job once again was to get home first and get our new home fixed up, painted and ready for all of us. This is where we started originally, and fortunately we were lucky to be back.

After a very difficult time Beth and I finally got our own home. It was an antique cape that needed a lot of work. We worked very hard and had a great place for the dogs, finally. The breeder from Washington had felt badly that Sarah was not show quality and worried about her name as a professional breeder. She felt she owed us a dog, so she shipped us another Old English sheepdog, free of charge, to Logan Airport. When I went into Boston to the airport to retrieve him, he was in a small cage with a note—*give me water in Chicago*. Well, no more cage. I named him Charlie and he road in my lap all the way home as we bonded immediately. So now we had the Three Musketeers; Sarah, Willie, and Charlie.

The three dogs grew close to each other. We finally had a great dog area for them in our barn, where they could come and go as they pleased. It was the best situation for dogs, we thought. They were very happy, as were we. One day Sarah escaped and got lost, but luckily she found a house where the people were kind enough to feed her. She was returned to us, thankfully. She was a wonderful dog. She would always love to jump in the car but after the engine was on, she would bark continuously until the engine stopped. Although she wasn't a great walker like Charlie, she was a character, and so lovable. She especially enjoyed falling asleep on the couch, or even in the tub! She failed all of the obedience training but did ok with us. The last obedience training class we took Sarah to was definitely one not to forget. Beth decided to have me ride in the back of the car with Sarah to keep her calm on the way to the class. I thought we could give it a try.

Well, the trip turned out to be noisy and dramatic, as Sarah was out of control. She jumped all over me in the back seat of the car. For a short while we were lost, trying to find the classroom in another town that we were not familiar with. Beth and I were trying to communicate over traffic, the dog barking, and then with no warning, Sarah messed herself! There was a lot of it, all over the seats and me! Yes, I went berserk with hardly anything to cleanup with. Beth and Sarah still went to the class and Sarah again failed her test. I had to wait in the car and then ride home with the stench and mess all over the place. I told Beth, "Do not say anything, just get me home." This was an unforgettable, nasty experience. We decided that classes would work out best if we did them on our own.

But one day, unexpectedly, Sarah had a heart attack and died. We buried her close to the house and talked to her all the time. She was ten years old. We enjoyed her, loved her, and had some great experiences with her. She was our first emotional loss at our home.

Willie also had obedience training and he failed as well, although he eventually became very obedient. Willie continued to run with me, but Charlie was not crazy about running; he preferred to walk. When you walked with Charlie, it was like a feather on the lead. Charlie was by far the most obedient dog I ever had. He was so relaxing to walk with, and so gentle and loving.

Willie developed cancer and we had the hardest time letting him go. The vet came to the house and our emotions were torn so deeply as he drifted away. Willie was fourteen years old with a story book of experiences and love that will always be in my heart. I buried Willie next to Sarah, as we felt he would have wanted.

Charlie later came down with cancer as well. He spent his last few weeks in our kitchen, and I felt I could not go through this again. I would hug him as often as I could and finally I had to let him go, as I had with Willie. Charlie was twelve years old. I have many pictures of those three wonderful dogs, and as I look at them I wander off, thinking of those fun times I shared with each of them.

The beginning of the most current threesome was Holly. We got Holly from a breeder in Canada. She and I didn't bond right away; she was closer to Beth and she always snapped at me. It was not a bite, it was just the way she greeted people, as she approached them. Holly is now about nine years old. We then got Joshua, who is now four, and our last dog of the three some is Abby, who is three.

One wonderful experience I recall took place a few months before we decided to sell our home. Beth and I had a system when we bathed the three dogs. I would give them their quarterly haircuts the day before, and then we took turns with the dogs, getting the hair dryers, towels, and blankets ready, as well as the rinsing buckets, brushes etc. After we got them all squeaky clean, they would eat and then would have to go out. I had had trouble previously with our next door neighbor because of her dog. Now Beth and I had just gotten them outside, they were all nice and clean and fluff-dried...and then our neighbor let her dog out! Inevitably our three dogs raced to the corner of the lot to bark at and greet the dog, and there happened to be a large mud puddle right there. Our dogs were instantly soaked with black mud. I was so mad I called the neighbor a variety of names, as I felt it was inconsiderate of her not to wait a few minutes for Beth and I to take care of our dogs first. The problem was, I knew she had done this on purpose.

When we moved from the old house to the home we reside in now, I actually dug up all the graves of our dogs before we moved. I put them in plastic coffins and brought them to our new home, along with head stones, and buried them on our new land. I could not deal with them not being on our property. It sounds crazy but my love for all of them is so deep I always want them close to me.

I love my dogs and have built the most unique houses for them. They are so spoiled but I enjoy all my time with them. They don't seem to take to baseball, but they seem to tolerate me hitting into the net or pitching balls to the target in our basement. We walk three miles a day, except for Holly, so we are all staying in shape. I tell them about the other dogs but I don't think they understand, although they do recognize the new burial site of our former dogs. They will also be there some day but I hope a long, long time from now.

Despite the crazy dilemmas, dog fights, and veterinarian bills, I would not trade any of it for the amount of love all of our dogs have given us in return. They are so loyal and only want to please you and be with you. I will always treasure each and every one of them, and hold all of the memories they have given me close to my heart.

Chapter Four

My First Job!

In junior high school I decided to get a job to make money for clothes, which were very important to me, being a young and impressionable boy. I had hand-me-downs for so long and didn't really care about clothes until then. I found a job at the corner fruit stand, less than five hundred feet from our house. I remember the family that owned the fruit stand were very mean. They never smiled and were so greedy, but it was a job. I started on a Friday morning at seven a.m. I immediately started unloading potatoes from a truck, then apples and fruits of all kinds, as well as vegetables. When I finished unloading I would clean and sweep, and then unload some more trucks. I worked until midnight. They gave me fifteen minutes for lunch, then another fifteen minutes for supper. Then on Saturday, the same drill all day long. Sunday, I continued the same type of work, same time off for lunch and supper, and then at midnight, I remember thinking, *gee, I worked a lot of hours – I must have a lot of money owed to me.*

I said to the owner, "Do you think I could get paid?" He looked at me like, *what – you want money?!* He reached into his pocket for a roll of money, and gave me one dollar and a pint of ice cream. My heart fell to the floor. The sweat was still dripping from my face and I was speechless and could not respond. I was in shock and went home.

My mom was so upset, so she and my brother Douglas returned to the fruit stand to argue with the owner. They violated every rule you could think of, as minimum wage was at least a dollar twenty-five an hour at the time. I was under age and could not get a job anywhere else, so I only wanted fifty cents per hour with no taxes. My mom didn't want me to continue working there, but this was a way I could purchase my own clothes and help her as well. Our family had problems due to my father's heart condition at the time, and things were not so good at home financially. I worked the rest of the summer and they beat me to death with work and abuse. That was my first real job. I was probably better off cutting lawns in the neighborhood, which was more relaxing at least!

I did have a paper route like most American teenagers, but I also cut lawns too. I had a regular route as I had about 27 lawns to cut. Some were every week and others were every two weeks depending on how burnt the grass got from the burning sun. So cutting lawns was definitely a great way to make money to buy my school clothes and then of course another way was to shovel snow but that was not a fun way to work. I think I never liked the snow conditions even to this day.

My friend Chester once again shared a new experience that goes down on our work resume for anyone that may be interested! In our neighborhood was a small restaurant/diner called pat's Good Food. It was a hang out for truck drivers as well as a community breakfast and lunch place. We'll Chester and I were there experiencing a favorite of our s hot chocolate and a blueberry muffin. Mr. O'Brien the owner and main chef there had this old door between the kitchen and the front of restaurant. Well this swinging door had this little peep hole in the middle and every time we were in there he wood peep through the hole to watch us and we would giggle. We thought that was really silly. On this particular day he came out and said what you boys are up to? We said not to much maybe some baseball later! He said would you like to do some work? We said sure! The rest is history.

We never asked how much money we would make until half way through the morning. We followed OB or Mr. O'Brien to the back of the restaurant as he lifted this bulked door with a horrible rotted stairway and like idiots we followed him down to this dungeon; what are we in for here? Chet and I looked at each other and thought! Wow. Well Mr. O'Brien said here are two boxes to sit on, a few potato peelers, and 50# bags of potatoes. Peel the potatoes and put in the bucket. I'll give you $.25 cents per hour and walked away! So our new career was peeling potatoes, just like on SGT Bilko the funny Army movie. We did not last long but we finished the morning anyway. I think we decided that there has got to be something better than this to make money at, so off we went to pick on his brothers for a while.

My next job was at Thorny Lea Golf Course in Brockton, Massachusetts. I became a caddy, and no, I didn't know a thing about golf. I learned as little as possible about the sport, as I was not very enthusiastic, mainly because I thought it was silly and boring. I looked at it as a game like bowling or cards. The main job was to carry the golf bags for people who thought they were good. This was hard to deal with. I would carry this big, heavy golf bag for an average wanna-be. I would watch them hit the balls straight into the woods, so I was constantly searching for their balls in the woods, rough, or water. They were hackers. They would smash their clubs against trees, and I would try not to laugh, which was so hard to do. The balls wood bounce off of branches and ricochet in all directions. People were always yelling out "fore," which meant, *duck – there's a ball flying around in your direction!* I found it especially hard to be supportive watching this fiasco. Then, they would give you a lousy three or four dollars for carrying that bag for eighteen holes. This was not a positive career for me.

Needless to say, my desire and interest to work there quickly diminished. Like a lot of things, you had to know the right people to get the right caddy jobs, and fitting in with the manager was a challenge, so I went back to cutting lawns until I was old enough to work at Fernandez Super Market. I worked very hard and started off with only eleven hours a week. I quickly got opportunities to work in other departments, which allowed me more hours. I was almost working a full-time schedule during the school year. During the summer I was working full time and none of the others my age were doing that. I was very fortunate. I was able to contribute at home, purchase clothes, records and take care and enjoy the pigeon hobby I had at the time. Life was simple with little pressure. Soon I would be finding friends from the eastside, and I developed an attitude in and out of school. At the time I didn't realize it but, as I look back, I picked the wrong friends, I was not involved in sports, and I took my job and my boss for granted. It was immaturity – how else can I put it? Those teenage years were especially hard for me to deal with, as I'm sure they were for most people.

Working for the supermarket was a great job in the fifties. My boss absolutely thought I was the greatest. I worked so hard and never said no to any overtime nor any dirty job. I did however blow it; I went with my friends who always hung out by the strip mall. There was a rich kid who had his way with the family home, new car every year and completely spoiled. No rules, no curfew for this kid. Well I went with him and two other friends to his house. He had a new GTO or 409 or something like that and we raided his Dad's liquor cabinet. It didn't take much liquor for me. I was delirious, staggering and being sick. That's just for starters. I was dumb enough to go to my job at the super market and see the female cashiers as I passed out on the floor in front of them and the customers.

That's not the worst; I called in sick earlier that evening so I could be off this particular Friday evening. True I ended up sick but I was not supposed to be free as a bee drinking. We'll needless to say I got fired instantly, lost my wallet as I was just paid for the week and I don't remember ever going home but I did because I was deathly afraid to come down stairs to breakfast after a night of being lost, drunk, broke and no memory -accept I lost my job.

This attitude continued for a while as my interest for anything and authority was drifting downward. I only had my friends who were also screwed up from their own problems and it was not easy to speak with parents as I thought but I never tried. When I nearly killed myself as another real smart friend and I had stolen a car went speeding and rolled it over. It looked like a wrinkled pile of aluminum foil after that. It was quite unbelievable, I had not died nor did my friend, as we were very lucky young lads. We ran through the woods and swamps till we came to safety. After this wonderful experience I knew I had to make a real positive decision fast, or I would have died in some manner.

High school years there was a lot of wasted time, poor choices of friends, hanging out at the pool room, drag racing on the highway and even down town for that matter and wasting time at parties and not spending any time on sports. I had many gifted talents in sports like basketball for example no one could shoot like me! Football I could have been a great half back as I could run, had the moves and could catch the ball but my heart was not there. I played on the high school team for a week as I didn't know the rules, how to play the game, never asked a question and was only there to get a free property shirt! I then of course, not was trying my baseball skills which I gave up pursuing, because of old operation, injury and terrible coaches. I was athletic and wasted time, skills and desire to enjoy the things I loved.

Our school the Brockton High School was one of the largest in the country, baby boomers you know! We'll in our town we were over crowded so we had double sessions. This meant that seniors went 8; 00 am till 12; 30 pm –mornings, and sophomore and juniors went 12; 30pm till 5 pm Monday through Friday. This was very ideal for working full time while going to school this was great meaning you always had a lot of free time and money for the weekends. The bad thing was it separated friends from friendships because you worked or went to school and eliminated sports. You were either going to play sports and have no money or work or have money. So the richer kids benefited here.

There were many pool rooms around town and naturally one very close to the high school. Great place to cut class and shoot pool. The way it worked was it cost for example $2.25 per hour for the table. Someone would challenge you and or you would challenge someone else to play a game. Who ever lost had to pay for the hourly rate so you tried a little harder to win! One particular day I had cut class and with my delinquent friends hanging out at the pool room when my Dad appeared there! I was shocked and a little embarrassed. He said rack em up! I did so as he beat me pretty bad in front of my friends.

This was an awkward time of my teen years Viet Nam going on, troubles at the high school cutting class, detention hours, then my Dad says if you are to smoke ,smoke in front of me or don't smoke at all. Then at home he did the same with a beer; I thought I don't even like beer but with your teenage friends on a Friday night its best to have beer on your breath than not fit in. The Army was looking pretty good for me daily in my thoughts. You know just about everyone in everyone's family in those days all spent time in the Military and waiting for the draft to catch you was not a good thing so volunteering seemed to be the way to go!

I was already a member in the Naval Reserves. I had a deal that I would spend two tears inactive reserves, two years active duty, and then my final two years in reserves to complete my six year obligation. Well I missed too many reserve meetings, over the limit; quite often I would be on extra duty mopping floors etc. I had really blown it this time. The Ensign said to me. Seaman Apprentice, I said yes. He said you are going into the Navy for four years, starting next week. I said, Navy, can I go to another branch. He said you have a week to do that. I then went to the Marine Corp of all places and they said four years young man. I drifted over to the Air Force and they said Four years. I crawled to the Army Recruiting office and gave my last effort there. They said three years." I said I'll take it".

He asked what I wanted to do., I said how about I drive a jeep; He said ok. I then was signed up for transportation school and rerouted to basic advanced training, and off to Korea. I would go in on a delayed entry program which meant I used up leave before I earned it. How stupid was I. I would go into the Army 21 December 1964.

The testing and physicals were scheduled at the Boston Army Base early December 1963! This was new for me to travel to Boston with the recruiter as we stopped on the way to pick up a few other recruits to test as well. The Boston Army Base was a long building a Government building and just as large as I was in awe of how big it was. It was actually more than a half mile long. After half of the physical in the morning we broke for lunch and don't you know the lunch room was at the opposite end of the building. This had to be a test as well to make you walk all the way there. I completed the test after lunch and I had a chance to visit my Mom because she worked there in the same building so I was fortunate to have a short coffee break with her. I then finished the physical and I had to return the next morning for the testing. This time I came in with my Mom because the testing was for all day. This was the written test!

On this day I had finished just before my Mom usually went to lunch so on this day I went to her office as I went to her small facility to have lunch with her. We went through the line and grabbed trays and silverware and found a table. Most of the women that worked with her all had a funny smile. I guess they thought "how sweet" and yes it was a mother and son get together. As this lunch had turned into a very relaxing, and for me this ended up being the only time in my life that," I would actually have lunch together with my Mother" ever! So, I think about that often. It may not have been a fancy rich restaurant or popular place, but for that special time it has been a special memory I have had through the years that I can reminisce.

This is as good a time as any to talk about other areas in the community. Everyone in this area has had some sort of experience at D.W. Fields Park. This place has numerous large ponds with a winding road circling all. One in which is a place to swim with a beach and picnic tables. They all have unique water falls, and decorative rock work that was done before and after World War II in the CC Camps. These camps were designed to keep people working. There was an observation tower built in the center about 6 stories high or so that you could visually see a lot of Brockton, a good part of the park and over look the golf course. This particular hill was quite busy during the winter months as hundreds of kids and adults would come here with toboggans, sleds, and slide down the hill. The snow seems to allow you to pick up incredible speed due to the vertical slant of the hill. We would do this for hours. This also was dangerous as being teenagers you would look for great targets to run over on the way down or occasionally have an accident or hit a tree.

This would all lead to a hot chocolate at the bottom of the hill at the Walsh's restaurant.

The other lakes in this park were for ice fishing, ice skating where thousands of people, families would come to ice skate, play hockey in between all the bonfires on the ice. Fire and police support would always be close by.

In the summer time, you would see many walkers and joggers on the roadways and hikers enjoying the scenic paths in the woods by the ponds and one particular pond would have an area where thousands of ducks and geese would congregate as the big deal would be to bring bread with you and feed the ducks. The Sunday drivers would pack the roadways also another place to show off the hot cars like corvettes and mustangs and off course the park had many parking areas that any red blooded American teenager had experienced there one time or another. Some people had a lot of time invested there! Gee how would I know this?

Main Street Brockton, Ma was another red blooded American past time, "Cruising the drag". I thought this was just a Brockton thing until I went to California and realized there were foolish teenagers everywhere. The drag, what is this? This term "cruising the drag" was very common, as you rode in cars, driving slow and checking out the girls. The cars were usually all girls in one car and all guys in another car. This is where the dating started. Some preferred to hang on the corners and meet the girls that were an easy way to meet new girlfriends. There were pool rooms in the town as well, also on the drag.

This drag area was a few miles long and truly a waste of gas and time but that's what the kids did in the 50's and 60's. Yea, blasting the radio, convertible tops down and being real silly. The young guys would have their hot cars all shiny looking for someone to drag race, go to the highway have their race and return. There were other places where a place in the next town had a fast narrow road with a quick bump they called thrill hill as when you picked up speed and hit this bump you would fly through the air for about ten feet, thus thrill hill. This was in nearby Bridgewater, Ma.

Here we go again with another job in my early life. This was fun as I was starting to grow as an adult and somehow find my way. My job was in Bradlees Department store. No, not the store itself but the luncheonette inside of it as many people in the mall would come for lunch, coffee breaks and also the folks at the beauty salon next door to the luncheonette. OK, my job was not fantastic but a job anyway. Lots of pretty girls came in there as I was a short order cook and at times cleaned off the tables and very frequently would mingle with the customers. They even put me in charge at times. How stupid were they hah. On Friday and Saturday evenings just before closing all of my delinquent friends would come in to wait for me and make a lot of noise and I would have to give them soda's and treats!

We had one very pretty girl who worked there with us. Her name escapes me now but she was a knock out! She went to a Catholic school and thought we were all "hoods" I can't understand why she thought that? My boss was pretty cool! He thought he could hypnotize us about several things but he found one area to gather our attention! He said he could hypnotize us to look through a paper cup and see girls naked. We fell for that and immediately asked to see our Catholic girl there but that never materialized! It was a fun place to work. I eventually got a few of my friends to work there with me so the fun really escalated in that environment!

There was a pretty girl next door in the beauty salon name Cheryl Ewing. I really liked her a lot as she and I became friends but nothing materialized accept that later, when I went into the Military she wrote me often and I lost track of her but I would love to see her again and share the news of our friends she knew that worked there. Some have died in Viet Nam and she was such a nice person the connection would be wonderful.

My first car was a 1951 Chevy as I really abused this car. I had no right even having a driver's license and I will be the first to admit that. I would let anyone use the car and forget who had it last. After it was beat up I would have my Dad tune it up and he would say where did all these beer cans come from? I would say you know how these teenagers can be. I don't know! After he fixed the car off I would go destroying it again. It wasn't that I was ungrateful or not. The fact that I was young and immature and not sure what I was doing in life as I was a confused teenager.

The Beatles are here! Yes the Beatles came to Boston and stayed in the hotel near Boston Garden and also while they were here their movie "Hard Days Night" was playing at the sky view Drive en out Door Theater in Brockton. So my friend Danny and I drove our bicycles and snuck in the back gate. We went through peoples yards to make our break into the rear of the out door theater. So we saw the Beatles on the screen as everyone was absolutely crazy there. This was Just a great experience, for Danny and me. This was probably the last time I road a bicycle as a teenager and yet so memorable.

There were numerous times when we had gone to these drive in theaters during those days as we would stack several friends in the trunk and after getting inside let them out! This was scary especially if there was a long line or a cop near by. Later, the movie theaters started to charge so much money for a car load so that eliminated hiding people in the trunk and took the fun away from us. There are not many of these theaters available anymore, progress you know!

Baseball, basketball or any sports were not an option for me as working part time going through high school gave me money to purchase clothes, and spending money for the weekends. As I look back, I should have been stronger and had the vision of being competitive as I learned later in life. I should have played sports, all sports and I should have buckled down and worked at my grades in high school. Going into the military at a young age and being sent to foreign countries was really not good for me as I was too young. In high school I didn't take part in clubs or go to proms or anything concerning school. I guess I was quite rebellious and lonely as well. I did very little dating until after getting out of the military.

Many of my friends had gone into the military as Viet Nam was in a dangerous state. I remember my friend Danny Goodwin and I would talk about our future and both of us very confused. He later went into the Marine Corp with my friend Roy. Most of my friends were in different branches of the Military but everyone looked to serve at some point.

I also felt that considering the Military was a challenge to the unknown and a step into adulthood.

I sacrificed my last three months of high school and went in the military early. I later would catch up and accomplished my high school diploma later as well as time spent at   Northeastern University not to mention the trade schools and military schools for further education later. If I had not left, I surely would have gotten into trouble which could have marked me forever in a negative way. Yes, I have regrets and missed out on so much in high school and built up letter writing with friends and girlfriends for a long while. I guess you could say the teenage years affect everyone differently but despite all of that I had turned out ok.

Chapter Five

Korea Service

In December, 1964 I decided to enter the military service. Yes, this was a tough time to consider something like this, but the way we were all brought up in those days, every family member spent time in one of the military branches. It was *duty, honor, and country*. So go early or go later, but at some point I would be called, as those were the draft years.

This decision was based on having made poor choices, always trying to fit in with friends and being so confused. I believed that entering into the military would probably force me to grow up. The problem was I had joined the Naval Reserves and went only to monthly meetings. I was a poor navy guy. I went through their two-week basic training course, and on their two-week cruise. Well, it wasn't really a cruise; we swabbed decks, and chipped paint on a tender at Quonset Point, Rhode Island. Some Cruise! I then started skipping meetings and the navy was just not for me. Because I missed too many meetings they were forcing me onto active duty for four years. I asked if I could go to another branch and they said, "Son, you have five days to make a change." So I went to the Marine Corps but they told me I would be on active duty for four years. The air force said four years. The army said three years; I said, "That will be fine." I asked for an easy job, like driving a jeep. Wow, was I stupid! I ended up in Artillery and Infantry.

I went in the army right after Christmas, with the dreaded bus-ride to Fort Dix, New Jersey for basic training. The ride was boring and very long. We arrived around three a.m. in the reception barracks. This is where the fun started. Our new drill sergeant marched onto the bus and put the fear of the Almighty in us, as we were all scared to death. We carried linen, blankets, and pillows, along with our little traveling bag, jokingly called an "AWOL bag," and went to the barracks and made up our bunks. Then just over an hour later, which was about four-thirty a.m., the drill sergeant came in yelling and banging on the bunks, and we all raced out of the barracks. To us inexperienced rookies, anyone in an army uniform was boss. Basic training lasted fourteen weeks, and then we continued on to advanced training.

I have many fresh memories from basic training, even to this day. When I look back I laugh, but things were not so funny then. A few men I remember from basic training were Bobby Rydel, Bobby Vinton, and Gary Lewis, who was the son of a famous actor. They were all in basic training at Fort Dix with me in my brigade. I would see them at sick call or other duty details. After four weeks we had a couple of days off, so we took a taxi to the air force beer hall for our 3.2% beer. We dressed up in "greens" with just a name tag, which was a pretty boring uniform. We sure had many laughs, though. Most of us got sloshed and returned to basic early Monday morning. The next highlight was having a northeast storm, or a "noreaster." Yes, we were out in the parking lot with army shovels – entrenching tools, as they are called. They looked like a child's shovel. That was terrible, when the accomplishment of shoveling snow seemed nearly impossible.

The next unique thing I saw was two guys fighting. They started upstairs in the barracks, went up and down the isles, then downstairs, then outside, then back inside, then in the latrine, and then upstairs again. It was the longest fight I ever saw, but afterwards they became super friends!

I have flashbacks of kitchen police duty, or KP. The mean old cooks really worked us to death for the long tedious hours we spent there. We had a group of friends; we were called the Terrible Ten. You had to fit in or you were in deep trouble. I was nominated to grab a guy who I actually liked, but the problem was, they thought he was not showering, so a GI shower was in the works.

But as I grabbed him he pulled a knife on me and then they really jumped him. They dragged him into the shower and took the hard long-bristled brushes and marked up his back. That was not pleasant to watch. There were also many blanket parties and other barracks's brawls.

On our graduation day from basic training, we had to turn in our M14 rifle. Apparently it didn't matter how clean it was; we learned very quickly that if you gave the armor clerk five dollars, your weapon was instantly "clean" and you were on your way to advanced training.

I went through the Light Vehicle Driving Course and it seemed those six weeks just flew by. There was more freedom and again several fist fights along the way. My strategy was—win a few and people will leave you alone. That did work out for me. The last few days were mind-boggling, as everyone agonized over whether they would be going to Vietnam (most were going there), or to Germany for three years, or Korea for a year. My orders were to go to Korea after my leave. I went home for a thirty-day leave, and then I flew out to the Oakland Army Terminal in Oakland, California.

Most of my friends from the service were either assigned to a different location, or they had just moved on after they completed their term in the army. I was then anxious to move onto another level in my life. My friend Francis was also home on leave. He was on his way to Germany and me to Korea. My mom took us to the airport, and I remember saying goodbye to her. The flight to California in a small propellor plane was very long and tiresome.

I arrived at Oakland Army Terminal along with five thousand other army and Marine Corps soldiers and a scattered few from the navy and air force. After a long, tedious check-in, we were given time off for nearly two days. There wasn't much to do, so a few soldiers and I went to San Francisco to see the sights. We went to Fisherman's Wharf, and the wax museum, and we saw the Golden Gate bridge. We took a ride on the trolley up that popular crooked street, and walked around the city, stopping at restaurants along the way. We even saw the well-known Haight-Ashbury district. There was nothing to see there, in my opinion; we just went there because of the popularity of it back east. There was one thing that stood out, though. There was a group of what I thought, in my naivety, were ladies, but I was quickly informed that they were men dressed up as women. I could not comprehend what I saw or why such a thing would ever happen. I remained confused for a while about that. The time off went quickly as we returned back to Oakland Army Terminal.

Our ship, a large naval ship, was the largest I had ever seen. I could not believe it was floating! There were sergeants with bull horns giving us all sorts of orders. First we were sectioned off into groups, then assigned a roster number. We were told before boarding to turn in an amnesty box—any weapons, alcohol, or anything illegal. Then there were barrels that we were told to put all aerosol cans, shaving cream, and cologne into. So we lost our favorite cologne. Before we left, there was a band playing music on the dock, and men yelling and cheering from the ship to their loved ones, and very soon that large heap of metal started to move and we were on our way. We sailed by Alcatraz, and under the Golden Gate Bridge, and before long you could no longer see land. We were to go to Hawaii, refuel, exchange cargo and personnel, and then head west.

The first five hundred men who boarded were selected to do kitchen police duty, or KP, all the way to Korea, and I was one of them. Since there were more than five thousand guys on the ship, there seemed to be a continuous chow line. We had three shifts of KP, but when you were off there wasn't much to do anyway. I tried an "adult" thing – I read a few books, which was a new experience for me, and for some reason I was proud of myself for doing that.

The total journey to Korea would take about thirty days or so. A few days into the trip we arrived in the Port of Honolulu. I couldn't get off the ship or even go outside. All I could do was look out a port hole and smell the pineapples. That was my one and only experience in Hawaii. We set sail once again in about four hours. Apparently we picked up naval passengers and some civilians, and we were planning on stopping when we were out at sea in a day or so to have a Naval Funeral. They had picked up a naval officer, and sure enough, a big ceremony had taken place with a twenty one gun salute of cannons and rifles, the remains dropped overboard, and a bugle playing Taps. All in all, it was quite an experience to have witnessed. *That naval officer must have been someone important for all that,* I thought.

The journey continued, the days going by very slowly, and then we approached the 38th parallel, the nautical line we crossed on our way to Japan. The 38th parallel has some sort of special meaning for the navy. Here at the 38th parallel, the ship stopped, and several naval and army personnel decided to dive into the ocean for a swim! *I don't think so,* I thought, *not with the entire unknown in the ocean.* The main point for this stop was a celebration ceremony for crossing the 38th parallel. The naval personnel had dressed up like Romans, complete with costumes and crowns on their heads. They lined up the army and had us take off our shirts. The next thing they did for this ceremony and initiation to the 38th parallel was throw gooey sugar and coffee grounds on our chest. I didn't have any hair on my chest, so it wasn't a big deal for me. It was a very hot day, so some opted for a quick swim. I just went to the showers. No swimming with sharks for me.

The journey on this large ship was full of anxiety and became more stressful by the minute. Soldiers were sleeping in stairwells, hallways, even on deck. The birthing area was cramped with bunks stacked six high with only a few inches between bunk mates, never mind the poor shower condition. But most of the journey was over and soon we would land in Yokohama, Japan. Once again, only sergeants could leave the ship. There wasn't much to see from the ship, just a lot of Japanese shipping personnel in the port. This is where the army and navy men heading for Vietnam got off. The remainder of the ship would continue on to Korea. The ship left once again after a few hours and now there were only a few days until we made it to Korea.

After a long grueling journey on this naval ship carrier, we were anxious to leave. The journey from Yokohama, Japan was not that long and we were very edgy looking into our personal new beginnings in Korea. The ship was so large that we were unable to go all the way into the Port of Inchon, Korea. Therefore small boats, I believe our naval boats shuttled us from the large ship to the port on this foggy misty day.

We carried our big duffle bags down the ramps stuffed like sardines in the open boat as all were quiet, nervous, and wondering what we were in for, in this new country we were entering. For the first time I could hear the Korean language and it did not sound friendly as I remember. We carried our baggage for what felt like miles but probably not very far. We went around a corner and there was our new ride; there stood a train, as it looked like someone had kept it under a blanket for 100 years. It was loud and sounded like it was ready to fall apart. Never the less we loaded onto it. The seats were small ripped and dirty looking. The car had smelled like no smell you have ever experienced before. This train was so dirty and smelly that you were worried about touching anything at all. The windows were smudged with unknown fingerprints and filth.

It was not very long as we would slowly leave the port of Inchon en-route to Camp Casey our reception processing point for the U.S. Army. There we would find out exactly where we would be stationed for the next miserable year. The train had bumped and choked and made all sorts of noises as it slowly developed speed or so call speed. There were no conversations as the unknown had scratched each others mind. Some scared and young like me and others who had done this before. That would be seasoned soldiers I am speaking of.

The sun came out and broke through the fog quickly as our ride took us through the new land. All eyes would constantly look at all sorts of scenery. This was not like a tour but a learning process entering a new culture. It was not long before my eyes had seen mud huts with naked children running around and sometimes and older person. The women would carry supplies in a large basket balanced on their heads. Some times laundry and chunks of fuel cubes or charcoal.

This was all so much for this immature eighteen year old from the streets of Brockton to handle but on the other hand other friends of mine were on their way to Viet Nam where their lives were definitely instantly in danger. So there was no real complaining knowing that. We were tired of this train and the thirty days on the ship so only too glad to finally calm down as we were finally our destination at Camp Casey came shortly. Being in Korea was a continued education for me. I was a rookie, and hated every second of that nomenclature. We now had arrived at Camp Casey, not far from the DMZ, or the Demilitarized Zone, maybe fifty miles or so, and this was the in-processing point. I then received shots, supplies, our venereal disease classes and a small introduction about being stationed in South Korea. The next thing was to be given our assignment to our unit for the next thirteen months. Another soldier and I were going to the same unit, so we rode together on a three-quarter-ton truck. We were then assigned to the 6th battalion, 80th artillery, or "Camp Knox," as they called it.

There were more sights to see as our trip took us through the country side and we went through so many small villages with so much to look at. My driving days were over, as I was assigned to an artillery battery. I became an assistant gunner on the 155mm howitzer. My job was to fire it, clean the breech, take it apart, and make sure the charges were set correctly, as well as the primer. I also had to spread the trails of the howitzer, set up and lift the heavy plates and hump ammo. It seemed no matter where you looked there was hard and heavy work.

We were very close to the DMZ. This was an area between North and South Korea where no military action was allowed. We were constantly on alert for field duty, so we were constantly training for the real deal. Meanwhile,

Vietnam was in full combat. We received the Stars and Stripes newspaper, giving us all the dreadful daily death reports of our fallen comrades. While in the field I soon began to sleep with my weapon in my sleeping bag. Pretty much everything else went in the sleeping bag too, because the farmers and Korean civilians would steal anything that wasn't bolted down. I soon joined the others, as it became common to count the days before we went back to the states.

On regular field operations it was very common to sit in the rice paddies and eat our chow. The problem was the farmers and starving Koreans would come nearby and watch us and hope we would give them our food. They even had wood bowls ready to take our food from us. That ruined my appetite fast. When we went to the line to clean our trays and silverware, the Koreans would try to get the leftovers from the barrel of garbage and the mess sergeant would hit them and kick them away. He was another nasty American.

I took guard duty very seriously over there; I had to because of the threat of war. My M14 rifle was always ready, and I walked guard with a shotgun ready at all times, no matter how cold it was.

One day there was a flood next to our compound, and a nearby bridge had been washed away, along with many mud huts. There was so much damage to the village. We were helping the civilians across the river to safety on pulleys and cables, and as they got off the ropes they were stealing our gear! I could not believe my eyes. We had a clear-cut mission to save them even though we were soaked, hungry and exhausted. This was my first indoctrination to the locals.

There was always guard duty either at the compound, in towers, on the corners, or walking a post by the barbed wire. When we were in the field, it was so incredibly dark, you could not see three feet ahead of you. We would refer to the enemy soldier as "Joe." Everything was Joe this, or Joe that, but that was not our only concern. In the rice paddies in the field late at night you could hear over a loud speaker a woman's voice echoing through the valley. I think her name was Kim, and she would call some soldiers by their names and try to get them to come to North Korea, promising the men they would be taken care of and get anything they wanted. From time to time some GI, who was weak, would take the bait and desert, and never be heard from again. I would get this eerie feeling every time I heard the voice late at night, and when I think about it now I still get queasy.

Every morning we would have guard mount, and all the guards would dress as sharp as possible, with their weapon clean. The officer of the day would ask questions, and pick one soldier as "The Man." This meant you didn't have to walk guard duty at all and got an extra day off..I won this award many times through the course of my thirteen months there.

We worked with Koreans from the Korean army. They were called KATUSAs, which stood for Korean Augmentation to the United States Army. Some of them were respectful and came from good Korean families, while others were drug addicts and we felt we could not trust them. On one occasion I was on guard duty and spotted one of these Koreans walking the post next to me, getting a fix through the fence from a civilian Korean. I reported him and he got caught with a briefcase full of drugs. I was glad he was gone; he was trouble even for his own fellow Koreans.

Christmas and New Year's Day was lonesome, cold and very depressing. I wrote a lot of letters home to Mom and Dad, and as many old girlfriends as I could think of. There was nothing better than a great letter with some perfume on it. I would like to thank all of them for writing me while I was there. Their letters meant so much to me at the time, and helped me keep my sanity. It was not real combat as it was in Vietnam, but yet there still were shootings from time to time, as they would pick off a guard once in a while. And most of the time we had no ammunition. The air force ran a program on the radio, known as AFKN, or the air force Korean network. They played oldies but goodies, and there would be requests for certain songs from girlfriends and wives back in the States, sending these requests to their soldiers.

On New Year's Day I was just walking around and I said to myself, *everyone is drunk, including the Battalion Commander. What a great time for the enemy to invade us.* Meanwhile our Colonel Battalion Commander had volunteered our entire unit to go to Vietnam. We all thought he was nuts, but he wanted us to be in combat. He was a POW in Korea and I think he wanted payback. They were looking for volunteers to go airborne and I volunteered, but nothing had happened with that. Who would think that many years later I would become a paratrooper?

We ran and stayed in shape, and had bayonet training every day. That's one of the themes of the 7th Infantry Division, or "The Bayonet Division."

They would say, "What's the spirit of the Bayonet?"

"Kill!" was always the response.

I sent home Korean pool sticks, paintings to my mother, and a camera for my sister. I even bought a suit made in the village, but I never had a chance to wear it.

Once in a while a North Korean would come over the lines and get shot in the street of the main village. It seemed there was always something going on. I remember seeing Koreans walking down the street and ahead of them were Turkish soldiers. The Koreans were absolutely petrified of them. They would run to the opposite side of the street to avoid them.

The Korean KATUSAs and the Korean army is disciplined beyond what you could imagine. There is incredible respect for the higher-ups, like the corporals and sergeants. One day in the mess hall a Korean sergeant came into the dining facility and one of his soldiers did not get up and give him a seat. He slapped the daylights out of him! Another day outside in the mess line a soldier did not salute his corporal and this corporal beat him so severely they had to carry him off.

The night club situation in Korea was quite exciting. The villages made a fortune on OB beer. When you went into any club there would be thirty to forty girls in there. Many were very pretty and dressed like American girls and would even use American names as well. We felt like Elvis Presley when we walked into any bar. They would attack you! On one occasion I saw the girls fight over a GI and one girl cut the other girl's hand severely with a butcher's knife. These were ladies of the night, so they were disowned by their families, but they made a fortune off GIs.

During one of my first trips into the village, a fellow soldier brought me and showed me around. We rode in the Kimchi buses, walked the streets, and went to the bars. But he was very nasty to the Koreans, and he even kicked an innocent girl who was selling pretzels into a ditch! There were drainage ditches on both sides of the streets in the Korean villages. Some GIs were respectful while others were hateful, and these hateful men gave most Americans a bad name.

We were always giving donations to orphanages, so I decided to see one, and that was so sad to witness. There were hundreds of children that looked like American kids but were shipped away to these orphanages because the families had disowned them. When you looked at a cute little blond girl and hear her speak fluent Korean, it was sad to see. I remember wondering what would happen to all these kids.

I met this black man named Will. He was a boxer and quite comical. He was big, and a very good boxer. He and I would work out and train just for the exercise. This was a routine for a few weeks. I played basketball with him and had a chance to play on the division team, but my first sergeant would not let me leave the unit to attend. Will and I took off one day over the weekend. Now, we didn't just go to the village—we went cross-country and really met natives in the mud huts away from the villages. Luckily Will spoke Korean fairly well. That was an education, to see the A-frames they carried, and how they fermented cabbage to make kimchi. The farmers in the mud huts would heat their little homes with a charcoal briquette from underneath the structure somehow, and many Koreans would die each year from carbon dioxide from this type of heating system.

We also witnessed a funeral. They would bury someone depending on how rich they were; the more money the deceased had, the higher up he was placed on the mountainside. They would drink and get drunk and carry the deceased in a very colorful coach. It had ornate handles on each side, as if they were carrying a king or something. They would drink, chant, and sway the casket coach from side to side until they reached their special plot on the mountainside. While on duty during a field exercise on the DMZ was very weird. We could see the North Koreans looking at us, since there wasn't that much distance between us. We were always wondering if war would start while we were still there, or even while we were sleeping.

My time in Korea was soon coming to an end; I would be returning to Camp Casey shortly, to out-process and go home. The week before I left someone stole a one hundred dollar money order from me, as well as some film from pictures I had taken there. Can you believe, eleven years later, someone sent it back to me at my address in Brockton, Massachusetts! There was no note, just the money order and the film. Tell me that's not a strange thing!

The day before I was due to leave, I broke out in hives from worrying about being stuck in Korea. I got so nervous, but when I woke up in the morning I was fine. So I made the long trip home…only to find my dog Ginger had died shortly before I had returned home. I looked for friends but they were all gone into the military. There was not much to think about back home. It was time to realize, *I'm older, I belong to the military, so try to think about anything but Brockton.* I was on Main Street when high school graduation services had just completed, and I felt sad when I heard horns toot, and saw kids celebrating. That could have been me.

I knew I had made a mistake leaving school early. Although I later made corrections by returning to school, it just wasn't the same. I had never gone to a prom or anything special. That was my terrible loss. The teenage memories were starting to drift away. At least I was still able to have a little fun before I was due to leave again, like going to dances on the weekends, collecting nickels and dimes so a drunk near a bar could purchase GI Q's for us, throwing water balloons, cruising the drag downtown, and chasing the girls. Vietnam was heavy duty at the time, and I still had a chance of going there. I would soon be going to Fort Ord, California for the remainder of my enlistment, which was something I was looking forward to.

Chapter Six

_____

California Dreaming

At Fort Ord, California, I was back in transportation, driving a jeep again. I was in this unit called CDCEC, or Combat Developments Command, Experimental Command. The base where I was stationed was about forty miles from San Francisco. Early Monday morning I would take a bus with many others to a place called Fort Hunter Liggett Military Installation. I would stay there all week and drive for officers or pilots, then return back to Fort Ord for the weekend. That was not bad at all.

I had a year and a half to go on my enlistment and Vietnam was still very much a possibility for me, but I never went. Call it fate, call it luck, however you want to put it, but it was not meant to be for me. If I had been chosen, I would have gone, and I would have been proud to serve.

I had many friends and I enjoyed my duty in California. Then things became very eventful. There were many good and positive things and definitely uneasy, sad things as well. I had a friend name Lanny. He had a Corvette, a 1965 Stingray. It was the most beautiful car. Lanny and I hit it off immediately. He and his wife, Rita, would ask me to their apartment for dinner or up to where they were from in Lodi, California, for the weekend.

Lanny had a problem with the commander on base. He had called him into his office and asked, "How does a private afford a Corvette, and I, a colonel, have only a regular car?" Lanny told him he had worked for it, and purchased the car before he joined the military. The colonel never liked him because of a small thing like that.

I dated Lanny's sister when I went up to Lodi, and on another occasion we went with Lanny and Rita, and two other girls, in his Corvette. We went to the beach in the morning and then to the mountains in the afternoon, walking under the redwoods in two feet of snow, in the same day. I had a blast with the two girls I was with.

He used to let me drive the Corvette all the time. That was so cool and so much fun. I have always loved those cars since, and now have a miniature collection of the last fifty years of Corvettes.

I connected with Lanny many years later when I was considering working out there in California, but it didn't work out and I returned home. Some years later I learned he died in a motorcycle accident. I was sad to hear of that happening.

While I was out there in California, I thought, *what about Disney land?!* But I couldn't find anyone to go with, so I decided to hitchhike there. I hadn't gotten very far from base when a car stopped and a guy I didn't know that well in my unit offered me a ride. He happened to live close to Disneyland! We had a long three-day weekend and I was able to not only drive there for free, but I also got a ride back. Plus I got a complete tour of Hollywood and still had a chance to go through Disneyland. I took pictures and had a great time.

I had numerous friends out there. Some were Mexican guys who were trying to get their citizenship. They served in the military for three years and were good soldiers, so I went to federal court in San Francisco and sponsored them. I did this twice and I felt very comfortable doing that.

On another occasion I went to Carmel, Big Sur, and Monterey, and saw some great sights on the tour. There was a funeral for one of the Hell's Angels while I was there and it made the news. I went to Cannery Row, sent home some salt water taffy, saw a lot of sea lions, and scuba divers, and was starting to like California. Having serious relationships, though, was tough with little money and no car. Even so, I did manage to have fun with the young ladies from time to time.

I remember meeting a girl on the beach and spending quality time with her, only to never see her again. We had a great time together, but with no car and no way to keep in contact, this became another happy memory.

The boys got restless and decided to go as a group to Santa Cruz, and the boardwalk loaded with fun. We hitchhiked down I-5, and can you believe we got a ticket from a state trooper for hitchhiking! He cut us no slack and we had to pay a fifteen dollar fine. When we got to Santa Cruz, though, I quickly forgot about that ticket until it was time to pay it. We chipped in and rented a cottage by the boardwalk and spent all the time on the beach, chasing the young women. I met this beautiful young blond and all she wanted to do was ride the roller coaster. We road about twenty times. I liked her a lot as well but we lost contact, and that memory faded away too.

There were incredible problems with drugs while I was there, but I was strong and it only affected me when I had to witness a close friend struggling with his drug problems. We worked during the week at the Hunter Liggett Reservation. That was brutal. The weather was hot, close to one hundred degrees every day. I also remember looking in my rear view mirror and watching the tarantulas spin like quarters down the road after hitting them with the jeep. I once got stopped by the military police for driving with my shirt off and got what they refer to as an Article 15. I finally got it removed from my record ten years later.

In Hunter Liggett, we had eight-man barracks. The soldiers had been so lax that they started separating; for example, the cowboys in one barracks, the blacks in another, the white guys in another, and so on. The racial problems had gotten worse for a while with fights and burning crosses, but eventually things got under control with a new first sergeant on board. He instituted a small shack called "The Red Dog." This is where, after-hours, we could buy candy, beer, pizza, chips and hot dogs. This helped to calm everyone's nerves and finally bring some peace. This first sergeant had a picture of Lana Turner (I think that was her name!) on his desk. He was real cool and had a MG sports car and was sharp all the time.

I decided to go home on leave. I was hoping to buy a car and bring it back to California. Once I returned home this proved to be an impossible task. Most of my friends were gone, either in training or in the service somewhere, or going to Vietnam soon. I went back to California with no car, but I stopped at Camp Pendleton to see my best friend Danny. He was in Marine Corps' advanced training, and he was going to Vietnam. He was an anchor of a friend. Tough as they come, but he was so brainwashed by the Marines training. I never gave a thought about his safety. There was something in his eyes that I can't explain, some sort of strength that made him seem invincible. I wished him well and wrote to him as often as I could.

I drove for a captain one time, and picked him up at the Hacienda, where the officers stayed. We then went to the helicopter pad. He was a pilot and we were to ride around in the chopper all day. That was so cool. I had never ridden in a helicopter. He was a hot dog, and flew straight at some cows in a field and scared them half to death. The cows would fall down, and although it was funny to see, it really was not a humane thing to do.

Around the holidays, the Hacienda had a Christmas show with the Lou Christi Minstrels performing for us. Not very far from this location we had a flood and I was driving a jeep. Suddenly, as I was driving where I though the road still was, it just disappeared! It was washed out from the flood. The jeep tipped and I jumped out and the jeep was totally under water. That was tough to explain when I returned without the jeep, but luckily the storm helped support my story.

At this point luck had switched gears for me. I was asked by two friends to go and have a few beers in King City, which was not too far from the reservation. I was going to go but changed my mind at the last minute. In a few hours we heard the news: the two guys I was supposed to go with drove through a railroad crossing and got hit by a train and died instantly. I was shaking, thinking that I could have been there.

I made a call home as I normally did on the weekends. This time it was different. My mom was not sounding right. I asked her what was wrong. She told me that my best friend Danny had died in Vietnam. I was so upset. I found this awful news just added onto the other things happening around me, and it was just too much to deal with. I didn't have anyone around to discuss anything with. This affected me for a long while. The last time I saw Danny at Camp Pendleton, I hadn't wanted to think that I would never see him again.

My best friend Daniel Eric Goodwin had perished in Viet Nam in 1967. This was so hard for me to deal with because as I had suspected that the possibilities were there to have it happen was so foreign to me. I was stationed in the Us Army at Combat Developments Command Experimental Command at Fort Ord, California when the news had broken to all. I had not served in Viet Nam as during the War I was on the DMZ Demilitarized Zone in Korea bordering North and South Korea. My unit was volunteered each month and after I returned to the states and at Fort Ord, I then volunteered once again but did not go. I guess my Mom's prayers were just too strong for the Pentagon! Through the years I had felt guilty not going there to serve but after being on the DMZ and spending my time serving in 13 foreign countries the quilt had left me especially when I had accomplished so much being a professional soldier and performing very honorable Military assignments in special operations.

Many friends and acquaintances through the years had either been stateside and were able to attend Danny's funeral and ceremony's during that dreadful time as well as going to the Wall at Washington DC to honor there as well. Danny's grave site was in New Hampshire as I visited his Grave after I returned home. Billy Brown and I had hitchhiked up there to visit and pay our respects. I can't remember why we had no car but we made it there and back.

Danny and all of our eastside friends had attended East Junior High School and after many friends got together they found a way to honor Danny by erecting a monument in front of East Junior High School and call it Daniel E Goodwin Park. There was a ceremony and dedication and a rock with brass plate put there in honor of Danny. I was able to attend that day. His memory will always be close to me forever!

Three weeks later up at Fort Ord, another friend wanted me to go to his home in San Jose and meet with his wife's sister for a date. I saw a picture of her and I really wanted to go, but again, changed my mind. He begged me to come but I chose not to at that time. He was on his motorcycle and got hit by a truck head-on and died instantly. He was only nineteen years old, with a wife and a young baby. That was very sad. And again, I could have been with him.

After these two major incidents, I experienced more turmoil from yet another friend's accident, and several overdoses on drugs by people I knew. The drug problem got so severe that eventually people started getting arrested. All I wanted was to be transferred to Fort Devens, Massachusetts, because by that point my mom and dad were ill and I wanted to be near them. The transfer was approved, but I had to pay my way home on that deal.

A friend of mine, a Mexican boxer, and I had put together our own private investigation on the drug problem. We knew all about the high-ranking officers involved. We submitted our findings to the congressmen, and we were told to deny everything we had reported. If I did this, I would be granted my transfer. If not, they would fabricate untruths and I would be put in the stockade. I said, *fine,* and off I went to Fort Devens. I found out thirty-nine years later, when I contacted my old boxer friend, that all those officers eventually got caught and went to jail. So I did some good in the process.

In 1967 I was stationed at Combat Development Command Experimental Command –Fort Ord, California. This was a special assignment that I had many interesting experiences with. One of my favorite stories is this one about my professional fighter friend, Leno Puente's from Socorro, Texas. Leno came from a poor Mexican family that he had five other Brothers and one Beautiful Sister! Their family had a regulation ring in their back yard so all male members of his family were good fighters and they all had a handle of Karate as well. Leno was basically a quiet person and concentrated on his goals, being a Black Belt in Karate as well as his Professional Boxing background kept him in great physical condition. So his sister was well protected as you may guess! I became friends with Leno and worked out with him often at the athletic complex on Fort Ord.

I must tell of this situation I had witnessed there. Leno was working out shadow boxing in the ring as I held a glove for him and I was going to shoot hoops but then we had some visitors. Three black men came to the edge of the ring and one guy said to him "man I can kick your butt" leno said I am just working out here, I don't want any trouble. The guy was persistent and repeated his big mouth and finally Leno just wanted to work out but had to get rid of this guy first! So, he said ok put some gloves on! The guy did and hopped into the ring and jumped around like he was going to do something and could not put a glove on Leno, finally after a minute and a half Leno knocked him out! The second friend said hey man that's my friend there I can whip him so I am definitely going to whip you. The same scenario again and less than a minute he knocked this guy out now Leno said I am not happy you ruined my workout as he gestured to the third guy and the third guy said hey man I want no trouble either. That was quite the experience to witness.

I talked to Leno 45 years later on the telephone and he and I had talked and he remembered me like it was yesterday but we never made plans to re-unite but it was nice to be able to speak with him. He worked as a guard for the prison system in Texas and ready to retire but continued his boxing and brought many young boxers from that area to television fights on HBO but unfortunately I was not able to see any of them, but I am sure they took place because he was a class act!

I stayed at Fort Devens for my last three months in the military. I bought a brand new car, a 1968 Camaro, turquoise with a black vinyl top and 350 horse-power with four speeds – that should get me in trouble, right? I miss California, but the sad events were tough to deal with.

I am now facing civilian life as I was just discharged from Military service. My first mistake facing the world was to spend the money I had saved for three years on a new camaro. Yes, I needed a car but really nothing like this. It was a beautiful Turquoise blue with a black vinyl top with chrome scoops on the hood with a powerful 350 engine. It was an eye catcher and surely would get me in trouble fast. Its probably a good time for me to get a job now don't you think?

I started off with a job at Lucy Shoe Company in Bridgewater, Massachusetts. It was an easy job of picking orders to ship out. The pay was not good so after a month I found another job a bit closer to home at the Fox borough Company in East Bridgewater, Massachusetts. This was a step up with more money, dress casual and a nice environment as there were a lot of young people there. I was still running tight for car payments so I was looking for something that would pay more and give me some freedom beyond the car expense.

After spending three months there I was offered two separate potential job opportunities. One was to work in Boston at the largest privately owned paint store in the country. This job was word of mouth from a friend of my Dad's. The other job was learning the printing business also in Boston, at the Boston Globe as this was an opportunity through my Mom's connection. I thought about my current situation and felt, let me try the paint store as I'm familiar with construction and maybe this will be good.

I went in to Boston for an interview and found the store as there was no parking and the busy Boston life would surely be an adventure was my first impression. I met with Mr. John A. Johnson the owner. He was a remarkable man as he was a Harvard graduate, as well as an officer in the (intelligence field) in the Army. He was not crazy about the Army but he was a Veteran and served his country. His families were all, from Norway as the family business originated in the back bay of Boston as horse and buggy had got them around but later earned their way to a store on Newbury Street where they are still very influential and prosperous.

I had a short interview with Mr. Johnson as he introduced me to my future co-workers and his three sons'. I had a tour of the store as" unique" and different was just touching the surface. I got the green light to start work on Monday as I would be riding with this little guy, a hippy to learn the route and

THE EASTSIDE KID

job. I was fascinated on how he knew the whole city. I fit in like a glove and through the years became very close to this family.

Mr. Johnson had done some unforgettable kind deeds from a boss; for me that will always remain special to my heart. When my Dad passed away he made a special trip to come to the wake as this was something very difficult for him to do but he did so because of me. One other occasion he let me take some time off to go to the baseball tryouts at Fallen Field in Roslindale, Massachusetts for the Boston Park League.

I went to the tryouts and did very well as I hit a few long shots about 380 feet but on the other side of the coin ,not so good for my fielding defensive skills, as a lot of time had passed since I last played. This was a much bigger stage than little league.

Little did I know that 35 years later I would be playing baseball at 60 plus years old and playing at Fallen Field again but now, still hitting the ball well but a more complete player as I became an ace on most teams I pitch for? This past summer was just that time when I pitched there at Fallen Field providing a two hitter for my team, along with 7 strikeouts and no walks. So I came a long way as the later chapters will explain.

The club I was trying for was made up of relatives and their team was all set so, I wasted time being there trying to make a club that had already filled their roster "but I had fun that morning playing baseball again. And the temporary baseball itch or fix was temporarily out of my system. I was back to work shortly. My family as I felt the Johnson's were; had always been supportive, the sons Robert ,David, and Nonny just like Dad happy go lucky, joking much of the time, but very hard workers. They would be after work treating the guys to beers, pizza etc on numerous occasions,. There were many trips then even Mr. Johnson would accompany us in the "zone" the Washington street red light district. This was another late night staying in on one of the leather couches in the back of the store. We all went to a bachelor's party in Revere together for one of the employee's. That worked out well, we had a brawl there in the nightclub. I'm not sure what happened now. Some of the guys hung out at the Kentucky Tavern a men's bar across the street but that doesn't exist today. There was another bar where they shot darts as a good crowd would come regularly there. One night, I won't mention names, but one of the bosses son's and an employee from the art store left the bar, but came back and streaked through the bar and out into the alley. That was so funny.

I started off like most of the help as delivering paint supplies, and artist supplies around the city. This was great especially at 9 am when there were thirty young college girls hitchhiking to class on Commonwealth Avenue or Beacon Street trying to get in class. It seemed, I always had room in the van to offer a ride, how could I refuse thirty pretty nice smelling beautiful young women. Girls filled in my van like sardines going to class. That was fun. I had a lot of speed dating in those days, as my memory comes to life. I had a basement apartment on Commonwealth Avenue two blocks from the Boston Common. This was a very great area but the hot summer nights leaving the window open was not always a great idea as you could see the feet moving by the sidewalk outside but a nice one room studio.

The Johnson's took care of all of their help, I can't stress that enough. You had a problem they were ready to help; Now as I mentioned, about maturity and making terrible decisions from time to time oh let's see," many mistakes concerning me". I take all of the blame. I had broken all the records in history. I got hired five times, and then got fired five times in seven years.

I left there to go to a less of a job, a really stupid job and always realized that leaving Johnson's was a mistake two minutes after the decision. Mr. .Johnson had taken me back so often but there had to be a limit for me being so spacey. I have absolutely no explanation about any of my decision process accept I was consumed by problems outside of work. I felt those problems were too severe and personal to open up for discussion. I decided to speak about the Johnson's because as they have been such a forceful emotion within me all through the years .I have so much to remember while in their employ; I would play basketball with Bobby and David and some other co-workers as their names escape my writers block but we had fun playing basketball after work I think this is where they had decided to call me "the jumper" Sure, I need another nick name hah.

When I had done well I had always wondered if they heard about one of my positive late in life accomplishments or not. My baseball book as I wanted was to share experiences and allow you as a reader to absolutely know John F DeCosta "The Eastside Kid" from all directions and with this yet another angle. The best way for me to describe my employment there is to sum it up as I had a chance in a lifetime at the fork in the road and I went left when "most all of me" wanted to turn right. I made wrong choices and I am very sorry for that. I was immature, and lost my personal dignity for a while. I am sure, they would be proud of me, if they knew how I turned out. I was young, dumb and made terrible choices but I have survived and faced the music.

My fault or wrong doing has been re-paid emotionally, as I am now the proper person that I always wanted to be. Yes, once again I have to thank the Johnson's for inspiring me and forcing me to challenge myself. I had left on not so good terms with them as I had regretted that all of these years. I should have been more accountable during that time.

During a troubled time in my life a time of confusion , as I had changed jobs I worked for The South Shore Meat Packing Company- in Brockton, Ma another eastside job for me. On this note the families that owned and operated this company were friends of mine during my young growing years as well as my Brother Steve's association with the eldest son John. I was closer to Maureen and Louis D'Arpino. Mr. and Mrs. D'Arpino, I had known from church at St. Colman's so I was immediately drawn to their generosity in hiring me so I had to show appreciation, with hard work and loyalty.

I had known this family most of my life, as they were much respected in our community. My job there started inside as I had worked making hot dogs, hamburgers, loading and unloading trucks, working in the freezer but my favorite odd job was unloading the cattle beef, sounds funny but that was a great physical workout! Unloading the beef was usually after hours and something that you volunteered for so that's what I did. My partner in this was Joe Bulman another worker there that we had become friends and did this job together. It would take us about 2 hours as we got $20.00 to unload the tractor trailer of beef. There were quarters that weighed about 225 lbs a piece and hinds that weighed about 175 lbs so you would have a hook in one hand, wearing gloves lift the hind or quarter up and off the hook, carry it out of the tractor trailer and there would be a rail on the ceiling with hooks dangling and simply re-hook the beef onto that as you would slide inside of the large cooler. Your memory of the Rocky movie with Sylvester Stallone would give you a picture in your mind of this. After we finished it definitely felt as if you worked out with weights and as time went on you got so much stronger. This would have been great training for my baseball workouts!

My main job as I later earned while I was there was driving their big 20"trucks with a reefer. I would deliver beef and meats to; Bars, Nursing Homes, Sub shops, Restaurants, Schools, Hospitals, Diners and hotels. This job was right up my alley. I would go to Quincy, Weymouth and Boston on

Mondays and Wednesdays and Tuesdays and Thursdays I would go to New Bedford and Mansfield, then the best was the whole Cape Cod area on Fridays. Louis D'Arpino and Kerry Masefield the son in law-married to Maureen D'Arpino had given me this job and stood by me. I had been so appreciative for their efforts in helping me.

It was a long hard days work for me but I was happy withy my job. I was working sometimes 12 to 14 hours a day and returned many times after hours late in the evening after dark and go to Mr. and Mrs. D'Arpino home to turn in my keys, cash and receipts.

They were always cordial and nice to me.

On another occasion I had gathered meat hooks out on the loading dock to move inside to store-They are very sharp! We'll the hooks fell and caught my finger as the blood was gushing all over the place as I grabbed towels to stop the bleeding and a sales person took me to the hospital as I got a lot of stitches an of course I was then out of work and a job but later I had worked for the Federal Government as a carpenter/and painter for 7 years.

Civilian life definitely was not working out well for me. I soon looked into going back into the Military where life seemed to be way less complicated. In the Military you were responsible for yourself good or bad as your career is set in front of you with an abundance of opportunity to choose from. Each place you are stationed was in fact its own little world sheltered from the extremes of home grown fun back in your old neighborhood. I grabbed my rucksack and off toFort Lewis Washington I went.

In April 1975 I made my return back to active duty in the U.S.Army. Because I was out of the Military since 1967 I had to have a refresher basic training, then communications school, then to Parachute school then to Special Forces at Fort Devens, Mass- and Fort Bragg, North Carolina. The mini basic training was boring but a necessity. I then went to Fort Gordon, Georgia for communications school for four months as that was just a stepping stone for me. While I was there I met some Spanish guys and we played some baseball as they know baseball and how to play the game. That was a fun experience playing pick up games with my new friends. I maintained staying in shape because I knew that Jump school, was my next stop.

I arrived in Augusta Georgia late in the evening, so I went to a hotel and got a good night sleep because I knew I would be running and doing pushups for ever the next day. The cab driver said to me," you going to jump school" I said yes as I smiled. He was not smiling and said, "You are going to run your ass off" I said I know "thanks"

Before the training actually got heavily started we had an orientation at the main auditorium; this was an experience I will never forget! The auditorium was as quiet as a mouse. We were told to come to attention, then we heard someone running down the middle isle and all of us afraid to look or turn our heads but the Colonel went in front an ran up the stairs and did a hand stand and walked on his hands to the microphone and gave us an incredible speech. During his run to the stage the song "blood on the risers" was playing basically a song about a paratrooper who didn't make it and died! This all got our attention very well.

The song of Glory Glory halleluiah, as a paratrooper wash pushed out of an aircraft and got tangled up and naturally blood on his risers. All were overwhelmed there and definitely put you in the mood but many had quit right on the spot.

The next morning I arrived early and got assigned a number, equipment and duties to perform. Then after that the work started as well as harassment and introduction. From that point on no one was nice and all day long total harassment, pushups, beating your boots otherwise known as knee benders and pull-ups. We ran every where and the start of each day we would be lined up on the cables early o-dark 30 or otherwise known as 5; 30 am. Immediately we would have a personal inspection, then pull – ups on the pull up bar and then to the physical training sandpits. There was murder as unbelievable physical fitness took place.

We had about 400 persons in this class from all branches of the Military. Then after PT Physical Fitness we would do our daily 5 mile run. The instructors would look for anyone limping or any reason to kick you out of the class. Very strict school. As I said we started with 400 and graduated just a few over 100 soldiers.

I was disappointed to see so many quit for minute reasons. Many made up reasons of fake injuries some actually had broken bones but men like Marine Corp really disappointed me because they just got out of their basic training and were not in shape for this and the majority had quit the school and training.

One funny note was, we had 5 Navy Seals in or class as this was their last training activity before their special graduation in their special operations course. They were funny as many had trouble with the pushups and exercise they were doing one arm push ups and laughing at the instructors. I became friends with one of them, Gerald Dorick E-5-Navy Seals.

In this school there was a week of ground activities such as a wind machine, so you would experience being dragged by a parachute after landing on ground. Then, the next station would be the swing landing apparatus, to feel and be able to pull risers to turn parachute and land on the ground" parachute landing fall. Then next week was tower week as we experienced the 34' tower and again with the 250' tower. The 250' Tower was as close to jumping out of a plane as you can experience. I thought it was more dangerous!

Jump week was fun as we jumped out of three –C-130 Aircraft then a C-123 Aircraft and our favorite C-141 Jet as this was our night combat equipment jump a whole new experience for everyone! Many got sick on the aircraft. The next day was our last jump and our graduation ceremony. You must make all jumps or you don't graduate! It was as simple as that.

The last jump was on Friday morning but by time we had all of our pre-inspections, loading and manifest call we did not jump until about 2; 00 pm. This particular jump was made with the new MC1-1 Parachute. This parachute had special holes in the canopy for balance and turning and had toggles to turn left, turn right or dump air, with many other functions. After I had jumped out of plane I checked my canopy and saw the holes and immediately got scared and pulled my reserve parachute. This was a lesson I learned the hard way and will never forget for the rest of my life.

I looked down and saw all of the instructors coming from all directions with bull horns yelling at me. I was up about 300' and could hear every word and see every instructor on the ground and felt my life was over! I hit the ground and started "S" rolling my parachute as I was taught but the instructors had me doing pushups and beating my boots, more pushups and I was so disappointed in my stupid mistake but definitely learned my lesson.

I eventually arrived at the turning point where there were families there for the graduation ceremony and we lined up and all got their Jump wings pinned on our chest. I was so proud of myself and my first thought was, if my Mom and Dad could have witnessed my accomplishment from the high heavens. Some paratroopers had what they refer to as "Blood Wings" which someone would push the wings and sharp prongs into your chest making your chest bleed. That was not for me! Just after the graduation, the Navy Seal cam to me, shook my hand and said John, you got your wings, your learned your lesson be safe I will see you when I see you! He then smiled and walked away.

After I arrived at the 10th Special Forces Group (Abn) Fort Devens, Ma I was assigned to Company C 3rd Bn 10 SFG. Sergeant major King was walking toward me in the company area and said to me. Specialist DeCosta would you like to go to Jumpmaster School? I said yes but I am a rookie with only 6 jumps so far. He said no problem Go to the class they are waiting for you!

I was all signed up for the Jumpmaster Course as I felt this is way over my head .What am I dong here? Then I was in classes and kept real busy and liked every portion of this course. This was a course that was not a physical harassment type course but thinking fast and making life or death decisions on the fly. You were responsible for every person on an aircraft and their personal lives as well as safety of the aircraft. E had about 200 soldiers in this class and graduated 29 as I was probably number 29 but very proud of this accomplishment because there was all sorts of people in this class, Sergeants, Master Sergeants and officers and for me such a rookie to complete all areas of this I was really proud. We would have to inspect three soldiers with parachutes m, weapons, weapons and a large bundle as well inspect all four in 2 minutes as they fixed the three jumpers and bundle with mistakes. You were not allowed any mistakes. One mistake and you fail and leave the course.

The last thing to accomplish was to jumpmaster 11 parachute jumps. You would inspect the paratroopers, inspect the aircraft, take control from the pilot hang outside of aircraft and look for identification on the ground and out loud recite the Jump Commands- Get ready, out board personnel stand up! Inboard personnel stand up, hook up, check static lines, check equipment, sound off for equipment check, stand in the door, Go! Immediately after saying go, push the jumper out clear the aircraft and jump yourself!

I was awarded my Senior Parachute wings with a star! I then went on to have 85 parachute jumps, 65 night combat equipment jumps , 5 jumpmaster jumps and then I received my highest award of Master Parachute Wings and my Commander then Major Bill Davis pinned my wings on my chest as I was really proud of this award. Major Davis went on to become Colonel Davis in Special Operations.

I went on to be a Special Forces Soldier, winter warfare, Training, Desert Training, received my Senior Parachute wings from the Country of Jordan in the Middle East and jumped in Germany twice and Jordan once. My parachute experience, I am so proud of!

Chapter Seven

Baseball Back In My Life

The time had passed quickly and I had been away too long from baseball. I continued to play basketball, as that became my new sport, although it is not a passion for me. I participated in a few pick-up baseball games on Sundays once in a great while, but playing on a team was history. When I was twenty-one years old, I had the urge again about baseball. I even wrote the Boston Red Sox. They must have had a good laugh at that. Then I tried out for the Boston Park league. I did great but they already had their team and I really had been away too long. It did feel good being on the field but this particular time was not the right time for me.

One of the last times I enjoyed playing sand lot type baseball in my early twenties was when my friend Paul Colombo and a group of friends that joined us at one of the junior high school ball fields to get a feel for the game as in hitting etc. We never had a full team so we played "lines" in which we usually only played the left side of the field and the other side were an out! It was baseball despite not being a real game situation but you could evaluate yourself and see where you were talent wise. I enjoyed that very much but I was at an awkward, age as there were no leagues at the time so only time for dreaming. I hit the ball well as I remember and even now I can go back and re-live my hitting as that was fun.

I met Paul playing pool but my main attraction was the way he and I were so competitive at the time. Whether was playing pool or hitting baseballs we tried our best. My other attraction was his sister Gayle that I had a very deep affection for as Gayle and I had spent a lot of innocent time together as she had Leukemia and died at a very young age, too young and that affected me though the years deeply.

Paul had wonderful parents as well as I enjoyed seeing them through the years. I guess I was drawn to them because of their unique warm and genuine personalities and they always treated me so nicely.

The years had gone by with turmoil, a time tunnel you might say, with so much disappointment, numerous deaths in our family as well as close friends, and many who were very close to me. I encountered relationships that were sour from the start and they originated for all the wrong reasons. My life was severely out of control, starting over way too often and never establishing any new secure foundations. The lifestyle I had experienced tormented my career fields, home life, and emotional being for a number of years until I challenged myself and overcame the problems that I allowed others to put on my shoulders. I am truly thankful I had the strength and character to overcome these difficulties and become the person I am today. I thank my guardian angel for that. The only positive portion of those years was the time I invested in the military. I was a paratrooper with incredible opportunities and experiences, which I will share a little later. With all that said, I vote we fast forward to more exciting, positive times!

It was August 1994, and finally, after years of being away from baseball, and being torn physically and emotionally, I finally found baseball once again. I also met the right person in my life to help guide me the rest of the way. That's my present wife, Beth. She keeps me straight and organized and out of trouble. We were married July 3, 1984, ten years earlier.

On this hot summer day in late August,1994, on the news I heard that a local Little League from Middleboro, Massachusetts was going to the Little League World Series in Williamsport, Pennsylvania. I spoke to my brother Douglas and we decided to drive down and see the series. Neither of us had ever been there before and only watched it on TV every year, so this would be a treat. Douglas had a pop-up camper, so we packed quickly and drove down. I think it was a ten hour drive, and after arriving in the area we hurried to the stadium to see our first game. The Middleboro team was playing so we were right on schedule. We both had Little League memories so this would ignite a baseball fire in both of us.

We found the Middleboro fan section, grabbed a program, hot dog and soda, and enjoyed the games. We picked up memorabilia, took pictures, and saw the sights. It was great. We saw the international teams as well as our United States teams. It was pure baseball, and the memories were right there in my heart. My heart was pumping as I wished I were young and had that opportunity, and I knew right then and there that when I returned home, I would check into coaching and possibly playing again.

Our four-day trip ended and after our return I immediately found an opportunity to coach a Little League team. During the same time I also found an Over 30 baseball league in my area, so I could play baseball. Life was starting to look very good again.

Prior to this, my activity was geared toward basketball, and running races. I ran to collect different T-shirts at each race and to meet other people. Basketball was competitive and fun, as I played all the time. I always had a hoop and I could just shoot around whenever. I did extra heavy duty training because of the heart attack I suffered in the military and my wife's dog Willie trained with me every day. He saved my life. He loved basketball. That was his joy. And so, the Little League World Series had brought me back to baseball with more intensity, making every moment count.

I met with some Little League people in Townsend, Massachusetts, and shared my enthusiasm and excitement to be involved. I assisted coaching a thirteen- to fifteen-year-old team in the Little League system. I had little control but I was back in baseball. I then made contact with that Over 30 baseball league for adults. I went to the batting cages, signed up, and practiced the remainder of the winter and anxiously awaited opening day. My skills were all still there, as if I had never stopped. I started off really well. I hit the ball and played defense well. I focused on pitching and played short stop too. My first season was a learning experience and I had a ton of fun. The next season I was given a twelve-year-old Little League team and I was the manager. Now I have the opportunity to design the training and have some baseball fun.

I went through the draft system, picked my players, and drew up plans for training and the upcoming season. This also would be my second season back to the Over 30 baseball amateurs team. I batted about three hundred that first season and pitched average as well, with still so much to learn. I fit in immediately and realized I hadn't lost a step. I could be very competitive in this league, as I was older but in better shape than most, with a heart full of desire.

Prior to having my first baseball practice for my Little League team, I made arrangements to use the conference room at the VFW in my town. I was able to do that because I am a life-time member to the organization. I had scheduled the meeting on a week night and invited all the team's parents. I had a tripod with illustrations and had the whole training process laid out. I explained how I was going to concentrate on extensive time spent on skills, and teamwork. In addition I stated that I wanted every kid to play every position, and that each kid could come to me and challenge another position. This way each chosen kid, at any given position, would work hard constantly and not take it for granted, for they could lose their position

I made it clear I would not tolerate any fresh kids – no kids bullying others, and absolutely no one was to say anything negative to someone if they made a mistake or struck out. I would send them home if they did that. I encouraged parents to participate. I made sure every kid received a signed ball from me during the season for their first hit, a home run, a great defensive play, or anything positive. I wanted them all to feel important. Most of the parents were great, and the kids were great, but after a promising season, it was time for me to move on. Our team, the Cardinals, made it to the finals but lost a squeaker in the last exciting inning. The previous three seasons the team had not made the playoffs. This was my total managing career in Little League baseball. They signed a ball for me and also a special card, so I left on a happy note.

Soon after my U.S. Army retirement, I was drawn back into my previous trade in construction and craftsmanship as well as high end painting and wallpapering. In addition I had done Faux Art work for the wealthy clients as that was quite popular in that era and was a money maker as well. Right time and place for me as it turned out.

I worked for as many good contractors as I could learning the trade at higher level and pick up as many tips as I could on the business end of things then I gradually went on my own and did not look back. I considered my self, fortunate, talented artist and craftsmanship and I made very sure I was on time and gave the customers more than fair and quality workmanship. If there was ever any problem whether things were my fault, product malfunction or weather situation on exterior work I always backed up my work even if I took a loss. My name and reputation was so important that I worked alone as there were not very workers to help me that I could trust. Like I said working for rich clients I could not take a chance on damage due to inexperience, neglect, drug or alcohol problems, smoking or a court history as that would destroy me! When or if your integrity, honesty or lack of quality exist during your work, "you are done" its time to head for the hills.

During the years I worked as a contractor I had more than 487 customers, many were constant repeats in hiring me. I worked at all the major hotels like, Ritz Carlton, Parker House, Four Seasons, Schools, Medical facilities, Hospitals, Law offices, Banks Condo's apartment complexes Restaurants etc. My major help in this was the many interior decorators I had worked for to get these type clients.

I did however have one friend I could hire which was a pure gift to me. My friend Randy Guthrie. He helped me on several jobs! We would start of having breakfast before going to the home where ever I was working, as it was nice to be able to talk about baseball with him and at lunch time we could have a pass with a baseball on the property where ever I worked, go back to work and then go home after a productive day. I paid him more money than average because of his loyalty, workmanship, manners to customers and he followed directions for quality of craftsmanship.

Being on the Over 30 baseball team in Leominster, Massachusetts was a huge challenge for me. Quite a few of the players had played in high school, college, and Legion. I had only played in Little League and at this point had a thirty-five year break from any baseball. With a heart condition (two previous heart attacks by this time), I sure had a challenge ahead of me. I did well my first year. However, I did question myself continuously. *Did I play my best? How much more can I improve? Do I fit in? Are my health and age always in question? Well, I batted in the top third of my team, and moved from batting last to lead off or sometimes the two spot.* I was pretty consistent and my defense would change constantly. I would be solid for three games, then be questionable for three games. But I did hold my own and I slowly improved every game.

This year, I batted even higher and my pitching came to life. Because of no training as a young kid after Little League, I was lacking proper mechanics and knowledge as a pitcher. Despite all that, I would come away with an average of five to seven strikeouts and very rarely walk someone. I did give up a few home runs and a lot of hits, but on the positive side of things, I did pitch a one-hitter but lost the game two to one in the late innings. I still felt it was an accomplishment.

One particular game, I was stopped in the middle of the game and taught how to stretch when a man was on base. Both my team and the opposing team, as well as the umpires, were very polite and understanding and handled it in a respectful way. I thank them for that, because I learned quickly and became a positive pitcher thereafter. There was a certain amount of embarrassment but I dealt with it properly. I was happy to learn correctly. I pitched about fifty innings that year, and progressed, as I became very serious about off season training.

I think you could label this," coming up short" My pitching performance has been in some ways stellar as they say and as I look at it, I am not sure. I absolutely hate to lose but that does happen and the sooner you get to accept that, then the winning should happen more frequently as well. That's what I am hoping for anyway.

We were approaching the end of the season and the playoffs in our over 30 baseball league in Leominster, Ma. I was on the Dodgers and my opponent was Big Jim Russell also from Townsend, ma. Jim was representing the Braves. There was not very much hitting in this particular game as Jim and I had pitched a gem to each others team. I had a no hitter going into the 6th inning as well as Jim. Very fast game, as no one was hitting either of us. The 7th inning however things started to change. My team the Dodgers were up and although there was a lot of activity we had not broken lose as of yet. There was a walk, a hit and run and a pass ball and later with a lazy infield hit we managed to push a run across the plate. Now, all we had to do is get three fast outs and go home!

It was a hot day in August and the Sun was shining brightly. I stood on the mound as the sweat and determination had moistened my face. I had one strike out and my first walk of the game. I threw the ball low and outside to the next batter as he swung late and placed the ball not far from the second baseman as it trickled off his glove and hit his shoulder and ricocheted toward right field. One run would score as we are tied up now and the next batter hit a line drive slightly up the middle and the 2nd baseman once again could not squeeze the ball in his glove and the other team, Indians found another run as it was a walk off game ended error. So we lost 2-1 in the last of the seventh.

So, I pitched a one hitter and lost 2-1 for a 7 inning effort with 1 walk and 5 strikeouts. The other pitcher Jim pitched a 3 hitter and got all the attention because his team had won the game. Then the next season I was on the

Leominster team as we played against the Legends, as this last game was for the championship game. This was another 7 inning war! There were lots of hits both sides but score going both ways inning after inning and down to the wire we lost also in the last inning but this to me at least ,there were lots of plays being made so this was baseball.

The more I played the better I got and many had noticed. I was not from this area at all so any compliments were taken respectfully. I started purchasing new bats, replacing equipment and really finding my way as a regular around the adult amateur baseball.

Baseball had returned to my life with a vengeance. I had been asked to play in both Over 30 and Over 40 leagues in Boston's MSBL, or Men's Senior Baseball League. I also continued playing in Leominster's Over 30 league. I'm now playing about fifty games each year. Boston had better talent, more traveling, and an opportunity to play more games. I remember playing a double header in Wellesley, Massachusetts, and upon completion of that game, I drove down to the Leominster league to catch their game. I was not thinking, as I had cooled down and relaxed while traveling to the second game. I got to the field just in time to go to the mound and pitch. I had no time to warm up or stretch, and after the second batter, I pulled a muscle in my rib cage and lost three games because of this. I should have known better, with my background in training as a paratrooper. *What was I thinking?*

I have at different times played with cracked and broken ribs, broken fingers, broken toes, and various sprained or pulled muscles, to go along with my heart attacks. The bottom line is, I play for the moment. I play any time I can, as often as I can, wherever I can. If someone needs an extra guy, I'm that guy and I'm ready to play. When I play, no matter what emotional situation that confronts me in everyday life, while playing baseball, everything disappears. My mind is free and clear of anything in the whole world. I am not better than anyone else, I am not a pro, I just love baseball, as I am a competitor in amateur baseball.

Upon my return from Williamsport, Pennsylvania, as I had gone to the Little League World Series to see the Middleborough, Massachusetts Little League compete there. This had made things very clear in my heart that for so many years I had deprived myself from the game I love baseball. I took immediate action and sought out in my area Little League Baseball. I then met a friend from Townsend who was the President of the league as I requested to become a coach. I then was lucky to be able to be assistant coach of the 13 and 14 year olds as it was called senior league. I did this for a year and then I got the opportunity to have my own team the "Cardinals" as I would be the manager. This was exciting.

I then found this to be so much fun watching a kid get his very first hit or winning a game or hitting his first homerun as it put me right back to when I was 12 years old. This was the 10, 11 and 12 year olds on my Cardinals team. I then found out that there was an over 30 baseball league in the area. I made some phone calls and actually had a tryout and I was immediately picked up by a team as this was my adult re-start in baseball. This was 1995.

I was so happy and excited that on a day that I had free time I decided to take a trip down to Brockton, Massachusetts and take a leisurely ride around my childhood ballparks and enjoy memory lane! I drove down to The Eastside Improvement Association where I last played in Little League in 1959. There had been many changes but as I drove into the new complex I saw a man taking a chain off the main gate. I said to myself, that couldn't be! I looked closer and walked over to the man and it was Mr. Richard "Hoagie" Trum.

Mr. Trum a had recognized me immediately as we shook hands and had everlasting smiles and grins. I explained that I was reminiscing and so pleased I was able to see him. He said do you want to see your plaque on the wall? I said sure! I knew it was there but I haven't been on this site for 50 plus years so a special warm feeling flowed through my body. My heart was pounding as we walked to the main hall as he shook his keys and let us in the facility. The facility was built about 1957 and since then there were numerous leagues, teams, banquets, dances and hundreds of awards place on shelves and all over the walls for all of those years. There was more memorabilia than Cooperstown!

He said, John your plaque is right down there on the right. Still looks great and you're played very well here! I saw my plaque as it was just as I remembered it, I touched it and ran my fingers across my name as it said MVP John F DeCosta and again several more times for most homeruns, most Runs Batted In, Best Pitching and Highest batting average. Other years maybe I was good or average but that particular year I was the very best of all in the entire league and no one could ever take that away from me. There were tears coming from my eyes as I was so emotional just looking back and especially touching it.

I thanked Mr. Trum for letting me see my plaque and showing me around and he said John any time you wish to come and see it please come ok. I said thank you Mr. Trum and off I went to see my family home and then make my trip back home to tell my wife about this beautiful day. As I drove down RT#24 and RT #128/95 I thought about that magnificent night when I received my award. Yes, the tears kept running down my face as I could hardly see as I was driving the car. I remembered being next to my coach and the 300 plus people packed in the banquet hall and the head table on the stage as guest speakers were there and it was a sit down dinner, then the awards presentation after dinner. I remember my Mom and Dad being there as I never expected to get the award so calling my name in front of all those people and saying so many wonderful things about my baseball abilities that the emotion just poured out of my eyes just like now but they were happy tears . That as I may have mentioned before was the most monumental moment in my life! I love that moment so much.

During a later time in my life at one of the ball fields were some ball field workers as they were working on the baseball field. They had replaced home late. I then took that home with me and this home plate I had scored a lot of runs, hit a lot of balls at bat and pitched a lot of great games there so now this home plate is the entrance to a flower garden at my home.

I think I could drive around to all of the adult ball fields I had played on and remember many games I played in. I just remember things like that. You know, game situations, the winning run, a great line drive or a diving catch. Its all in the memory bank .I just need a visual to reconnect with my memory and that is easy.

I played for a friend of mine who was the manager of a team called the Orioles, Bob Major. We played in the MSBL league in Boston over 30 and over 40 year old league. I played there for about 5 years. Bob was a very smart coach as he really knew baseball. It was always so much fun. Other members on the team were, Glenny, Frank, Jon held, Danny, Bill, Coop, and so many others on the Orioles. There was great team chemistry!

We played a game in Somerville, Ma- and were losing in the 7th inning 11 to zip as we only played 7 innings and we had our last time at bat to do something. There were two outs and our team all were hitting like crazy as we came back and won the game 12-11. What a great comeback that was.

Then in our over 40 league we had a game at Jefferson ball field in Jamaica Plain, Ma- as we were also down in the last inning and I was at bat with bases loaded and bunted down the line as a run scored and then my teammate Dan bunted as we scored again and won the game as that was really cool! We played after rain delays in mud, played in the heavy rains and baseball was always fun.

Chapter Eight

_____

Tournament Invitations

One Labor Day weekend, I was invited to play down in Cape Cod, Massachusetts for an annual baseball classic on the college fields, in Chatham, Yarmouth, Brewster and Falmouth.

There were about twenty teams in this particular tournament. The teams came from New York, Connecticut, New Jersey, New Hampshire, Maine, and Massachusetts. This was geared for Over 30 baseball. The unusual element was the fact that a few ex professional baseball players were playing in this tournament. The only rule was they had to have been out of professional sports for at least five years. Rich Gedman from the Boston Red Sox, a man from the Los Angeles Dodgers, and another big guy from the St. Louis Cardinals were all on this team. So stacked teams were common, in tournament play.

There was so much talent that at first I didn't play much, but after the second game when opposing players kept asking for me to pitch, finally my team took notice and put me in. I pitched seventeen innings without a man on base. I pitched real well, and made a lot of friends. The fact that I got to play where all the talented college players play, in the Cranberry Cape League, was a new memory for me. This was a great experience and my first tournament.

I wanted to pitch to Rich but by the time I got into the game, he was out of the game. I didn't even care if he hit a home run, it was the fact that he was a professional baseball player. I did get to meet him anyway.

I continued my regular seasons in Over 30 baseball; I played in Boston in the MSBL Over 30 baseball, and the Over 40 MSBL too. Then, after five years of playing in the same leagues, I decided I needed more. The Leominster league closed down and I found out about Lowell's Over 30 baseball league. I made it just in time for the 2000 season.

There is no comparison to regular league play, no matter what state you are from, compared to tournaments of any age with the average tournament format. Let me explain. Your average leagues are full of players that are either gamers, average athletes, or some who haven't much experience at all playing baseball, but love to go to the water cooler on Monday mornings and spread the word that they play. Their co-workers are amazed and their ego is inflated. The team, however, suffers from these particular ballplayers. These are the ones who never practice, never stretch, are late coming to games, and are never really in the game, no matter how intense the game may be.

Now in tournament play, things are different. Two hours before the game, the players are in the batting cage hitting or doing soft toss. Others are hitting pop ups, grounders, or playing pepper. When there are double headers, after the first game, they take a quick lunch and a water break, and then the players are back at it in the cages, dealing with more hitting and sometimes with a sandwich in their mouths! They can't get enough baseball. During the game, players are running to the coach's box, chasing foul balls, and clapping, jumping and keeping everyone in the game. That's how it is and that's especially why I like being with this type of ballplayer. I feel right at home and usually the chemistry is a great comfort zone for me.

The Phoenix World series Tournament is unique in its own way. Yes, its tough getting from field to field as the distance is like 30 to 40 miles between daily double headers so that makes it difficult as other tournaments, you just move to the next field 200 feet away. Phoenix has the hot sun, cool nights and beautiful fields. There are several age brackets to include father and son tournaments and sometimes father, son, and grandson are competing. There are more than 300 teams that participate out there in Phoenix during the month of October/November. The talent level in every age groups is some of the best baseball in the country.

Las Vegas has its over 50 and now over 60 year old tournaments. They are fun and again beautiful and I must say fantastic fields. Greg Maddox has a field names after him out there and royal Grande Complex and many other complexes. Two games per day enjoy playing baseball then you have the Las Vegas strip, the shows, entertainments and so much to do out there. If you make the circuit Las Vegas, has to be on your list. I always make an appointment for a massage in the middle of the week. This is the time of the week that you are broken down and beat up so the massage will bring your muscles alive and get you through the week of six double headers. Between games and sometimes after a double header the guys from both winners and losers will go to a back room pizza shop in one of the breweries and have pizza and beer. Socializing with other ballplayers is the greatest thing to do. The guys talk about their families, baseball leagues back home, more baseball talk their career fields and back to baseball again. I will talk again later about tournaments and variety of ballplayers to compete with. The more tournaments you go to more baseball friends you meet. Then, when you go you are considered seasoned and experienced and like magic everyone knows your name and where you are from. It doesn't end there for they start inviting you to other tournaments around the country. If you are rich there are enough baseball tournaments to have a complete schedule year-round and fantastic ball fields tourist are and family enjoy the tournaments as well. Definitely if you love baseball this is the way to go.

Play at the Plate is another route to competitive baseball tournaments. They play in Las Vegas also but in Canada, Louisiana, Multiple places in Florida, to include West palm Beach, New York's Central Park, and other places of interest. Its like a fantasy camp atmosphere.

Baseball International has a Florida Tournament in January and has been held at Sarasota, Florida but has been at other stadiums there as well. This is another four day double header each day tournament. They are known to travel to China, Japan, Australia, Europe, Russia, Italy and France. They do Cruise ships from Island to Island and lots of baseball and tours.

NABA Is National Adult Baseball Association; they have Tucson, Phoenix, Las Vegas, Florida and several Cruise opportunities to play competitive baseball to add to your list of interesting places to go.

Roy Hobbs is another held in Florida another World Series type of competitive baseball. There are so many places to play that maybe there's too many to choose from.

Greg Wagner's Wooden Bat Classic Baseball held at Terry Park at Fort Myers is a unique place to play baseball. Terry Park is one of the oldest in the country. Old timers like Ty Cobb, Babe Ruth, Mickey Mantle and Jackie Robinson have all played there. The tournament people mix up the schedule of playing fields for their games at the Red Sox Player Development Complex as well.

Chapter Nine

Basketball Tournaments

I need to back up the bus a bit and give a health report. I had a heart attack on active duty just after a parachute jump June 3, 1987. Therefore I had to retire against my wishes from United States Army (Paratroopers) Special Forces. My life had changed right there. This is when I trained so hard with my dog Willie the sheepdog. I was thinking I could get in shape and return back to Special Forces duty. The military said, "John, retire and enjoy your life."

I had always enjoyed basketball as I most always had a hoop in the yard no matter where I lived. So I always was a good shooter. My heart was damaged enough to be forced to retire. I inherited the bad genes from my father's side of the family and it seems I got the worse dose, compared to my two older brothers and one sister. They seem to be fine. I later had two more heart attacks after retirement, but I went right back to playing basketball, and after I had found baseball once again in 1994, I continued to play actively, in three-on-three basketball tournaments. I continued doing cardio kick classes, basketball and baseball. I was really enjoying sports as much as possible, because it was so much fun.

While I was in junior high school I belonged to a very unique and strong eastside basketball team. We played in the Boston Garden for the state championship but lost very badly to an Everett, Massachusetts team. I had played regularly, and also played in church leagues, the YMCA, summer leagues…almost as much as baseball in those days.

I worked for the Veterans Administration in the early nineties and at lunch time played basketball. I was a three-point threat, as always, and this was a great way to pass the lunch time and stay in shape. So there I was, once again, competing against younger, faster and more energetic competition.

Basketball has been a great off-season workout for me. I sometimes feel so confident that I am playing so much better than when I was young. In fact I enjoy any sport at this stage of my life. I understand the sports better and my drive and determination is so much more focused. I love to shoot the ball. I like to be the one at crunch time that has the ball with a few seconds to win the game. Basketball three-on-three came to me somehow and it was organized with international rules, which made it a very fast game. I played about three times a week, so this was a great way to stay in shape for baseball.

Like all other things I have done, I jumped right in, head over heels. I had a list of potential players and the notifications for tournaments were available to me. I brought a team to the basketball hall of fame in Springfield, Massachusetts, to compete. We won a bronze medal and just got nipped by a Boston team. We played three separate three-on-three games at the Springfield Hall of Fame basketball court. That was unique in itself. There was actually a crowd in support of all the guys, no matter what team they were on, mostly because of their age and ability.

This team that beat us became a rival. It's not them winning that bothered me. It was their attitude and dirty play that bothered me. They had very poor sportsmanship. I got my revenge at a later tournament. This time it was full court basketball, and five-on-five. It happened to be on my birthday. I played the first game and scored eighteen points, and my team won. The second game I scored seventeen points, and the third game for the championship of the tournament, we played the bad boys from Boston once again. This game was a *game*. They played as dirty and hard as they could. They elbowed us as we drove the lane, or they would step on our ankles when making a move to the basket. I got twenty-two points this game, with five three-pointers to win the tournament. My team was strong and we played really well. I was happy to beat those guys.

I went on to compete in New Hampshire, and I also won a three-point shooting contest there between games. I got thirteen out of fifteen three-pointers. In addition I played three separate three-on-three games, but my team came in third place. I received a gold medal for the three-point shooting contest.

I played pretty consistently until my fifty-fourth birthday. That day I had a complete heart check by my doctor, including EKG, stress test, echocardiogram, blood, urine, x-rays and a few other things, and said the check-up was fine.

*Well...*I had a heart attack just after playing several games. I was shooting like Larry Bird; it was my birthday; and then the heart attack started. I was sweating, dazed, delirious, but somehow I was able to drive my car the thirty miles to the emergency room where I knew my doctors worked. I called my wife and she prepared the emergency room and I believe my guardian angel got me there safely. I was very near death and never should have taken the chance at all. I was in the emergency room for hours, then was transported by chopper to Boston's New England Medical Center. I had another stent installed in my heart. Nice birthday, huh?

I've been zapped from playing basketball due to my heart problems. It's very hard for me to say no, but I know it would strain my heart and I would rather not take the chance and be able to play baseball. When I do play basketball I love to just shoot, as I shoot very well. I won a three-point contest one time, scoring thirteen or fifteen, shooting for a gold medal. When I play I play hard and that's when the young guys get mad and want to hurt me because I shoot so well. Maybe if I were taller than my present five foot eight, I wouldn't get so banged around.

What I do to fill my appetite is shoot around whenever I get the chance because when I'm in the zone, it feels pretty good shooting and hearing nothing but net. I know all the ball fields and usually there is a basketball hoop at a park next to the ball field. I go early, hit some balls off, tee, exercise, stretch and bring my basketball to loosen up, and I enjoy being in that zone just for a few quiet moments. I feel so relaxed, and gather my baseball thoughts and then, I'm ready to play some baseball.

Chapter Ten

Opening Day at Ryan Field

My 2000 baseball season at Lowell's Over 30 baseball league was to start in the spring. I just barely had time to recover, train and get ready for the season, and not tell anyone of my medical problems. I went through the draft system and got picked up by the Twin's team. My very first game, I had an RBI, or a run batted in, two singles and a double, and played well defensively. During the game, after I hit a double, the next player made an out and killed the inning.

I was walking towards the dug out, and said to the coach, "You better send someone else out to play third base."

He said, "Really?"

I then said to two teammates, "Someone should call 911 right now." I then collapsed and in a short time the rescue ambulance was there and I was at the hospital soon there after. So that was heart attack number five, with four stints in my heart, and counting. Great way to start the season, wouldn't you say?

So I've had yet another comeback, and it gets tougher each time, but I deal with it. I have played at this same field so many times and each time I have the flash backs of that fateful opening day. Comebacks are unique, and so many eyes are on you, and you wonder what your friends really are thinking. Are they afraid of playing with you? Did you put a scare on them so that they dislike you for being there? There's a lot to consider.

Well, three weeks later, I was back in uniform, ready to play. My very first at bat, I got hit by a pitch in the head! I continued to have a rough season as I got hit four more times and never could be comfortable. I struggled through the season and realized my heart attack in front of my teammates was difficult for them to deal with. The team also already had two starters for pitching, so it was time to move on.

I trained through the winter and made myself appear to be upbeat. I was in good shape and this year I would be on the Phillies. I would have to start over, prove myself once again and go from there. I maintained cardio kick classes, aerobic classes, but no basketball – that's off limits to me. I can only play baseball, which is great. I'm using fitness equipment and I appear to be in as good of shape as anyone in their thirties.

I batted much less than I was comfortable with. I played well and they called me the energizer bunny for my hustle and desire. My batting average dropped to two hundred and eighty, but my pitching had stepped up a notch, as I had three wins, all nine-inning completions, but again, I needed to move to another team. I was not getting enough pitching there, since there was already too many pitchers on the team.

I finished the season fine and again went into the draft for yet my third team, the Red Sox. So I trained very hard and I became a regular with them. I was one of three starters and I also pitched in Boston to give me the innings I desired. I am now playing about seventy games per year and pitching on average about one hundred innings.

My batting average has bumped up to over three hundred and I know I am better than that, so I hit the batting cages more often with more desire. This Over 30 league in Lowell is a metal bat league and Boston is wood bat league. Bouncing back and fourth every other day is difficult, with very difficult pitching. I had played all over all the parks in the Boston area, night leagues, and my Sunday metal bat league. There was plenty of baseball, a lot of at bats, and my pitching had surprised me as I had grown to a higher level, with a lot of self-confidence, and respect from ballplayers.

Chapter Eleven

Winter Baseball

With another season in my rear view mirror, there were leaves to rake, plans for the upcoming cold winter and the Christmas holidays before me. My wife had given me a baseball tournament in Orlando, Florida. I would be playing with the International Baseball Tournament at the Royals Professional Baseball Complex. This trip was a wonderful Christmas gift.

This tournament mixed up ballplayers coming from several foreign countries, so it would be fun baseball. Our games were played each day at this complex. They had eight beautiful fields, a minor league stadium and the major league stadium. We played two games at the major league stadium. My team came in second place. We had a great and unique bunch of guys. There was one gentleman who was eighty-three years old, who had traveled down with his fifty-four year son, who had paid for his trip as a gift. They were great and fun to be with. I pitched about eighteen innings and did well.

There was one moment that requires mentioning. This was vintage John DeCosta. I was pitching at the major league stadium and my foot was on the rubber. The umpire called, "Play ball!" but I was looking up and around at all the box seats, enclosures, and press box way up high. I got lost in the thought of *what this must be like for the professionals, playing in front of a big crowd like this...*

Finally, the umpire said, "Hey pitcher! The game is down here!" Everyone broke out laughing and I finally began pitching. I struck out five batters in three innings. That was so fun. I pitched really well throughout the tournament and had a great time.

My next season at Over 30 baseball was very positive. I had several wins and completed three full games and won them all. I had a total of thirty-nine innings with thirty-nine strikeouts and nine walks.

I had an additional thirty-five innings in Boston, as everywhere I played I was more trusted and they all had more confidence in my effective pitching.

September just before the regular playoffs there was a home run derby. That was fun. I didn't win anything but I did well. I hit about seven balls out but they were foul balls. It looked good and felt good so not a bad day for the old guy.

The league had a banquet with awards and dinner, but I was out in Las Vegas participating in an Over 50 baseball tournament. This was great – I played for two separate teams with a total of twelve games in a week!

I played for the Texas Padres and the other team was the Red Sox. One night my wife and I were at this Italian restaurant in Las Vegas and an older man there came by with his accordion and played "Take Me Out to the Ball Game." That was a treat. Just after that some people from the next table over asked what team I played for. Without thinking, I told them I played for the Texas Padres. They thought I was a professional player! I tried to correct them by saying I was out there for a tournament, but they insisted on thinking I was a pro. I still don't know if they got it straight or not.

I played in Las Vegas's Over 50 baseball tournaments four years in a row and played about thirty-nine total games out there. I received three Most Valuable Player awards, so that was rewarding and productive as well. I did so well due to playing with my same age group. I had usually played with thirty-year-olds all the time, so that was a positive rebound for me.

I usually managed the teams, came up with a team breakfast at Caesar's Palace, a team dinner at Batista's Italian restaurant, and capped off a couple of nights at Crazy Horse, a nightclub near the strip that provided a lot of entertainment and laughs. The tournament usually provided a banquet during the week and after games the guys usually met for beer and pizza to recap the games and talk about the next game.

Near the end of the last tournament out there I was racing out of one ballpark to play in the finals at another ballpark. I still had my cleats on, and yes, I got pulled over by a motorcycle cop and he wrote me out a ticket for ninety-five dollars! I managed to get to the game on time but had no time to warm up, so I went directly to the mound and started pitching. I had a good game with seven strikeouts, no walks, but we lost two to one. The trip was over now, and a long journey home was ahead of us.

This concluded all tournaments and all leagues for the year, and I had pretty good statistics. I played fifty-six games, two hundred and five at-bats, seventy-three hits, twelve walks, twenty runs batted , twenty scores and nine strikeouts. Defensively I made two errors, one hundred twenty put-outs, and my pitching had improved drastically. I pitched ninety-one innings, eighty-seven strikeouts, and thirteen walks. Now I can start corrective training during the winter. The reason I mention these statistics is because of the tough talent I was playing against and especially my heart disability that taunts me. Most people who have heart problems aren't playing baseball at the level I am. Therefore, I am proud of my accomplishments, but truly thankful for my health.

This is also a way to measure my abilities so I can prepare and accomplish more the next season. Believe me I am my worst critic, as I am very hard on myself with my discipline and training. If I do badly, I will make myself train harder to correct whatever the fault is.

When the season is over I usually give myself a few days and then I'm having baseball blues and have to get started right away, correcting deficiencies and elevating my positives.

Besides cardio kick classes, aerobics, and working the machines at the health club, I have adapted throwing programs for myself. I use soft baseballs that weigh about three ounces less than a hard baseball. I have a bunch of them. I practice in a tennis court against the plywood wall. I make a strike zone with blue painter's tape in the form of a small square. I also put small x's in strategic locations for change-ups and curves. In addition to this I throw weighted balls once per week to help me increase my speed. The long toss helps that as well.

I warm up by throwing about seventy-five pitches. I start at forty feet and work up to sixty feet. I then extend to one hundred and twenty feet and back to sixty feet. This takes up to one hundred and fifty pitches to accomplish. I then pretend I'm having a game and throw to imaginary batters. I throw for control and strikes and the total amount of pitches comes to about two hundred and fifty to two hundred and seventy-five. I do this workout twice a week, plus I try to hit the batting cage for hitting. I throw so much that I am very ready come spring time or if I go to a winter tournament.

I even tried to throw with my eyes closed to see if I could hit my target and I was so surprised to see how well I had done. Sadaharu Oh would have

THE EASTSIDE KID

been proud of me. I concentrate on my mechanics, I look for things I see the professionals do that might help me and I incorporate that into my chemistry. Sometimes it works and sometimes it doesn't.

Winter baseball does not end here. I go to batting cages to hit with five to seven other friends that feel the way I do about baseball. Some are even on other teams. We usually do live pitching in the cages for it is more realistic and you can correct bad habits quickly. When the machine throws the ball, it comes in the same speed, same manner, and very unrealistic to a game. The balls are even different so I usually bring my own balls that I keep in the house near a heater. The balls at these batting facilities are usually heavy, cold, and not lively at all. These heavy balls that are a variety of weights are very bad for throwing too, in my opinion.

I refer to the notebooks I have made on skills in pitching, fielding and batting. That puts me in the right frame of mind. The older I get I find preparation really helps, although maintaining the necessary skills is very difficult. Some of the players practice two weeks before the season starts and they are good to go. Those same guys are the ones who don't practice, and show up two minutes before the game; *where am I playing? When do I bat?* They are fair-weather ballplayers who couldn't care less if they win or lose and basically want to go to work Monday morning at their water cooler and say, "Hey, I played baseball Sunday!" Wow – whoopdedoo! They have no idea what baseball is all about.

The winter baseball options are International Baseball, at one of the Florida professional baseball facilities, lasting usually four to seven days. There's a tournament registration fee, which covers all of baseball, then you're responsible for airfare, car rentals, hotels and your choice of food. Usually guys bring their families or the ones that go alone sometimes split cost in large suites at the hotels to help the financial burden. Other winter baseball opportunities are in late October, in Las Vegas, Phoenix, Roy Hobbs in Florida, MSBL, NABA, Play at the Plate, and Wood Bat Classic. Yes, plenty of baseball in the off season, not to mention here in New England all of the indoor baseball facilities. There are even places with a dirt infield inside of a large building. There are bubbles much larger than a football field, and batting cages in nearly every town. So, if you like baseball, there's plenty of it. Besides, it's always great to get away from the snow and cold weather, and get a jump on things before spring time.

Chapter Twelve

Pitching

When I'm on the mound I have picked up a few tricks from my friend Bill Lee from the old Boston Red Sox. First I set the rubber and clear the dirt on and around the rubber. This is mine while I'm out here and I own certain parts of home plate as well. The batter doesn't know this but it's true.

When I warm up I get five feet to the rear lower part of the mound and throw pitches from there to warm up, establish my distance, and make sure I'm not throwing in the dirt when the batter steps in. I then go to the rubber and try far left, and if the batters are watching sometimes I move to the far right just to screw with their heads.

I usually watch very carefully the demeanor of the batter. I size him up: *Have I pitched to him before? What did he do? Is he a contact hitter? What is his weak area? Is he crowding my plate? What kind of foolish stance is this? Does he respect me as a pitcher or is he very cocky?*

Sometimes when I get a batter that is on every pitch I throw and I don't know what to throw anymore, I will do a double windup just to throw him off. Sometimes that works and sometimes it doesn't. It's worth a try at this point in the at bat.

I have picked up baseball savvy and confidence from Bill, through his pitching thoughts. The guy loves baseball and has such great tools, but he is a lefty and I can only use some of his help for my abilities. Then there is Jeff, my batting instructor who has major league experience. There is Mark from Wesleyan College in Connecticut. I attend their weekend baseball camps when I can afford them or if I need immediate help with one of my skills.

Mark runs a camp in July, as that is a great time to catch you on the verge of losing confidence, or as your batting eye to complete your season on a high note. Mark has helped me tremendously, catching for me at one of these clinics. His positive feedback from a real college coach has been super.

The Connecticut camp is similar except that they stay in the dormitories and also attend a minor league baseball game during the weekend. So if you're slumping, losing confidence, or feeling like you could be better and need a little instruction, this is recommended. The people who work there absolutely care about baseball and are there for the love of the game and not to take your money.

Just prior to this busy fall a friend of mine, Brian Ansara, had a Korean acupuncturist interested in the works of baseball and wanted to film us pitching, and batting. I said, "Sure, why not? Just another baseball day." Brian met me at a park over in Chelmsford, Massachusetts. Soon after we arrived, the acupuncturist showed up with his son. After our introductions we chatted, and he and I had much in common. He was Korean and I spent a year over there. He was a Rock Army soldier in the Tiger Division during Vietnam. So one Veteran to another, we got along fine. His interest was making a DVD for his own instructional use. My interest was playing baseball with possibly something to learn. He filmed while Brian and I hit balls from both sides of the plate off of a tee and into a circle he had drawn in the outfield. He also wanted us to stamp our foot as a karate move when swinging. I didn't see any future in this at all, but I understood his thought process. This was just another day of baseball. He offered me free acupuncture treatments but I'm happy with my own acupuncturist.

I would grab every opportunity to have a new experience, try a new type of training, work out with other pitchers and baseball was consuming me completely as I loved it. I guess you could say I had brainwashed myself. During the process of trying everything and anything related to baseball, I was constantly learning. I would fall on my face many times and would get batted around the park but I knew underneath all of this I had God given talent that would eventually turn into a positive thing, in my life. I would never give up as my confidence level was constantly increasing and gradually I would grab attention and develop believers in me. I began to have more managers and ballplayers trust in my abilities. I knew there was light in the tunnel somewhere.

Between tournaments and leagues I found a guy who was older than I, like twenty years older than I. All I would hear is do you have a change up. God I would hear that all of my life. I asked myself what the heck is a change up? Finally this older gentleman who said he played in the majors. Well that's questionable, but he did how ever show me how to throw a change up. Yes I finally figured out what a change up was and why you would want to learn how to throw one. Well at first I was uncomfortable as I could not find any control and could not find confidence either. I practiced, and practiced and finally it just came to me. I held the ball like a two finger fast ball but lifted my middle finger and threw with the same motion as my fast ball.

I had instant results. I got better at it all the time. I threw it so many times in practice so I would be confident when I threw it in a real situation in a game. I remember when I had a hitter up one who hit a home run off of me in the past. I had him foul off two balls and threw him my change up and struck him out. Many took notice at first as they thought I was just getting weak with my fastball, but I would come back with a fast ball to them as I had them on their heels. My confidence would continue. This was a memorable time for the change in my mechanics and the start of new training for me.

I started heavy duty year round training and soon found others interested in working out with me. Yes I was older than most but I looked younger, I was quick on the bases for my age and had a good strong bat. I always had a good bat but inconsistent which has bothered me. Batting is the hardest thing in baseball to perfect and stay away from slumps. Slumps happen to every ballplayer to include the professionals.

I always had a great curve ball but I would run into trouble by the third inning most of the time. When the players went around the batting order and I would see them for the second time that's when I had trouble. I use to throw this lazy curve ball which moved slowly level across the plate. This was big time trouble.

I finally watched the Major Leaguers on television and listen to the announcers describe the pitchers curve balls. That was enough for me. I learned how to throw and release the ball at a twelve six direction which became un-hittable. Now I had this devastating slider, a change up and I could mix my pitchers well.

The few problems that hurt me now was this; I needed a smart catcher who could work with me, know me, understand exactly what I had in my arsenal.

No you don't have to be fast at all. Its nice to have power but more important to trick the batter by changing speeds and pitch's. I spent a few years' having good games and bad games. I was learning all the time. I now had a good take on being a pitcher I was learning how to operate on the mound and not afraid as I was confident all the time.

I began working on long toss, weighted balls, throwing as often as I could try to build speed up. I also thought I needed to concentrate on accuracy and not to walk a batter. I had this thing in my head that if you walk someone, they usually will score as I believed that nearly 80% of them do but I don't know absolutely if that's true it's just my mind set.

To add to my work outs and training activity I would concentrate on control. I would go to a school or a place where there was a cement wall early in the morning before work and throw the ball against the concrete to improve speed and accuracy. I would make a strike zone and passersby's would give me strange looks but I didn't care I had a mission and journey.

During off season in my mid years I started a new practice that I still engage in. I go to the health club and get a private racket ball court; I would get those soft baseballs that were the same size as a real baseball but soft. I would get painters blue tape and make a small strike zone and then to the right I would have two spots about two feet apart. I would warm up with about seventy five pitch's throwing to the left then to the right, Back and fourth maintain accuracy not speed. Then I would move over and throw to the strike zone and one in the left bottom corner, then right lower corner, one top right, then top left and one in the middle. I would call each set of five a series. I would go through several series of curve balls, changeups, fastballs and then do an imaginary game. This is how I improved my accuracy to the strike zone.

I carried on this type of training for the past bunch of years as it has helped me tremendously. I have either led the over thirty league with least amount of walks or I placed second or third but always did well. I have improved in pitching every year because I care. I am now very accurate but play with the umpire and batters. I give them nothing to hit but some are now being more patient than the past with me. I make them go for bad pitches that are two balls on the outside of the plate or two balls on the inside of the plate.

I like to come inside and brush them back, and I take control and I am not afraid of any batter. It's exactly like this; the batter and I are half of the equation therefore "we are one". You get it! My half and their half equals one. Therefore one beats the other an equal chance for both of us.

I am not afraid of any batter. I beat the best and stuck out the best. Sometimes they beat me and hit a homerun or long drive but either way I'm ready for the competition to begin. I watch them closely as they are in the batters circle or especially when they approach the plate. I watch intently how they approach my plate, and if they crowd my plate? If they are too far away from my plate, and whether they are open or closed with their feet. I watch their pre swinging and also if they are aggressive. Sometimes they open their mouths and speak out loud over confident with the old guy. (Me). I love it keep the mouth going I have something for you. I'll immediately come near their face to let them know I can put the ball anywhere at any time with precision.

I have learned to be professional, confident, and demonstrate to the batter and their team that they are not going to have it easy, that they will have to earn their hit or go home. This is only done by the practice sessions I have developed, my determination and the love for the game to allow me to be a step above my personal expectations. This is when I am having fun. The hard work extra training, work ethic and mental approach all work together to lift your confidence or my confidence to be successful in a game. The more effective practice the more games the more you challenge yourself allows you the special reward that you so want.

Chapter Thirteen

My First League Home Run

It was a very hot Thursday evening and I was playing at Doyle Field in Leominster, Massachusetts. It was an Over 40 baseball league, which I was part of for five years and then later left for my current Sunday league. During my time in this current league I have never hit a home run, but I hit five off the fence. I've come close, but no cigar.

During this game at Doyle Field, I was playing center field. Outside the fence was a very pretty girl strolling around the track for exercise. I could not help but notice her. She smiled and waved.

This game was relatively close and I was right on the ball. My first at bat, I hit the ball right center gapper for a double. Then my second time at the plate I went up the middle for a single. The pitcher was a friend named Lenny. He said he used to pitch batting practice to Ted Williams the short time he was a professional baseball player.

Lenny was on the mound, I slid into the batter's box, set myself and felt very comfortable. He threw a pitch a little high, then the next pitch was a curve ball outside. There were no strikes and two balls. The next pitch was a curve that hung over the middle of the plate and I got all of that and set the ball deep over the left center field fence. I watched it all the way and when I stomped on first base, that felt great. The whole team came out to greet me and that was cool. It felt just as it had when I was in Little League playing ball and hitting my home runs there.

After I hit this home run my friend Mark hit one right after me, which made things even more exciting. When I was retrieving my home run ball outside the left field fence, I was also looking for the girl I had seen walking around the track. I jokingly thought she should sign the ball, since she inspired me moments prior to hitting the home run. This was all in fun, and just a good memory of my first league home run.

The next season I hit two more home runs, and I started to gain serious confidence at the plate and still maintain that ability. My hitting has excelled. My confidence and all around skills in baseball have continued to increase, as I am truly getting better and better playing baseball, despite my age or disability.

I am not safe, by any means. I have a quarterly check with the doctor and usually there is bad news. My heart has enlarged quite bit, therefore more danger and physical concerns to deal with, as well as more medications and more testing. People look at me and I can hear their thoughts loud and clear: "You're still playing baseball?"

I basically say to them, "Baseball is keeping me alive." I live and breathe baseball and I think there are little baseballs in my blood stream! People don't like to hear that stuff but I am right on it when I say it's keeping me alive.

Heart disease is a dilemma. It's a progressive killing disease and I'm doing all the correct things, like diet, exercise, medication, testing and so on, only stabilize and slow the process a bit, but in fact it is a disease that does not rest. I do have to face it and deal with it, and the best way I know is to play baseball, play harder, train harder and enjoy myself as much as humanly possible as long as I can be an affective, positive player. I'll be there taking grounders, catching fly balls, hitting and pitching. Those are my thoughts on the dreadful disease.

I'm usually a regular at my acupuncture doctor. Every time I come in with a new injury, she says, "Have you seen a doctor yet?" I simply say to her, "You are my doctor!" I go to see her several times a year. Getting hit by balls, broken bones, torn ligaments, twisted muscles, strains and pulls – you name it, it's happened to me. I try really hard to be a good patient in my rehab process, but sometimes it's hard to be good. I fell off a ladder and landed on my back on cement a few years ago, but besides my back being black and blue, I was fine.

The DeCosta family, 1955

Mom and Dad, 1965

My sister Joanne, Dad and me, playing ball in
the yard, 1956

Dad, ready for a day of fishing, 1962

THE EASTSIDE KID

Illustrating my wood bat skills to dad, 1955

Mom, Joanne and me, 1951

Chester Perry and I in our Cub Scout uniforms, 1956

Fishing on pier Onset Harbor-Onset, MA, 1965

THE EASTSIDE KID

22 Massasoit Avenue, Brockton, MA - our family home

John and Edward Perrota and myself with our skyscraper, 1957

Trying to be Elvis Presley, but decided to stick with baseball

East Junion High School City Champions, 1961-1962

Brockton High School Graduation, 1965

Mom, on her way to church, 1962

Mom and Dad, 1945–I was being planned...I hope!

THE EASTSIDE KID

Beth, on her way to horseback riding, 2007

Willie, a former sheepdog of ours

Abby, our sheepdog

THE EASTSIDE KID

Joshua, another of our sheepdogs

Charlie, my former baseball dog

Ginger and me, 1957

My pigeon coop

THE EASTSIDE KID

Beth and me, 1986, Fort Sam Houston, San Antonio, Texas
(Beth graduated from Officer Basic Training in the United States Army)

Operational Detachment (ODA 336), 10th Special Forces Group,
Fort Devens, MA, 1977

Just prior to a parachute jump at Turner Drop
Zone, Fort Devens, MA, 1976

Coach Jim Costa, another coach from Keene State, me, and a
catcher from Keene State, NH, 2005

Rudy

A group picture with my team and some German locals saying
goodbye–Operational Detachment "A," Flintlock Exercise, Germany, 1976

10th Special Forces Group, a winter jump at Turner Drop Zone,
Fort Devens, MA, 1976

THE EASTSIDE KID

Running from third base to catch a ball near
home plate, Hohokam Stadium, 2005

Playing third base at Doubleday Field,
Cooperstown, New York, 2005

Stacey Coporasso and my wife Beth at a game
in Cooperstown at Milford Field, 2005

Pitching for the 2005 Over 58 World Series,
Hohokan Stadium, Tempe, Arizona

Eastside Improvement Association Little League Baseball, 1959 Award
Winners: President– George "Scoop" Gustafson; Most Home Runs–
Billy Fulcher; Highest Batting Average–Ricardo Diniz;
Best Pitching Record George Phelan; Sportsmanship–Norman Benoit;
Most Valuable Player–John F. DeCosta

Eastside Improvement Association Little League, 1959

Downey Little League, Brockton, MA, 1958

Downey Little League, Brockton, MA, 1957

Hitting a line drive for Over 30 baseball in Lowell, MA, 2004

My birthday basketball game—Competing in the Over-50 Cedardale
Invitational Tournament, December, 1998. We were awarded the full-court
Champs for a 3-on-3 game, with 22, 19, and 17 points in three games!

Springfield Hall of Fame, 1998—Competing in the Over-50, 3- on-3
Tournament. My team won the Bronze medal in the Senior Olympic
Games, Four Horsemen!

THE EASTSIDE KID

Rochester, NH, 1998–I won a gold medal for the 3-point Shooting Contest.
I shot 13 out of 15 shots with an average of 23 points per game!

Jeff McKay and Bill Lee, Middlebury, Vermont, 2004

Yours Truly in catcher's gear at Middlebury, Vermont

I am pitching to Bill Lee at Middlebury College

Bill Lee giving his "Spaceman'" instructions

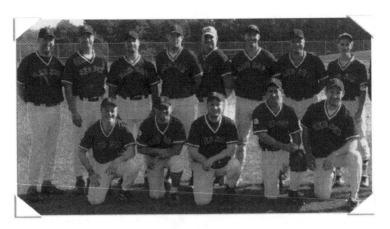

Over Thirty Baseball, Red Sox, 2004

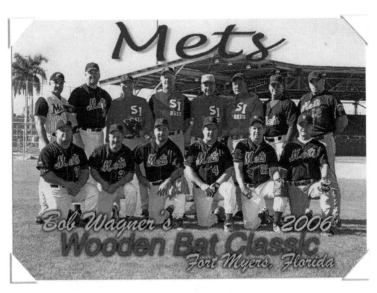

2006 Wooden Bat Classic "Mets"., Terry Park

Homerun derby at LeLacheur Stadium, Lowell, MA with friends
Mike Gilronan, George Peavey, Rob Ortiz, John DeCosta and Bill Keefe

Homerun derby at LeLacheur Stadium, Lowell, MA with friends
Brian Cole, John DeCosta, Bob Emerson and Frank Kavalowskas

2007 Over 30 baseball, "Phillies" National League Champions

Washington Nationals team at Cooperstown, New York, 2007

On deck waiting to hit, Cooperstown, New York, 2007

Brian Cole and Jeff Allison Homerun Derby winners.

Author, John F DeCosta

THE EASTSIDE KID

Beth with her horse, "Chocolate Truffles"

Beth preparing for her dressage competition.

THE EASTSIDE KID

Beth with Joshua our Old English Sheepdog-Taking a break on a walk.

Beth and a Frisian horse name "Bravo"

Mom at work Boston Army Base-1964

Johnny D-Pitching at Roger Dean Stadium Juniper, Florida

Johnny D-Pitching "closer" Burkholder Field-Las Vegas, Nevada
Over 50 Baseball Tournament 2010.

Long Island Braves in 2009 and 2010 World Series-Phoenix, Arizona

Lowell Millers from Lowell , Ma- Las Vegas Over 50 Tournament 2010

NOTB; Night Over Thirty Baseball; Champions 2009

Las Vegas Tournament, waiting to finish off last batter.

Phoenix World Series, waiting for ride to Baseball Complex.

THE EASTSIDE KID

Roger Dean Stadium, waiting to go to the mound!

That's me! 2009 OTB Banquet. MVP of All-star game, MVP of Team,
First Place Hitting Contest at Minor League stadium "LeLacheur"
and Manager's award.

Herby Jones, My mentor and Legend from Downey little League- Sept 2010
This was a reunion since 1957 another great memory!

John DeCosta, Eric Campanelli and Daniel Eric Goodwin
Danny had been KIA in Viet Nam 1967 Marine Corp

My first new car-1968 Camarro Super Sport Turquoise wi Black vinyl top

My friend Roy Andrade from Brockton- Sharing some memories!

Here I am Black Hat Drill Instructor for Parachute School Fort Devens, ma

In the bush, in the Black Forest, Germany 1976

Here I am in 1976, Black Forest-Germany in the bush! On patrol.

Elizabeth and I in our photo for 25th Wedding Anniversary.

Chapter Fourteen

Paratrooper Brotherhood

"AIRBORNE ALL THE WAY"

What separates them from the rest
these men with silver wings,
troopers from the sky above
in which devotion springs?
What spirit so unites them?
In brotherhood they say
their answer loud and clear:
Airborne, all the way.
These are the men of danger
as in open door they stand
with static line above them
and ripcord in their hand.
While earthbound they are falling
a silent prayer they say,
Lord be with us forever;
Airborne, all the way.
One day they will make their final jump;
St. Michael will tap them out.
The Lord will be waiting.
He knows what they are about.
And answering in cadence
He'll hear the troopers say
We are glad to be aboard, Sir!
Airborne, all the way.

I have read this poem many times, so all can hear. The setting is usually a grave site or funeral home. The atmosphere is always solemn and with intense emotion, so real and close to my heart. Many soldiers are currently deployed overseas, serving our country honorably, yet no active duty here to speak of in the United States.

I served twelve years of honorable service as a paratrooper, and I worked for the federal government as well. I am a life member to the Disabled American Veterans, the 82nd Airborne Association, Special Forces Association, The Legion, and Veterans of Foreign Wars. So I guess you can see how involved, dedicated and patriotic I am. With all that said, it is why I participate in parades, ceremonies, dedications, and attend funerals for our departed heros. I feel it's a small service that I can still provide, but yet something.

My friend and airborne brother who served in Europe in the paratroopers and who now resides in Onset, Massachusetts, started an airborne reunion a few years back and invited seventy-five of his closest friends and airborne friends from all over the country. He provided a large free buffet at his restaurant, and we all had a wonderful afternoon and ceremony. This started six years ago and has grown to over three hundred and fifty people attending this wonderful brotherhood. He personally cooks, and offers free buffet to all veterans and the local public.

He further helps the homeless and the needy during Thanksgiving and Christmas season and is such a unique person, I decided to write a story about him and his good deeds to veterans and everyday people. The story I wrote was published in an airborne magazine.

I wrote several short stories and had them published. Then a few opportunities came my way. First there was Buck O'Brien. I went to a ceremony in Bridgewater, Massachusetts two years ago. This man, Buck, was a paratrooper from World War II . He also had four other brothers who served during World War II at the same time. Buck became a POW but luckily escaped. After the war he raised a family, and worked for the post office for the next thirty years until he reached retirement. Yet he never received his well-deserved Prisoner of War medal from the government. Two weeks before he died, the U.S. government sent him his award...but the box was empty!

Twenty years after Buck's death, his family was finally awarded his Prisoner of War medal. During the ceremony one of the relatives read my baseball story that was published in the newspaper and there was a lot of positive feedback from the family. The family then asked me to write their story, and I was delighted. In my research I found that the uncle to the five brothers and two sisters was Walter "Buck" O'Brien, a pitcher for the Boston Red Sox back in 1911! He opened the season against the New York Yankees and won in extra innings, eight to six. He was also the first major league player to pitch for the Boston Red Sox in Fenway Park. I had done up the story nicely and put it in a booklet, making several copies for the O'Brien family.

This led to other stories and opportunities. Later I established a close relationship with a friend of mine and a World War II hero, Berge Avadanian. He was a paratrooper legend. He made five combat D-Day parachute jumps. He and I began a relationship similar to the men in the story, *Tuesdays with Morrie*. During that time, he asked me to re-write his life story. I did so but unfortunately, he passed away before he could finish the story with me. I completed the story two weeks after his death. He died on the D-Day anniversary. He was quite the man to admire. I respect him so deeply. I presented the completed story to his family too.

The stories I wrote about Berge Avadanian, and Buck O'Brien, were both published, and I also sent copies to the 82nd Airborne archives, to share with other paratroopers. In a short while I received numerous phone calls from paratroopers from all over the country. Some wrote or called me, asking to republish the stories in other magazines and organizations for veterans. I gave the ok, but in one situation a military retiree in Fayetteville, North Carolina published one of my stories and took the credit for it. He later apologized to me.

I did receive a lot of recognition and one particular man really got my attention. He was Jim Costa from Claremont, New Hampshire. He had known Berge Avadanian and was so emotional and appreciative of my writing. We talked, exchanged emails, and spoke on the phone on many occasions. Jim and I became good friends. We exchanged several stories from our lives. Jim had written a book called *Diamond in the Rough*. He sent me a copy and graciously signed the book. He later changed his book cover, changed a few items in his book, but signed the new version and sent that to me as well.

As I said, Jim and I shared stories, and when I mentioned baseball, a whole new relationship was born. Jim was a Minor League baseball player, and due to military service, being a combat veteran, he had lost his leg in the Korean War. Jim lost out on baseball but with a strong family unity and the will to succeed he had gone into the machine shop business and was very successful. He raised a fine family and now, being a grandfather, wanted to share with his grandchildren and children his talent in baseball.

Jim asked if I could come and throw baseballs to him while he and I were being videotaped for a DVD for his grandchildren. I thought, *yes, I will be glad to help.* I was planning on going to Vermont in another month at the time and I thought, I would leave early and spend the morning pitching to him and getting reacquainted. Then off to Bill and Jeff's baseball weekend in Middlebury, Vermont.

Jim had set the time early that Friday morning so I would still be able to go to Vermont. I went early and met Jim for a quick breakfast in Keene, New Hampshire. This is when I met the Keene State College coach, who was one of Jim's friends. We soon went to the college field. He had another gentleman come from college with a video camera and sound system, and there was also a college catcher to help out.

He administered some soft toss to help get Jim loosened up. Keep in mind, Jim is seventy-six years old, with an artificial leg! After he signaled he was ready, the coach took the field and I took the mound, with a few buckets of balls. I pitched four buckets of balls to him and he did very well, scattering balls all over the field.

Jim hit some pretty good drives but I think he was disappointed about not hitting any out. I said, "Jim, it's been a lot of years since you have picked up a bat or held a ball, so don't be so hard on yourself. You did great and better than a lot of young guys that I know. You hit some nice drives, and I'm sure your family will be very proud of you."

Jim finally finished and I got a chance to throw hard to the college catcher. That was fun, as I surprised them all with my varied speeds, control and pin-point accuracy. We took a lot of pictures, and then I packed up and continued to my planned baseball weekend at Middlebury College. My arm was sore when I got there from throwing so much!

_____

Chapter Fifteen

Port Charlotte, Florida
Winter Baseball

On December 5, 2004, I turned fifty-eight. How about this—that day it was about fifty-two degrees, the sun was out, it wasn't windy at all, and a perfect day for baseball. I made some calls and had three friends join me at Hadley Field in Chelmsford, Massachusetts to hit some balls. Things could not be any better, playing baseball on my birthday in New England. We all hit two buckets of balls a piece, threw the ball, and then after we collected our gear, we went and had pizza and soda. That was the first time I ever played baseball on my birthday, since it's in December and it's normally freezing outside. This was definitely a great preparation for my tournament at Port Charlotte, Florida in January the following month.

When I arrived with my wife in Fort Myers, Florida, we quickly went to the baggage claim. My only concern was my baseball bag. Everything else could be replaced. We soon grabbed our rental car, and off to Port Charlotte, Florida we drove. The homes in all the cities and towns along the way had incurred incredible damage from Hurricane Charley the previous summer, from uprooted trees and twisted metal posts to demolished homes. When we arrived in Port Charlotte, it was not impressive at all, but the fields at the sports complex were great. My team was called Egypt. We played a total of eight games and played well together. I established friendships and solid bonds with most of the players and still maintain these friendships, hopefully forever. We played a tough tournament and again, came in second. I pitched about twenty-two innings this week, and during one game, I went ten innings but we lost four to three in a thriller. I hit the ball well, and even in the tenth inning I came through with a hard shot up the middle, but no one hit after me in and we lost. It was truly a pitcher's dual and I held back my emotions, for it was such a tough loss.

The pitcher and I have squared off before and we will meet again. He is quite the gamer, and we will reunite on the diamond, that's for sure. Whenever any ballplayer comes to Florida for any baseball tournament, you can be very sure that you will play on terrific first-class major league fields.

My Christmas present that year, a stealth baseball bat, had allowed me to continue my hot hitting streak while in the tournament and I was fortunate I had done so well. I was invited to attend with this baseball group to another tournament at Doubleday Field in Cooperstown, New York in September and November. I was not only invited and recruited, but one of the guys had airline miles and paid my way to the Phoenix Baseball World Series! So that year was starting off very exciting for me.

Snow back home ended up delaying our return to Boston. It was too late to enter the Fort Myers Tournament but I would do so the next year. So back to the drawing board, to buy more updated baseball equipment, plan out tournaments for the year, get ready for the upcoming baseball season, and start right away at the batting cages, staying sharp.

The routine I use before every game is like this: The games start at eight thirty a.m. on Sunday, for example. I get up at four thirty a.m. After eating breakfast, showering, feeding the dogs, and getting my baseball equipment ready, I do a lot of stretching, usually for about thirty minutes. Then I head for the nearby high school. I then get my batting T out and hit about fifty to seventy-five balls into the backstop. Now I am loose. My next move is going to the field. Usually all the baseball fields have a basketball court nearby. I then get my basketball out and shoot hoops for a half hour. More stretching and then throwing warm-up to two or three players to make sure I am real loose and warmed up correctly. I do this before every game.

With my age, my disabilities, and the competition I face pitching, and hitting, I need all of this workout and then some.

My team the Red Sox has had this guy come to all of our games. He is eighty-three years old and our most loyal fan. He loves our team. I got all the guys to chip in and get him a Red Sox uniform shirt. His nick name is Pickles, so on the back of the shirt is the number eighty-three, for his age, and his name, Pickles. Everyone felt good about that. I guess we are his baseball family.

I made the all-star team two years out of six so I'm happy for that. The team votes for that. Each team has two, and we have sixteen teams. I also made the all-star team for the Boston Men's Senior Baseball League and pitched a few innings in their all-star game.

This season, yes, I was totally ready for. I was in shape, hitting the ball well, and very accurate, with better velocity to accompany my super control. The first game, my first at bat, and then the first pitch came and hit me in the upper rib. I was in severe pain but played the rest of the game. I still ended up with three hits. Towards the end of the next day, I was in excruciating pain. I went to the hospital and discovered that I had a broken rib! I had to wear a brace, intended for la cross, but it worked for me for this purpose. I managed to go to a batting practice two weeks later and my friend and competitor, Brian, hit me with a fast ball and almost broke another rib!

I came back to play but I wasn't one hundred percent. Three weeks later I pulled a muscle in my upper thigh. I rested and went to acupuncture for the two separate injuries—a broken rib and a torn muscle in my thigh. I had hopes to play better baseball injury-free. Then, three weeks later I got hit by a line drive pitching and almost broke my leg! I spent the whole season dodging injuries, and recovering.

Despite being hurt I went to Connecticut for a weekend baseball camp. Jeff and Mark ran this camp at Wesleyan College. It was so much fun pitching to a real college baseball coach. That was a treat. I still communicate with him from time to time.

I caught a minor league game while I was there and that was super. The teams playing were Norwich angainst New Britain. It was nice to be in a professional atmosphere once again. In September I went to Cooperstown, New York and played nine games there and had a spectacular time.

The excitement of any tournament is beyond imagination. If you're talking about Cooperstown, wow—an amazing dream land. As it is when playing at the plate tournaments in Florida, Roy Hob's, Wooden Bat Classic, International baseball, Phoenix World Series, MSBL Men's Senior Baseball League in Las Vegas, or Over 50 Baseball in Las Vegas. The atmosphere, the demeanor of the players, the skills, and everyone's love for the game are all beyond comprehension. If you were to listen to a conversation between ball players, you would think you were listening to professional players. They are serious, love the game and can't get enough of it.

My Port Charlotte experience with Baseball International has proven to be so rich, providing me with many rewarding friendships. I met Mike, Ron, and Ray, among many others. I made future tournaments and whether playing with them or against them, our molded friendships will last forever. They have the fever I have been talking about: The passion of baseball.

Chapter Sixteen

Doubleday Dreams

I'm watching the Little League World Series and relaxing, but always thinking baseball. While I'm watching the Little Leaguers I can't help but go back in time and reminisce about my experiences playing at Downey Little League as well as The East Side Improvement Association and all the games, friends, and experiences I had during that time. To watch this on TV is quite amazing, and the kids' talents are so spectacular now, compared to years ago.

Cooperstown, New York – it doesn't get any better than this. This is where baseball began. I can still remember my walk up the old wooden ramp leading into Doubleday Baseball Field. My wife and I had walked up the steps and instantly everything was in slow motion. I could hear the crowd, the noise of ballplayers, the sound of wood bats cracking against the ball, and this beautiful authentic ballpark before my eyes. My wife was talking to me but I didn't hear a word she said. I was choked up and so overwhelmed with all I was taking in: the history, the hall of fame down the street, the sandlot statue by the street, the batting cages. Wow!

The thought of me pitching, playing third base, hitting the ball, running the bases…I could not wait. This was truly a dream. There are homes on the outside of the fence overlooking this field. I thought, *I hope they are baseball enthusiast or they should move.*

The maintenance crew was unbelievable. To think that they play an average of three hundred and forty games each year, four games each day, and the field is immaculate and so perfect all day long. There are no divots, no pebbles, and no bad grass. It's so soft, like a mattress. I know this because when I was lying down to stretch I could not believe how comfortable it was. Fenway Park in Boston only plays eighty games per year, as compared to this complex, if that gives you further thought.

While I was playing on the field, I had to keep myself alert because it was so easy to drift, dream, or just look around and not pay attention to the game. Concentration was very tough here. The dugouts were different, down under with a steel beam at eye level and nine out of ten players hit their head on the steel beam as you step down into the dugout.

They do not allow camera crews on the field. If you're not playing you can't be anywhere near the grass or dugouts. When the game is not on, players have to be careful where they walk as they have a ton of rules. I guess that's how they keep it in such good shape.

The dirt is shipped in from out west, processed and reprocessed before being spread onto the field. I did manage to "borrow" some red dirt from Doubleday for my collection of special baseball places.

The village at Cooperstown is quite unique and full of memorabilia, and everything to do with baseball is there. You immediately melt into the baseball magic instantly when you arrive. Not very far down the road is a place called Dreams Park. This is a baseball complex for Little League baseball teams to compete in tournaments. That is quite interesting to look at.

The Legends of Baseball tournament that I had played in had three fields. The first one, of course, was Doubleday, then the second was Beaver Valley Campground. This was a field of dreams. It had the corn stalks out in the outfield and players would put on or take off their shirts as if they were in the movie "Field of Dreams." The third field was Milford Park, another extremely well-groomed baseball field. All three are some of the best in all of the Northeast part of our country. If you don't visit and share this experience, you're missing out.

The Hall of Fame is also here and a must-see. The tournament I had participated in was held in September, so no school kids, no lines, and nine games with the possibility of playing eleven games in five days. I pitched twenty-three innings and played well, bought a few Cooperstown bats, and enjoyed the fantastic energy there. Will I return and play there again? You bet I will.

Chapter Seventeen

Terrorist Training

The radio station I was listening to had a guest speaker. This was not a normal guest but a voice I could not forget. This was Colonel David Hunt, a TV and radio Middle-East analyst. How do I know him? Because while stationed at Fort Devens, Massachusetts, I had left Special Forces duty to be reassigned to the Post Garrison unit for an opportunity and challenge to be an operations and training non-commissioned officer. I took this job as a ticket puncher in my career in the military. Colonel Hunt was my commander there and I remember him well.

Colonel Hunt wrote a book called, *They Just Don't Get It*, and was promoting his book on TV and the radio. He was also announcing a book signing session at Borders Book Store in Portland, Maine. I thought to myself, *I should go see him, and purchase his book*. I then drove up to Portland – yes, a very grueling drive, but I still arrived early. I therefore went to the nearby mall and sporting goods store to kill time, and then went to Borders and sat in the front row.

I could hear his approach as his voice is a voice I could not forget. He went to the podium and gave a thirty-minute talk and took questions from the crowd. He looked at the different folks in the crowd and very often glanced at me, and I could see his wheels turning as he thought, *where do I know this guy?* I had a miniature set of parachute wings on my light blue dress shirt, and I'm sure he honed in on that. After the question and answer period, I got in line with the others to have him sign the book I had just bought. He was very positive, recognized me immediately and was very thankful I went through all the trouble to drive up to see him. That turned out to be a nice experience, for I had never been to a book signing prior to this.

Colonel Hunt, as I said, was my commanding officer. He was prior Special Forces, so he and I had shared stories and memories, as well as having similar backgrounds in the military. I had an enormous amount of respect for him, and I was very proud to have served under his command. One particular day I was in the middle of paper work in my office, and all of a sudden thirty guys dressed in black clothing raided the hallways, clearing all rooms, and securing the building with weapons! They were anti-terrorist FBI, assault swat soldiers.

The next day I questioned him on the training that had taken place, and he immediately said to me, "Would you like to come and do some training?" I said, "Yes, sir, I'm ready."

The mission was as follows: we were to operate a training exercise at Boston's Logan Airport for anti-terrorist training. This mission was for real life training for the Summer Olympics back in 1984. We had an airplane, a group of small buildings, a wing of the terminal; I would provide about twenty volunteers to be hostages on an aircraft. I was an organizer of the operations and coordination of this exercise. There were a total of one hundred and fifty personnel involved. There were FBI agents, Boston swat teams, Boston police, undercover police, military police, New York swat teams, and secret service.

I also had to obtain a moulage kit, which makes people look like they were shot, bleeding or a had bad wound, all of it being artificial. I had to obtain transportation, meals, weapons, 45 pistols, Uzi machine guns, etc, as well as plastic bullets. After all this was organized, I then became a terrorist with five hostages in a small building and our mission was to barter for food, and whatever it would take to get to the aircraft and apprehend it. I was to be a bad terrorist. This exercise took half the afternoon and all through the night, as we finished at about five a.m. the next morning.

We traded hostages for pizza, and after trading so much, near the end we only had two hostages left. There was a touch and go point when, during the training, I had to put a light on to show that I had a hostage holding a gun to his head, with a mask over my face. At that particular time a Boston patrol vehicle slowly drove by but was not alerted to the training and picked a great time to come by. My plastic bullets would not have saved me. They were notified and the mission was completed. It had turned out to be a great experience for me.

Near the end of the exercise we ran out of time and hostages to trade, so we made an attempt to head for the aircraft. As we walked back to back holding weapons, the special marksman put the lasers on us and we were gone. That ended the training.

One of my female soldiers said to me the next day, "Staff Sergeant DeCosta, you looked very real during that operation and I was scared!" I said to her, "Relax. It was training and everything will be ok." Soon after, I received some recognition from Colonel Hunt. He got reassigned to another unit, and I went in another direction. That was twenty-two years ago.

Chapter Eighteen

Phoenix World Series

The tournament season was in full force at this point, and I was going to Phoenix, Arizona for the World Series. There are over three hundred and fifty teams with thirty different divisions flying in and out of Phoenix during the months of October and November each year to participate in this tournament. There are as little as fourteen men on a team to as many as thirty-two. They all want to win, so sometimes you may see former professionals, or "secret weapons" flown out for free, to compete.

I got recruited for the Virginia Silver Eagles in the Over 58 Division. My friends Ray and Ken wanted me to come. They are both great, as we played together in Florida as well as Cooperstown. Ray made arrangements for me to use his sky miles to attend. That was so super. I am grateful to him to help me with that. Otherwise I would not have been able to attend.

I left my family to play ball, and my baseball gear had been packed for sometime now. It's always hard when I leave home, especially for my wife. She is a nurse and is always worrying about my health when I'm away from home and across the country. I try to assure her all will be fine. Her loving support means so much to me. While sitting at the airport all checked in, like a little kid I was thinking, *I'm going to play some baseball!*

I was spoken highly of and expected to do wonderful things, therefore I was hoping I would be as good as others had spoken about me. I just did my best, played hard, and the skills took over. My friend Ray and I are both from the north–New York for him, and Boston for me. The rest of the team was a softball click that played together for years in the Virginia area. Therefore we were considered Yankees. We could definitely sense that feeling throughout the tournament.

I ended up being passed around as the team's ace, and although that felt good, there was a lot of pressure to be "lights out." I had noticed at our first game how many people were watching me, scouting for other teams. They also had a mini reporter for the small news report after the games each day. Things were like other tournaments in the center of five fields were massage therapists doing quick twenty-minute massages for the injured. There were hot dogs, and memorabilia, bats and hats for sale, and families for support.

The umpires arrived and I was ready. I received a nice brand new World Series-stamped baseball, with a loud voice saying, "Play ball!"

I pitched a great game. I pitched a four hitter, with nine strikeouts, no walks, and no earned runs. We still lost three to nothing. My team was terrible—couldn't hit, couldn't throw, couldn't catch the ball, therefore I was wasted.

The next day the team that won had a pitcher that was terrible, with no strikeouts and several walks, but was the "winning pitcher" and got a huge write up. If I had won I think the write-up would have been rewarding.

We won the second game. I played short stop and played well. How we won, I have no idea. The next game was played at the Hohokam Stadium, our only stadium game. There I had my best baseball game. I played short stop, made about fourteen put outs to include a relay from left field, and I threw a guy out at the plate. I also ran all the way in past the catcher to retrieve a high pop up which they captured on film. I closed out the last two innings pitching with four strikeouts, but it was too late, as we lost three to two. I must add that up in the sky box an announcer introduced all the batters over a loud-speaker, so it was great when he announced, "Number twenty-two, John DeCosta, will now hit." That was very cool. And hit I did—I hit a line drive, stole a base and scored a run.

I played well the rest of the tournament but we were out of contention. Later in the tournament we played at Surprise, which was an incredible stadium built down under the ground level, with eight well-groomed fields on the surface. When I say down under, I mean just that. The whole stadium would be beneath your feet if you were standing near the outfield fence! The best thing we could do was enjoy playing the last few games, and not spoil things for the other teams.

We had a few team dinners, one of them being at Rustler Roof. That was at the top of a hill overlooking Phoenix. When we walked in the front door we saw a corral with a live bull in it. Then we walked through a rock hallway, and there was a real metal slide we had to slide down in order to reach the hostess! Rattlesnake was on the menu, but not for me.

Our last team dinner was at Don and Charlie's, another must-see baseball restaurant with an unimaginable amount of memorabilia, which was so neat to see and talk about. This was so appropriate for a baseball trip.

Ball fields out in Phoenix are very nice and super groomed. After all, they have been winter baseball facilities for so long. While I was playing I couldn't help but think, *what old baseball players have stepped in the same place I have stepped, and played in the hot sun and felt such love for the game as I do?* The sun sure was bright, and I was there in November when the temperatures were in the low nineties. The locals there said it was cool compared to what they were used to!

I finished up the trip after our last loss and went to a mall nearby to get Beth some wine glasses for a gift. They arrived safely at home a week later. When I travel I always try to bring home a gift or mail one home to my wife. She doesn't usually accompany me, since she does not like sitting in the hot sun watching baseball.

In January 2006, I traveled to Terry Park in Fort Myers, Florida for Bob Wagner's Wood Bat Classic. More baseball for my future memory lane is always a dream in itself.

Chapter Nineteen

Terry Park with the Mets

On January 22, 2006, I participated in Bob Wagner's Wood Bat Tournament at Terry Park baseball facility. Mike Caputo, or Mick Number Seven, my Mets Manager, has been a super teammate and great manager in the past with me. We played in Florida and then he was a manager up in Cooperstown, New York. During the holidays I had special-ordered a complete Mets uniform for this and other future tournaments with the Long Island boys. They are a great bunch of guys and I always look forward to this tournament in January.

Terry Park is in the Fort Myers, Florida area, and was built back in 1896. It officially started in competition games around 1925. Such players as Babe Ruth, Lou Gehrig, Bob Feller, Willie Stargell, Roberto Clemente, Jimmie Foxx, and of course, Tyrus Cobb, all played there. Can you imagine digging in the batter's box, throwing off the mound, scooping up ground balls, running the bases or flying after a ball in the outfield? What I'm saying is, playing baseball in the same spot as these legends was a dream come true. Yes, once again, I collected a small jar of dirt as a keepsake from Terry Park on this trip.

My new uniform, number twenty-two, had my name on the back. This uniform had just arrived from UPS, from Mike, and I had been taking real good care of my wood bats as well. This cold New England weather is always tough on my bats, so they are safe inside and ready to play.

The flight from Logan Airport in Boston went as planned and I arrived at JFK Airport and soon met Mike in the terminal. We then boarded the aircraft for Fort Myers, Florida. Soon after we left baggage claim, Rich, one of my new teammates, picked us up and we then raced to Terry Park, field number three, as we had a one hour time slot for our team to have practice. We accomplished a lot in an hour and I was well acclimatized from that practice. Many had known me from other tournaments and there were new players, and very good ones that I had to prove myself to once again. I am used to that, and I look at it as just another challenge. Meeting the new players was fun and inspiring. I liked the idea that most of the team was better than me. That meant I was full of challenges to play harder, and luckily my personal skills always seem to improve with better talent.

I hit the ball well, showed my defensive skills, and now the pitching coach wanted to see how I threw the ball off the mound with the other pitchers. I was not on target but I threw hard. Therefore I was the number two pitcher. The big left-hander was the ace, which was fine with me. He went the distance and won the game. We won four to nothing. Then, during our second game, against the Hurricanes, we lost eleven to eight, as the pitching coach pitched badly, and it was too late to recover. The team had played badly on this day.

In the third game I pitched eight innings and we won. I pitched well, therefore, for the remaining tournament, Jim the left-hander and I would do all the pitching. Jim and I were unstoppable and we regained our lead in the tournament. I once again pitched and this time it was in Terry Park. During this game a funny thing had happened. There are usually some family, friends and a small crowd at most games, but on this occasion, as I was on the mound, directly behind the umpire was this very pretty girl. She had long brown hair, was smiling away and cheering for our team. Like a dummy, I thought she was looking at me. It didn't affect my concentration or accuracy, but she got my attention. When the inning was over, she moved near the dugout with her small sun blanket and shades, listening to music.

I said to my short stop, Mike Baltieri, "Hey, did you see that girl?"

He had this big smile on his face and said, "John, that's my girlfriend." I turned a few shades of red, and then we laughed. There I was pitching, with mike playing short stop behind me, and she was looking at him and smiling, not at me! It became a very fun joke on the dugout bench.

In the middle of the week I was able to go to a nearby spa and have a deep tissue sports massage. I then went to a gift store to get Beth a music box.

Our team was quite unique – there were lawyers, police officers, nurses, car dealership owners, stock brokers, people in the jewelry business, landscapers, real estate brokers, and such a variety of baseball players. At these tournaments we only talked baseball. The other unique thing about this group was they organized and did pranks on each other the whole week, which took the tension off the players, and helped us play so well as a team. It was like we had always played together. That was a fun group.

There were sixteen teams in this tournament and at one point we were six wins and one loss. If we won the next game, where Jim would pitch, we would go to the finals. I would then pitch against Bill and his Knights. Unfortunately we lost, so that game would never happen for us. We, the Mets, ended up with six wins and two losses, so we did well in the tournament. My friend Randy, from Massachusetts, was working near the Fort Myers area and came to see the game and have lunch at Shoeless Joe's Café after the game. I did, however, continue my tradition and collected a jar of Terry Park red dirt.

We had a team dinner, and this was funny. Everyone on the team was there, and near the end of our meal, we were waiting for dessert to be delivered in this fine Italian Restaurant. It was, of course, very busy at the time, so it was completely filled up with a line of more customers patiently waiting at the door to come in. Well, all of a sudden the lights started to blink slowly as if there was a power surge. Then the lights finally went out for good. The whole place started looking around, and then the hostess walked in, carrying a small piece of cake with a candle on it. She went directly to our manager as if it were his birthday. Everyone in the restaurant started cheering and then they all sang "Happy Birthday" to Mike.

Mike went along with things, with a grin from ear to ear. The problem was, it was not Mike's birthday! His birthday was not for six more months. This was a prank by one of the teammates on our team and no one would own up to it. That was hilarious. There were countless pranks the whole week long. That kept everyone very loose and as a result we really became a team with energy and chemistry. That was one of the best teams I have ever played with.

I enjoy crunch time the most. When the game is on the line, I like to be the one throwing the ball. I liked it in basketball as well, with a few seconds left and I'm the one who takes the shot. I like being on the edge. I want the ball to pitch, or I want to be at bat. I feel confident, and I like the idea I am consistent and trusted by my teammates. This only makes me work harder off season because it gets harder to compete all the time. My progressive heart problems are bad cards I was dealt, but others I have met in competition baseball also deal with disabilities such as artificial limbs, kidney transplants, cancer, lung problems, and many say nothing about their ailments. They all love the game of baseball and we all share a very common bond.

I look forward to playing with this group again. We all may get together this coming winter if I have the funds. First, before the holidays, I will play at Shea Stadium in New York, for a charity event. And then I will play in the International Baseball Tournament in Sarasota, Florida's spring training complex, then The Wood Bat Classic once again at Terry park, and finally, in April, it's Play at the Plate Tournament at Roger Dean stadium in West Palm Beach, Florida. This is my present dream list. I would love to do more but hey, I'm not rich.

Chapter Twenty

Middlebury, Vermont Baseball

Columbus Day Baseball Camp, at Middlebury College, Middlebury, Vermont–this is where the original "extra innings" were formed by Jeff McKay, an ex paratrooper and a very knowledgeable baseball batting coach. Jeff has been a batting coach for many years, from the college ranks through the professional ranks. He has lots to boast about but does not choose to do so. He has been a batting coach for UCLA, UMASS, University of Washington, and Middlebury College, as well as coaching professional baseball in Cincinnati, and for the San Francisco Giants. So he is one to listen to.

Jeff, because of his experience in baseball, and being an alumnus at Middlebury College, had many contacts, including Bill Lee from the Boston Red Sox, otherwise known as "The Spaceman." They together had brought the idea of having this baseball camp during Columbus Day weekend. College baseball season was over for the college; usually it is homecoming week while this is going on, with an important football game and several soccer games that the college hosts each year at this time. This is a very busy time for the college, with so many events in and around the college and the township. As the fall is settling in the area, nature paves the way for winter, which is a nearly perfect time for baseball. The scenic setting, the mountains, the fall colors, with sixty-five degree weather, while playing baseball on the beautiful college field – is this the best or what? When there is rain or any type of weather related problems we train in the "bubble." The bubble is larger than a football field. That was an option for our group last year as half the weekend was destroyed by rain. We continued, made the best of the situation and thus the camp turned into another successful weekend baseball trip.

The camp starts Columbus Day weekend each year, and usually meet-up time occurs on that Friday during the hours of two p.m. to four p.m. on the baseball diamond. Who comes to this event, you might ask? Well, anyone who loves baseball – office executives, past college players, some young women who actively play baseball or softball, people from all age groups that want to get away and clear their heads, improve their personal baseball skills, and meet others with the same drive and inspiration. Some have a father and son weekend, others go for the love of the game, and yet others are just gamers. The group usually consists of about fifteen participants for the weekend. So the ages run from fourteen years old to sixty-five. When each person participates they are there for their own personal goals.

There is an incredible amount of one-on-one personal instruction, so there is no competition between the participants. This is where you learn to coach yourself, in the future.

I usually start out early in the morning and take a leisurely ride up to Vermont from my home. It's about a four-hour ride, so I stop on the old country roads and at an old fashion diner on my way there. I usually arrive in the Middlebury Village around noon. I browse the shops and pick up a sweat shirt or novelty for Beth. Sometime she might come with me, but she likes the Middlebury Inn or five-star hotels, which are tough to find in this area.

I then go to the beautiful ball field, walk around enjoying the scenic mountains and breathing baseball. Usually there is that sweet, soft, fall breeze in the air, noise from the soccer fields nearby or occasionally the playing of the college girls' softball team holding practice for their tournament play on the softball field next to the baseball field. I usually do a lot of stretching, hit some balls off the tee, and my other favorite thing to do is look for lost baseballs. Sometimes I'll find forty or fifty of them! I even found a football in the woods one time. I'm a sports scavenger at times, you might say. I have about four hundred balls at home and I give them away to kids who appreciate baseball. Sometimes I find bats, gloves, and I just save the extras for someone who doesn't have much or can't afford things. The richer kids will just get a new one, right?

Finally the new group is starting to arrive. Jeff appears with equipment, and the college coach or college players lend a hand to assist, and then Bill

Lee arrives. You can always tell when he's around because there's always a lot of chatter, baseball bats flying out of the trunk of his car and everyone wanting his attention. Bill Lee sells baseball bats from his company, The Old Bat, and they are pretty good, I must say – very distinctive with a big knob.

Jeff usually starts off with introductions to all, and forecasts the weekend before us, and then we stretch, run the bases lightly and take positions in the field – one person at bat, one on deck, another hitting off the tee, and personal instructions start. You do observe and see where people are and it's really fun to see how well they progress in two and a half days. It's truly amazing.

When all have hit about fifty balls, and Jeff remembers how to approach each player, he has a plan in effect. The main thing is to not let Bill lose your concentration. He is Mr. Baseball but from time to time he has you in hysterics. He does a lot for baseball, so much for youth, and he believes (as I do) that there should be no Designated Hitter either (DH), nor artificial turf, nor metal bats. He feels it's not real baseball. I agree with him one-hundred percent, but I don't think those things will change. You will learn a lot from Bill, but truth be known, he does not like right-handed batters, or right-handed pitchers.

The plan at this point is to meet at a downtown restaurant, for example the Ice House, and enjoy a get-acquainted meal time. When dinner and drinks are completed, we caravan over to Lake Dunmore at Dunmore Acres and then are assigned cabins. There are about ten cabins there and a large meeting hall with an enormous fireplace and game area.

The cabins are located on Lake Dunmore, as this is a beautiful lake. Some of the participants run around the lake while they are there. There is a basketball hoop so you know what I do. After settling in, there's more baseball talk, and then we all meet at Rosie's Country Restaurant in the morning and have a great, enormous breakfast. When breakfast is over we head for the field and immediately start skills and drills all day long, and repeat everything from base running to batting, fielding, bunting and situational baseball. Bill usually takes aside the ones who are interested in pitching and starts off by saying such things as, "The portion of the rubber I use on the mound is mine. I also own home plate, I don't like batters, especially right-hand batters, and my best pitch is a strike." That's Vintage Bill Lee!

We break at noon with sandwiches, either on the bench in the dugout or in a nice conference room at the college, but we are always all together. The afternoon is tough and with so much baseball training, it's coming out of your ears. This is Saturday and usually this time of year is when the Red Sox and Yankees square off in their divisional playoffs. Somehow we manage to find a TV somewhere, despite having to deal with the poor reception due to the mountains.

During one playoff game between the Red Sox and Yankees, trouble had started in the game, as Pedro Martinis pushed Don Zimmer to the ground. Well, when that happened Bill Lee flew off the couch with excitement and started screaming at the TV and calling Zimmer a gerbil. It was so funny...I guess you had to be there. This is usually at the big lodge out at the lake with a roaring fire going. Everyone gets involved with baseball at its purist. We talk for what feels like hours about baseball. Everyone has a story and we learn even more about our new friends that have joined us there.

During all this, pictures taken during the day are developed and shared by all. The hospitality of the college alumni is super and makes an enjoyable weekend. We have a catered pig roast with salad, vegetables, and blueberry crumb cake with vanilla ice-cream. I'm not even describing it as wonderful as it was.

Jeff provides some fun awards to all who have come and some baseball stories that are so funny. Bill can go on and on with stories. Jeff recites a baseball segment from Sadaharu Oh, the Japanese "Babe Ruth"of Japan. It's quite intriguing. More baseball stories continue and then it's off to the cabins.

I would like to now share a portion of David Faulkner's story Sadaharu Oh, the Babe Ruth of Japan as this informative and inspirational account of his last Major League Baseball game "A Zen Way of Baseball" anyone who loves baseball that can put your mind and body in the stands and witness this special moment in life will appreciate the respect and loyalty of this amazing person, Sadaharu Oh one of my favorite baseball players; Just a few years ago he was the Manager of the Japanese team that won the last World Baseball Classic in which Boston's pitcher Daisuke Matsuzaka was featured.

Sadaharu Oh

"A Zen way of baseball"

Sadaharu Oh, The Japanese Version of our Babe Ruth; this is a small portion written about his very last major league baseball game;   By Author David Falkner

Outside, the warm autumn sun shone on the grass. The grass had yellowed during the summer and was dying now. White clouds floated in the clear sky above. The light of the sun, so particular now, carried a hint of winter. The sounds of the crowd filling the stands came to me like the low rumbling of island surf. The game would be starting soon. Everything was as usual, accept;;;

The sound of the crowd, the clear colors of the sky, the warmth of the sun the light of winter coming.

This was my last game, my very last game, twenty- two years leading to this moment- a whole lifetime. I could realize that I was standing alone in the locker room. I had not meant to linger behind, but I had-and now I was by myself in an empty room that seemed like a warehouse; row of lockers, empty trunks of equipment, signs of life everywhere but not to be seen. I felt enclosed in this space, as though in a dream just before waking, unable to stir myself past those final restraints of sleep. Why was I standing here? I wanted to follow my teammates, but I didn't. I became conscious of how foolish I felt standing there alone. I moved to a bench and sat down.

My uniform number was #1, one-all the years I was in high school, and all the years I was a major league ballplayer. Number One, people made something of that. Big One the press blurbs read. "Big One"! What is a "Big One"? I don't put that down. I enjoyed it too much. But I know who I am-or who I've been. I am ordinary, no larger and no smaller than life size. But my number matters to me.

I blinked; I looked down and saw that I had been gripping my cap so tightly in both hands that I was in danger of tearing it. I wiped my face, I had been crying, so strange. Why was I behaving like this? Get up, go out there and join your teammates! But I was not ready.

I am a professional ballplayer, I told myself, a professional. The word has meaning for me as few others in my vocabulary do. There is a standard of performance you must maintain that at any level of consistency. No excuses for the demands, of your ego or the extremes of your emotions. It is an inner thing. I held myself to that standard for twenty two years. It is my proudest achievement.

I saw my face in the locker room mirror used for shadow batting. A kind of mirror I had stood before for perhaps thousands of hours in my pro career. My face looked odd to me, eyes a little swollen, the expression open and easy, almost as if I were a child again rather than a man of forty.

Get yourself together, Number One!" "Easy give the man time. He has it coming". My voices, for me, the tough one, the hard one nearly wins out; it is November 16th, 1980.

You are in Fujisakidai Stadium in Kumamoto, Kyushu. The opponents are the Hanshin Tigers. Your teammates and the fans are waiting;

"This is your very last game, last time you will swing the bat. This game is for you, just you. There is something in it for you. Take your time, be kind to yourself…" I have been a pro baseball player for so long. More than half my life on earth, I barely had the time for my boyhood just to myself. I hit 868 homeruns, more than Babe Ruth or Hank Aaron, more than any man, on either side of the Pacific. I was a homerun champion for fifth teen years, thirteen of them in a row. I hit thirty or more homeruns for nineteen consecutive seasons. I led the league in Runs Batted In, thirteen times, in batting five times. I won the Triple Crown back to back in 1973 and 1974 and was the leagues MVP nine times. I walked more than 2,500 time's in walks eighteen straight seasons. In 1972, Japanese professional baseball introduced fielding awards- "The Diamond Glove"- equivalent to the Gold glove awards in America. I won a Diamond glove thereafter for nine consecutive seasons till I retired.

But I am not Babe Ruth or Hank Aaron. I cannot compare me with them any more than they might have compared themselves with me. I am the Japanese Sadahara Oh, and I should qualify that, too. I am only half Japanese! I take my records seriously, off course. Athletes are very fond of saying that they look forward to having successors come along and break their records.

There have been two figures that have been a constant inspiration for me throughout my career, Lou Gehrig and Miyanoto Musashi. Gehrig was a homerun hitter but his greatest achievement was as "iron man" playing 2,130 consecutive games. This is not just an athletic record (which it is and will be most likely forever) it is more an event of the spirit. It is impossible to play through fourteen straight seasons simply as a body showing up. You must be filled with something in your soul that enables you to withstand bruises and injuries and pressures of boredom and fatigue. The stretch of so many years and so many games leaves you with that one game, that one day where you simply sit down. But Gehrig never did. There was something in him-not necessarily physical strength – that enabled him to endure. The Japanese word of spirit power is "ki" It's both spiritual and physical. They are not to be separated.

Thus the quality of Lou Gehrig's play during that incredible stretch was as much determined by his spirit as by the "iron "in his body. He was a man whose great talents were enhanced by spirit-discipline. He wanted to retire later than he did. His physical body betrayed him. His spirit never did. On Independence Day, 1939, knowing he was dying, he told a fan in Yankee Stadium not only how lucky he was but also that he was truly happy. It was his Independence Day.

"Mr. Oh, it is time!"

'Yes, I'll be there"

The crowd in Kyushu, like the weather, was warm and encouraging. This was a good day, in a good atmosphere, to end it. At this time you could hear, now "Batting Fourth, Number One, Oh Number One Oh.

This was my Last time as cleanup hitter, my last time to swing my special Ishii bat, last time to try for one more, just one more.

Our opponent that afternoon was our traditional rival, the Hanshin Tigers. It was the bottom of the fifth inning. The newspapers, the day following, said it was exactly 1; 56 in the afternoon. The Tiger' pitcher- Norikazu Miyata-was young and inexperienced, and he threw me a ball I saw well. I hit it into the bleachers in right center field. I circled the bases for the last time. (By coincidence, my very first hit as a major leaguer had also been a homerun).

Yes, this was the way I wanted to end it. But, then, a curious thing happened. As I crossed second base, heading toward third, I saw players on the Hanshin bench leave the dugout and come toward the third base line. By the time I reached the bag, they were lined up from third base to home plate. Some of the players on the field had also joined them. Even though they stood formally, at attention, there were expressions of genuine affection on their faces. I was much moved. I slowed my trot so I could shake hands with each of them in thanks. As I approached each player, he took off his cap, bowed to me, and shook my hand. At home plate, the manager of the Tigers presented me with a large bouquet of yellow autumn flowers. The crowd cheered, I waved to them, and bowed to the stands and the other players and then I went out to the mound to encourage the Tiger pitcher and to wish him well in the future.;;;

My opponents lifted my spirits and in doing so, reminded me of something that I had spent twenty two years learning. That opponents and I were really one. My strength and skills was only one half of the equation. The other half was theirs. And standing there that day in Kyushu as my past became the future in a single moment, the years dropped away and I was a young boy again, coming out of high school to this strange, exciting world of professional baseball.

How full of hope and strength and eagerness I was! I saw in the faces of the young players near me on the field the same look of expectation. In their eyes was the same will to combat, the same dream of creating records; and to me, because I was a celebrated old timer now, they were kind enough to pay respect for a job well done.

My job is not done, it is only the beginning-and where the future will take me I do not know. I learned as a boy, because fate put me in the way of a master teacher, that practical training in skills, if done in a certain way, was a method of spirit and discipline. And in combat, I learned to give up combat. I learned in fact, there were no enemies. An opponent was someone whose strength joined to yours created a certain result. Let someone call you enemy and attack you and in that moment they lost the contest. It was hard to learn this-perhaps I am only just beginning to follow its lead- but baseball career was a long, long initiation into a single secret; that at the heart of all things is respect. We are, each of us-harmony with it, not in conspiracy against it. To respect by being in harmony with what surrounds you is to be reminded that the humblest of life's offerings is as treasured as the greatest in the eyes of the creator.

When listening to this story one must feel a very strong will to get out there and play some baseball. This man was so devoted to the sport and if you are lucky enough to get this book Sadaharu Oh, A Zen Way of Baseball-by David Faulkner you will appreciate the determination, desire, devotion and work ethic above and beyond most human beings to achieve greatness and love for playing baseball. His story surely inspires me to push myself to higher levels to dig down deep and find all I have to give. I would truly love to meet this man or his trainer, Miyanoto Musashi.

Sunday morning arrives and it's breakfast at Rosie's once again. We usually take up one long table. The same routine continues, only this time we play a game, a real nine inning game. One year we played against a team of Over 40 players going out to Phoenix, Arizona to the World Series. Our little group beat them pretty good.

By the end of the day, it is so good to look around at our group to see how everyone is more confident, their skills are improved, and their confidence renewed. When the game is over, we take group pictures, some seek out autographs from Bill Lee, others shake hands, say their goodbyes, and we all leave for home. This is a great baseball weekend for anyone, especially a great thing to do before going to a baseball tournament. I like to call it a "baseball tune-up."

I have attended this annual baseball weekend for five years. It's a great way to double check your mechanics and skills and make adjustments, and see where you are on Sunday when it's over. Your skills, confidence, and attitude toward the game of baseball are much improved. I have been to many camps but now I seem to be right on with my mechanics, making great contact, and my confidence could not be any greater. I am in control of my game and that is a wonderful feeling.

Chapter Twenty One

My Feathered Friends

Once again the Eastside Kids take on a new hobby. In my junior high days at East Junior high school there were about twenty five kids that attempted to raise pigeons for a hobby. Some had Homing pigeons, others had Rollers. Homing pigeons were larger, stronger and designed for racing long distances. The Rollers tumbled backwards while in flight, as many rolls would look like a fireball coming down from the sky before your eyes. Many eastside kids had their own coops and encouraged each other and developed many friends as a result of this hobby. I think as I look back it taught young people respect and responsibility towards many animals as well as birds.

This type of hobby was very popular, as I indicated earlier. Many have continued throughout the years or some just enjoyed for a few years and went on to other things. Here in New England and all over the world, we are acquainted with many animals and birds. Pigeons are thought of in a negative fashion when they come to an average person's mind. I would like to make an attempt to make you, the reader, become more aware, knowledgeable and informed about our feathered friends. I would recommend an open mind, so here we go.

Birds and many animals instinctively prepare for the winter, as they seem to be a step ahead of us and have a better grip preparing for the long haul. I'll focus strictly on pigeons, as we look into habitat. They seek protection for their young, the elements, and the upper food chain. That is, hawks, falcons, cats, raccoons, and most animals. They look towards holes in attics, buildings, abandoned houses, high cliffs, etc. There are several breeds, just as there are several breeds of dogs.

Pigeons have been a part of our lives, dating back thousands of years. Back in the Roman days of war, pigeons were used for communication, as well as in the Prussian war, World War I, World War II, and the Korean War. The British Army started using paratroopers first. As they parachuted in combat operations into the battlefield, the commanders would send operation reports, intelligence reports, and other messages in the area of operations. There was a capsule attached to the legs of the bird, and also a plastic packet attached to their chest, as the birds were strong, with little visibility, adapted to the terrain, and could be counted on.

In England, blood was transported by pigeons from one hospital or clinic to another. They would attach a plastic sterile blood bag to the pigeon's chest and the bird would make remarkably efficient time, beating traffic and saving valuable time.

The Homing pigeon, or what most people refer to as "homers," is what I'm describing here. There are breeders, clubs and organizations throughout the world otherwise known as "fanciers." This is like many sports, where you discover many other activities the more you investigate, thus the more you are aware of, concerning a particular hobby or sport. Like horse racing, for example, the pigeon fanciers race their birds for big cash awards, and again money is the issue derived from something that started out as a simple concept. They have anywhere from one-hundred mile races to six-hundred and even one-thousand mile races. The training is quite expensive and time consuming. They usually start training the pigeons at about eight weeks old. They familiarize the bird to their loft, then after a week start releasing them one mile to the south, then the next day to the west, the next day north, and finally to the east. Then the distance is moved from one mile to five to fifteen, etc.

Some breeders work together, helping each other with training, trading, purchasing from each other, and usually a good friendship develops. There are shows, similar to 4H, and that's when deals are made and information shared with one another. There are numerous breeds of pigeons and more people involved than you can imagine. The winnings can be large cash prizes as well, in both shows and races.

To further your knowledge on pigeons, consider this: most domesticated pigeons have a common ancestry with the Dove. It is said that Noah's Dove was a racing Homer, but who really knows for sure. Homing pigeons, for example, are very fast in flight. They are known to fly and have been clocked at over ninety-two miles per hour on an average during a four-hundred mile race! They have been known to fly seven-hundred miles in one day.

Their heart does much better than mine. Their heart beats about six-hundred beats per minute, as the pigeon beats its wings ten times per second while the bird is flying over a sixteen-hour time frame without rest. The US Army liked that idea. These pigeons are truly amazing. During a long flight they tuck their legs back to the rear, holding onto their short tail feathers to save energy and rest their legs. It's also noted that their keen eyesight is so impressive they can see as far as twenty-six miles on a clear day. I have trouble seeing the opposite side of a ball field! In several studies at universities it was discovered that pigeons have a very smart brain and are one of the most intelligent in our animal kingdom. So when you hear remarks about *dumb pigeons,* tell them it isn't so!

In the 1800s, pigeons were introduced here in the United States. In 1880 the first five-hundred mile race took place, which started an ongoing tradition of racing birds. The pigeon's hearing is extraordinary, as they can sense and detect storms, earthquakes or any type of electrical storm by vibrations alone.

Pigeons do mate for life, unless you separate the cock and hen, or if one should die. The point is: when they are bred, the hen will lay two eggs in about a week. The cock will sit on the eggs during the daylight hours and the hen all through the night (See? The cocks are like men trying to do their part!). The eggs will hatch in about eighteen days. The cock and the hen will both feed the youngsters or squabs, as they call them. They regurgitate a liquid from their own bodies and funnel the liquid form in the mouths or beaks of the squabs. The squabs grow very quickly and are out of the nest in about five weeks and on their own with minimal flying at six weeks old. They are usually banded after a week old for identification purposes. Some pigeons will feed young birds in the same manor whether they are the parents or not. Being a foster parent is common. This is encouraging for thoughts of parenting, wouldn't you say?

To continue and expand your knowledge on pigeons, here are some more interesting facts: the average racing homer pigeon is twelve to thirteen inches long, while the Roller pigeons are nine to ten inches long—much smaller. They eat all sorts of grains and minerals, and like any other animal or human, their intake has to be controlled or they can get fat and lazy. They can live as long as twenty-five to thirty years old, if they stay away from predators like cats, rats, raccoons, or hawks. They actually have to worry about every animal or human. When the cock and hen are mated, they stay together for life. They set a great example for the rest of us.

There are of course numerous breeds, different sizes, an assortment of colors and body types. Some are average, some are strong and full of vigor, and some look ridiculous. The US Army has a Hall of Fame for pigeons. The civilians also have a museum in Oklahoma as well.

To many, it would appear to be a strange hobby – breeding, racing, training, or the showing aspect. The pleasure or profit, how ever you choose to view this, is not common knowledge at all. In addition, there are very inspiring examples of well known people who you may relate to that have explored this hobby. Here are some examples: Yul Brynner, Walt Disney, Andy Devine, Marvin Hagler , George Foreman, Wayne Newton, Gypsy Rose Lee, Roy Rogers' Happy Trails Loft, and Queen Elizabeth II, whose Royal Lofts in England are still being maintained today. They also say that Elvis Presley developed his leg shake from pigeons!

On the eastside of Brockton, Massachusetts there were numerous kids that participated in this hobby. When I look back, this was great to have this sort of interest as opposed to being on the streets getting into trouble. There still are many who think pigeons are annoying, or a nuisance, because of the large numbers surrounding our cities. That is somewhat true but that is also out of control and not part of the actual hobby. Those birds are not cared for, protected, fed properly, or cleaned. There is a lot of responsibility in this hobby, as well as knowledge, and incredible time spent in caring, training, and the human touch. There are pigeon clubs, shows, races, and meetings. It's like any other animal hobby – they argue, bet, trade, and each feels they have their own fortune. The pigeon lofts are sometimes small, sometimes very large. They separate the cocks and hens and only breed for the exact amount for racing or competitions necessary to maintain control. They allow for nesting, breeders, flyers, ventilation, warmth for the winter, they are kept dry from rain, just as you would for a dog or pony, or some other pet.

Rollers are a smaller pigeon. They have more choice colors and are very attractive looking birds. While in flight they tumble backwards. When they do this repeatedly it visually looks like a fireball coming down from the sky.

That's the attraction of this bird. They are daring, fly very high and maneuver quite quickly. Roller fanciers fly their birds in competitions. They usually fly about twelve to twenty birds in competition together. The birds fly in a tight group together and in their case stay close together, roll together, and land together. It becomes very involved. To make a long story short, they get timed for flying a certain time together, and rolling together. They fly for thirty minutes to an hour, and sometimes longer. The racing homers fly for hours as they fly together and roam the countryside, always returning home. There are many other finer details as you get more involved with this hobby.

There are show birds of all sorts, some that even tumble on the floor. There are Fantail pigeons that have trouble walking around because of their weird body type. But racing Homers are the biggest interest of all. Racing Homing pigeons are larger, stronger and require heavy duty training. Cleanliness, inoculations, and extreme care are a necessity in this hobby. This hobby has been around for hundreds of years, and require a lot of work and expense, I must add.

Squab raising is another interesting facet of the pigeon hobby. In the south it is even on the menu in restaurants, and they are considered a delicacy as some would say. There are commercial poultry and manufacturing plants in South Carolina, as well as in Pennsylvania and in California. There are more than you would ever imagine.

Very soon you will see how my life seems to go full circle with three areas: carpentry or construction, parachuting, and baseball. It seems even when I get off the subject, I share in all three at one time or another. This is also true again with pigeons. The US Coast Guard trained Homing pigeons to locate orange life vests – what a neat achievement. Pigeons were used so much from World War I, World War II, Korea and other conflicts as well. Their success rate averaged ninety-eight percent and saved numerous lives. English and British soldiers had tested and used pigeons in combat first, and later, the United States Army also made great use of them.

The paratroopers had a special basket located above the reserve parachute about waist high in a basket strapped to their parachute harness. The soldier, usually a communications specialist, was always close to the commander to be ready in the event needed to send an important update or message about intelligence, security or operational information. Many of these heroic pigeons were called "sky soldiers." The Israeli and Chinese Soldiers use them as well.

Pilots that crashed had pigeons with them, to release and give their location to the good guys. The CIA, OSS, and FBI also found use of them. The Military has an Honor Role for Pigeons. One bird, named Cher Ami, was attached to the New York Battalion 77th Division. This bird was released during combat, and after being wounded flew an entire flight of forty kilometers and saved a lost battalion.

Another bird referred to as GI Joe received the Dickens Medal for saving the entire town of Clovis Vechia and a thousand British Brigade soldiers that had occupied it. The Mocker was another pigeon awarded the Distinguished Service Cross as well as the French De Guerre, another superior award.

I think now you can agree, since you have a much clearer insight into the capabilities and understanding of the pigeon. So when you are in a park or a city square and you view many pigeons, consider them possible lost heroes who are gentle, misunderstood, a bit shy, and loyal to mankind. Many pigeons are protected by breeders, and they are the lucky ones. They are intelligent, trusting, and honorable companions. Now when you're walking down the street or country road and you see one land near you, you can ask yourself, *Was this a sky soldier, a lost bird from training for a race, or is he or she from the CIA watching me?*

Chapter Twenty Two

Fire and Ice

It was January 1976, and my unit, the 10th Special Forces Group, Charlie Company, Third Battalion, was in Fort Devens, Massachusetts. We were the Paratroopers, Soldiers from the Sky, Ski Troops, training in cold weather environment, survival techniques, along with many other soldiers' duties. Our direction for this survival winter warfare training program was in the White Mountain area of Vermont, and very close to Mount Washington and numerous ski areas.

There were hefty weather reports, not in our favor: cold, heavy north-easterly winds and blizzard conditions were heading for us. We would prepare for the worst and concentrate on our current mission for training, and for all future soldiers participating in winter warfare, and similar areas of operations.

The upcoming training was very demanding. Therefore we had an increase of physical fitness daily. We had a variety of exercises, like judo, karate, and running. We were all in great shape. One day during training, we had partners. I got stuck with the Captain. CPT Larry Neidringhaus was a Vietnam vet with a competitive edge. He and I were paired off and as he came towards me I pulled his hands, fell backwards, and jammed my knee into his chest as the momentum knocked him flat on his back. I said to myself, *oh no*. He looked at me with fire in his eyes and tossed me around like a rag doll. It was really good training. I don't know where that came from, my quick reactions, that is. It must have been from a movie like Davy Crockett or Daniel Boone, but it worked.

We packed rucksacks for weeks, packing carefully cold weather equipment, personal clothing, personal items for hygiene, books, writing paper and pens. We were heavily packed from head to toe. We had cold weather gear, candles, essentials like a steel pot, full rucksack with sleeping bag, air mattress, snow shoes, skis, c-rations for a week, water, and lerps for two weeks supply. Lerps are dried food that you mix with water, no cooking involved, but light and easy to carry. One thing you learn is: "Travel light, freeze at night." There was also shared team equipment, radios, weapons, mc1-1 parachute, also reserve chute, all tightened down. The parachute and equipment was inspected by the jump master of this C-130 Hercules Military troop transport aircraft.

It seemed we had flown for hours, bobbing and weaving, tilting the wing tips, and soon we landed and would be boarding in our prospective trucks heading towards Crawford Notch in the White Mountains. The jump had been cancelled due to high winds, although we had jumped in these conditions numerous times in the past.

Our daily chores began at Black Mountain Ski Area. Early in the morning, the first duty was to go to the "goat house," as we called it, where our skis were stored. After the morning rituals of shaving and personal hygiene we would head for the goat house, and scrape, melt, and re-wax our skis depending on the temperature.

This was time-consuming, and upon completion we would go to the edge of the trail and ski down to the main lodge where the military had prepared their usual chow line.

Upon completion of breakfast we had a safety briefing, as always, and then we were divided into seven-man teams with an instructor. My instructor was a sergeant and also a friend of mine. Initial instruction had taken place and we went through the basics: snow plow, heron bone, turns, and stopping. When this Bad News Bears squad was a little bit ready we attached ourselves to the ski lifts and the fun began. The sergeant would lead us, as one by one we would play Follow the Leader. He would veer off the trail and zig zag through the paths and woods and out onto the main trails. The speed would pick up and visibility was poor and many of us would fall face-first, head-over-heels into the snow like a cartoon show. Despite being well clothed with a ski mask and goggles, the icy wind and snow was unbearable most of the time. We had progressed after repeating the runs. We also had to ski with our rucksacks on, which was difficult.

Most were fortunate to use civilian skis on the downhill trails but we also had to maintain our long, wide military cross-country skis as well. The military skis are the ones that needed so much maintenance, hot waxing with a household iron, scraping, and re-waxing. There were different colored wax sticks. They were labeled, as certain temperatures required a certain color wax. The weather was constantly changing throughout the day so waxing was important.

We finished our downhill instruction after two weeks, and had a fun contest and party at the end. There were no awards coming my way, but I did learn to ski and manage my turns and stops with no broken arms or legs. We then practiced on our "white stars," which were long wide, military skis with wire bindings, using our military boots to slip into the bindings. There was quite often time spent skiing without poles. Our feet were always *so* cold. We had lamb's wool, which was also called "lambskins." They slipped over the top of the skis and then we were able to climb straight up the hillside. Sounds neat but very rigorous, I must add.

The next day we moved into formation with our rucksacks packed heavily to endure fifty miles across the White Mountains countryside. We arrived at the top of the mountain, got off the chairlift and bonded with our training squad. We would play Follow the Leader down about fifty yards at a time, and each time do a different turn or stop or something. We would be critiqued and then continue down and get in line again for the chairlift. We did this all day every day for two weeks. We did stop briefly for warm-up breaks, hot chocolate, water, and lunch.

The third day many of us were more confident so the instructor was dying to venture into new things. He had us continue the follow the leader game and we picked up speed and momentum and he would sharply turn off the main trail and onto this narrow winding trail shooting downward into what was to be a ramp.

This is where we all crashed and burned, due to lack of experience and loose bindings. There were bloody noses and lots of embarrassment to follow. This was also getting old.

There were civilians around us up and down the slope and in the lodge having a great time watching us crash and burn. Our muscles were sore, and many got hurt. The weather was extremely cold, bitter cold I must say, with lots of snow.

One soldier fell off the chair lift, another was at the bar in the lodge and climbed the fireplace stone wall and fell and broke his thigh bone. There were also broken legs and numerous injuries to follow.

Our Captain, CPT Larry Neidringhaus, had his dog Chinook with him. Chinook was a Siberian husky and was equipped with a backpack to carry his own water, dog food, and I think the Captain's rations as well (what do you think?). Chinook was neat to have around.

We started our journey bright and early, all of us excited for the challenge. This was survival and we would fight the elements like you would not believe. I am not sure of the exact area we traveled but I know it was near Crawford Notch in the White Mountains area within the vicinity of Maine and New Hampshire. The snow had started falling again and the radio reports were calling for blizzard conditions for the next week in our area.

Yes, the Blizzard of 1976 was here, three separate large snow storms, back at the Fort Devens area, and we were to receive more snow. All I saw was rough terrain, ice, and snow. Breaking Trail was the nasty word of the day. Allow me to explain.

There were about eighty men in Company C, 3rd Battalion 10th Special Forces Group, Airborne, from Fort Devens. Also included were support personnel and staff officers. The work was shared with all. So starting from the front, the first man stepped with skis walking forward as if he had snow shoes on, then the second man followed in the same manner, and so on. By time the tenth man stepped on the two-runner trail, the remainder of soldiers continued to glide with their skis. Breaking the trail in this manner, with one-hundred pound backpacks plus snow shoes, weapons, etc. was quite grueling, as you can imagine.

There were five teams of twelve men in each. Each team had an "archio." An archio is very similar to a canoe. Therefore all the rucksacks, supplies, demolitions, rations, and tents were packed firmly into this archio. Then three men in a line six to eight feet between them pulled this archio like a sled dog team. There was also a man to the rear with a rope working as brake man.

During the fifty mile cross-country venture we would stop for a break for ten minutes. The experienced soldiers would have the stoves lit and hot chocolate steaming before the inexperienced got their rucksacks off. The break would be over and the inexperienced would learn a valuable lesson on preparing for chow breaks.

Our first night was quite stormy. We all shared guard duty for safety of each other during the night. Some had tents, while others built snow caves or lean-to's. There were wild animals, like fisher cats, coyotes, bears, bob cats and what ever you could imagine in the New England wild. Waking up during the night to get the snow off the tents was a trick. The snow in the area we were at was more than six feet deep under our tents. The wind was howling, forty to fifty degrees below zero. Believe me, I thought to myself, *I'll be glad when this is over.*

Our World War II troops had fought in Europe in similar conditions. This training was geared to future combat situations with experienced soldiers to carry the torch and teach others the cold weather basics and combat strategies.

In the morning, no one was very energetic about getting out of their sleeping bags. I managed to find a few other soldiers willing to get up and get a fire going. Later we had a strong blaze and began to throw logs on the fire. We had chickens for survival food–*live* chickens, that is. They were barely alive and actually climbed up on the logs on the fire to be warm. That sure was a tough way to die for the chicken. Some soldiers thought they were like Rambo, and bit chicken heads off for the ego boost. When men get together, a lot of crazy things take place.

The conversations were constant while we were trying to stay warm, cook up some hot chocolate, and see if you could outdo your friends with stories. Seldom did they talk about sports– it was usually military stories, paratrooper stories or women.

The convoy had continued through the forest, along the river sides, crossing over rough terrain and watching everyone crash and burn on skis. The archios were hard to pull and often would be ridden down hillsides and hard to control as well. There were many accidents and run- away archios, as one could imagine.

We had traveled many miles up to this point when I suffered from frostbite conditions. They realized how serious my injuries became and decided to evacuate me. The problem was, helicopters could not fly, snow mobiles could not get to us, and the nearest road was thirty miles away! The soldiers made a litter out of my skis and wrapped me up and two pulled me with one soldier as brake man. They skied and pulled me along through rough terrain for about three miles, where we found a cabin and stayed there until the weather had broken a bit. During the movement of me in a litter, I wasn't sure if we would make it or not. I was wrapped tightly in this litter and could not move at all. If I had tipped over and slid into a river, I was toast, or I should say, "ice cubes." We awaited for a snow mobile to take me many more miles to a road for a connection with a jeep to take me to a hospital. This took three days to evacuate me. I stayed in the hospital for three days as well. I was then released, and it was back to Fort Devens.

The only problem I had while I was in the hospital was the diet they put me on immediately. The first shift of nurses were not nice, so I was glad when the next shift arrived and the nurse regime was gone. I said to the new nurse, "I have been starving for days!" Finally I convinced her to get me ice cream, Jell-o , a sandwich and soda. I even asked her out, but that didn't go well either.

Winter warfare was now over and an experience to remember. You never know when you're in a dangerous, life-threatening situation, until it's before you. Living an experience of any type that has danger and you survive becomes a memory that lasts forever. There is survival in the desert, the forest, the ocean, like running from a forest fire or storm, or dealing with avalanches or blizzards. Whatever comes to your life, if you have the opportunity, try to prepare with supplies, knowledge, and listen to someone in the know.

Chapter Twenty Three

Flintlock

It is spring, 1976, and as a member of the Special Forces team, I had orders to participate in a training exercise, code name Flintlock. There was meeting after meeting, intense planning, and training everyday to test preparedness of our unit. Our teams consisted of twelve men known as an "A Team."

The task before us was loading equipment, rations, radios, team equipment boxes, parachutes, riggers equipment, weapons, ammunition, personal duffle bags, and rucksacks onto five-ton trucks with canvas and bows for the top. This was a forty-five minute ride by normal car, but with the military, stop and go caravan and convoy style, it took two hours. Our Special Forces unit, command and control elements and support had arrived closely together. We soon saw our transportation, a C-141 Jet Aircraft. This bird would fly us to England. We waited for what seemed like forever. You know the story – hurry up and wait.

Finally, we were loaded completely, and the big bird took forever to get off the ground. Then we had a long nine-hour flight to enjoy. This was very uncomfortable, as you claimed areas to sleep on, like on top of the ammunition or a space on the floor. We were heading for RAF Mildenhall Air Base in England, not too far from London. There were many stories during the flight, as usual, as well as books to read, but sleeping took up most of the flight time. Despite being paratroopers, many like me did not like the idea of flying over the ocean. I would prefer to jump out of the aircraft over desert or mountains in an emergency, as opposed to the ocean, full of sharks and the unknown.

There was a refueling stop in the Azores off the coast of Spain. We had a delay for a few hours to refuel, and then we were off again. When we finally landed in Mildenhall, we were secretly convoyed to a barracks. We had two days to enjoy London and the sights and then we would have an operation order. The soldiers went in all directions of London. We checked out the NCO night clubs on base, we tried the double Decker buses, made an attempt of the red box phone booths, and saw So Ho Park. We went as a team on a few occasions and had uplifting dramatic laughter. Then of course, as they say – what happens in London, stays in London. That's the best philosophy.

When our free time ended, we formed up and we were then selected to go to isolation for three to five days for planning of an operation in route to the forest in Germany. The detachment commander explained our mission and responsibilities, and then we were secretly hidden from everyone to begin our serious planning of this mission.

In the middle of this isolation period, we all got on each others' nerves. After all, there were no windows, no fresh air, and we were all cooped up in a small two-room enclosure working around the clock. The last day after investing long hours of research and calibrations each of us had specific portions of this mission. The group Commander then wanted each to effectively explain to him, by maps and pointers, their part in the mission. When my time came, I was quite nervous, but after several missions it became easier each time.

In my early days in Special Forces, I was told to give a class. I had a terrible time being in front of just five men, but after team members helped me I soon got the hang of it. Later in my military career it was no problem ever being in front of forty men or even over three-hundred men and women in an auditorium. I had gained experience and confidence.

Our pilot team, which was made up of advanced personnel that would go in first, parachuted into Germany at, say, drop zone Alpha at 2200 hours, which was at night. Upon their safe landing they would link up with guerrilla forces, local populist, and a liaison to assist our team. Then, two days later we, the remainder of the team, would parachute into drop zone Bravo at, let's say, 2100 hours, and hopefully be greeted by our pilot team. They would then organize our transportation, and bring us to a safe house. Usually we would end up in some farmer's barn, unless we were met by enemy forces.

The C-130 Aircraft, called a "blackbird" in specifics, which had very high security, flew us at low altitude under the radar most of the time, banking the plane and causing many men to get air sick. One lieutenant barfed in his helmet. That was not a pretty sight. Later, when we were ready to jump and he had to put his helmet on...woo!

The rumble of the aircraft filled our ears, and there were no lights of course. Just a dim red light illuminated the interior, and you could look out the windows and view the radar dust as periodically it would spray about. We were flying about five hundred to eight hundred feet and the lower we were, the faster it felt.

The time came when we needed to dawn our parachutes, and hook up our reserve parachute, rucksack and weapons, and get inspected by the jumpmaster in preparation for this parachute jump. There were two jumpmaster checks and "all ok," as they say.

The red light just came on and the jumpmaster gave the signal, "twenty minutes!"

We sat there, looking at one another, wondering how the jump would go. Hopefully no one would get hurt but numerous thoughts went through our minds. The next command was "ten minutes!"and the final and last warning was "six minutes!" Then the jumpmaster continued the remainder of jump commands as such: "Outboard personnel stand up, inboard personnel stand up, hook up, check static lines, check equipment, sound off with equipment check, from rear to the front, all ok!"

The doors opened as the jumpmaster checked the door and the edges of the aircraft for any safety problems. He continued to look outside the aircraft until he found the signal from the ground. He was looking for the daily code. Because this was a night jump, he was looking for fire pots on the ground in the shape of an inverted L to signal to the jumpmaster that the drop zone was safe. The air force signaled that it was a clear night with wind gusts of three degrees. They also informed us that the drop zone was an open field.

Gee, the air force was wrong again—who would think that? The green light went on as the jumpmaster said "Stand in the door!" We shuffled to the door and handed the static line to the jumpmaster as he said "Go!" and we exited the aircraft. The aircraft was so loud and noisy, and it was pitch-black outside. Soon after I exited the aircraft and as I was descending, the night was so peaceful and so quiet, you could hear a pin drop. I could see the other jumpers and all looked safe. I checked my equipment and focused on facing to the north of the drop zone where we were to link up. I saw what was to appear like shrubbery, but what I was seeing were the tops of a forest. It happened so fast—I heard screams and branches cracking and soon I prepared for the worst myself. I crossed my arms as I was taught, with my hands under the opposite arm pit for protection, and my feet and knees close together and my chin to my chest. The branches of this large fern cracked and broke until I came to a sudden stop. I didn't know how high I was or how close to the ground, so I carefully checked for injuries, adjusted to the night light of the moon and began to climb down my parachute to the ground.

I pulled my parachute from the tree and packed up. I gathered my equipment and went to the infiltration rally point and parachute turn in. When everyone showed up we loaded in trucks that were apple trucks with canvas hanging down, hiding us. We rode for a few hours and were left on the side of the road. We rallied up and went into the woods and walked about two clicks, or two-thousand yards, and thus found and claimed our temporary base camp.

From this base camp all operations would start and hopefully return here. There were no fires allowed. One reason being the German folks were very particular about the treatment of their forest. There would be no cutting trees or destroying branches unnecessarily. The second reason was for security in our war game training. From this base camp we would target areas to blow up, like radio sites, strategic enemy headquarters, petroleum storage facilities, water storage tanks, and of course, the enemy. Therefore we would go daily to analyze, reconnoiter, and basically spy on certain locations. For example, we would watch a bridge for hours and see how much traffic went by in order to plan a raid, ambush, or to blow the bridge.

The patrols were fun and exciting for me. Walking with stealth and sneaking around—it was amazing to be able to go within just a few meters of our own American forces and not be heard. There were three thousand American forces in our area of operations, who were our enemies for this game, and all against our one twelve-man team.

During the reconnoiter periods we would watch for hours and document all noises, like dogs barking, voices, vehicles traveling, the number of troops, the weather, the distance to a target and descriptions from different view points. We would gather our information, with usually two of us on this task, and return back to base camp and report to our team sergeant or lieutenant our intelligence report and plan effectively thereafter.

If the lieutenant happened to be in charge of a patrol, well, look out, I'm afraid we had a great chance of getting lost. Most lieutenants, on too many occasions, had a reputation of having a personal battle with the army compass, map, and protractor.

Two other soldiers and I had just been given an oral order to pick up a downed pilot about ten miles from our location. We had an operation fund, so most of the time we would be in civilian clothing to blend in with the locals. We also had rented cars in order to really fit in. Our plan was to go to a road marker two clicks from an intersection and wait for ten minutes, no longer, and the downed pilot would come out of the woods by a clearing where we would pick him up. It was a rainy day, drenching downpours and when we saw the down pilot, he was soaked; we took off and left him.

In the scheme of things he was supposed to once again appear at the same time, in the same location, twenty-four hours later. As he was a potential threat, we thought we would have fun with him and make him stay another night.

We reappeared twenty-four hours later and picked the pilot up. He was happy to be saved from the elements. We scurried him back to base camp and upon his entry he was blindfolded and tied up. We brought him to a safe house up on the third floor, as I remember, and he was fingerprinted, his photo was taken, and had a dental inspection to accompany the identification he provided. It took three days to find out for sure if he was friend or foe. We knew this British pilot was friendly but this was the process. We spent the three days sharing c-rations and talking army stuff and paratrooper stories and soon he was cleared by intelligence. Moments later we were invaded by enemy forces; there were two jeeps and a five-ton truck coming into our location.

I knew I was not going to be a prisoner of war, so I grabbed my M16, threw my rucksack out the third floor window and jumped. Fortunately I did not get hurt. The British soldier did not follow me.

I was officially on my own. I knew where I was on the map, and I knew where the new safe house was, so I booked across country, down winding forest roads, hopped a few fences and found the farm house where my other teammates would be.

As I said, we were in civilian attire most of the time and we worked the farms during the day, keeping our eyes open for the enemy. I worked in the long barn where the chickens were. This was the egg farm. I picked eggs and loaded the baskets every day. It was kind of fun for this city boy. Other chores included shoveling cow manure and chopping wood. The farmer and his wife provided us with much-needed hot showers and great German food. When I looked at these nice people and wondered to myself, *what if the war went the other way? Would Americans treat German soldiers as nicely and warmly and respectfully as we were treated?* I seriously didn't think so. I felt honored to have met those folks – another very nice cultural experience for the Eastside Kid.

We stayed in the hay loft and heard the bats and mice making noises through the night, but most of the time we were quite busy so, being tired, we didn't care about the critters. In a few days we would move to yet another hay loft on another farm and link up with guerrilla forces, or German paratroopers. There were about twenty of them, and we were to teach basic tactics to them and share responsibilities with raids and ambushes. They were reserves and a pretty wild bunch. This was their weekend duty.

We moved to a camp site out in the woods. Then we heard vehicles coming. Immediately we were thinking *enemy* but what was happening was the German paratrooper called their friends and family members to bring them meat, cheese, bread and beer! There were about three Mercedes and two BMWs loaded with food and beer. I guess these guys weren't that bad!

The German paratroopers became instant friends. We exchanged berets, jump wings, addresses, took pictures, and had a bunch of laughs. I received a German paratrooper knife from one of my German friends but they took it in customs when I returned. We wrote letters for a while, but with time and distance, that became just a nice memory.

The next morning we were raided by enemy forces and we were on our own again. We carried our rucksacks for what felt like many miles and then settled at a camp site by the Black Forest, ready for another adventure. Our next objective was to blow a bridge and a radio site. We had reconnoitered both areas for two days. We decided to casually hit our target that evening and carelessly walked down a road to the bridge with our demolitions ready to set. The bridge was guarded heavily and we were surprised by enemy forces all around us. I dashed through the wickets of the forest and broke through electrified barbed wire for the cow pasture within. I saw some brush and hid myself for over an hour.

The enemy soldiers were within ten feet of me but did not see me. Soon they were gone and my teammates had all separated in all directions. My team sergeant was captured by the enemy and now I was on my own, with no map and no compass. I had no idea where I was in the country of Germany. I walked the streets and neighborhoods, and this time I had fatigues on and I was carrying an M16 – it was hard to hide the fact that I was a US soldier!

The operation would be over in two days and I didn't want to be left behind, so what did I do? I went to the German Police Department! I had a card that explained in German that I was a US soldier with a telephone number on it for emergency. I talked to the police officer and he let me stay in a jail cell (with the door open) until someone came for me. I stayed the night, which was another experience I did not want to repeat. Luckily they were very nice and laughed at the situation.

In the morning I was picked up by our team liaison, an area assessment team member, and he brought me back to the town of Bits where the farm house was by the village. There was a big farewell party geared up for this evening for all the soldiers and farmers at the guest house in the village.

Some of my teammates and I had gone to the guest house early to grab a beer, which we anxiously looked forward to. The big German man at the bar had talked to us for a while about every little thing, and then he took us around back where the cow was. He took his pistol, shot the cow between his eyes, hung him quickly, slit his throat and drained the cow's blood into a steel pot. They quickly put the blood in the kitchen where they make blood sausage, or "blood worst." The rest of the cow was slaughtered and the whole process, despite being interesting, was also disgusting too. There would be steak tonight, as we hoisted our beer. The Germans sure know how to eat. Many drank the blood from the cow. It appeared that this was a delicacy and a normal cordial. That was definitely not for me.

The party carried on late into the night, and in the morning several were still feeling the affects of the drinking. We had a large picture taken with the whole crowd. There were lots of hand shakes, and hugs, a sad yet happy occasion. I still have that picture at home in a frame. The German family gave us "schnapps," which is like tequila or scotch or just plain "firewater." Our team was loaded up and then we took the long ride to Stuttgart Airport in a five-ton truck full of gear. All of us were wasted and the Dye Wee, another name for our captain, had passed that dam bottle of schnapps around and made everyone partake in it. It was hard to fake a swig and the taste was unforgettable – horrible, to be exact. The ride became longer the more the bottle was passed around, and no one escaped. The captain had an evil, evil eye about that stuff; he felt everyone should be part of everything.

Finally, we boarded another C-130 Hercules aircraft and flew back to RAF Mildenhall in England. We were debriefed and at last free for the time being. We had one more shot at visiting London for a day to pick up souvenirs or just see the sights. When all was done we loaded the aircraft once again but had to clear customs. That's when they grabbed my German paratrooper knife. We arrived at Hanscom Air Force Base in Lexington, Massachusetts and soon returned to Fort Devens for some R&R.

As you can imagine, my mail was backed up after five weeks, there was lots of laundry, catching up with my friends that stayed back, and thinking about our next trip. I think I needed a break from flying; it did get old, especially when I didn't jump regularly.

In 1976 I had quite a busy year. I attended nineteen funerals, as I was an honor guard for each of them. In Boston, when the Queen of England visited, I was honor guard in which she was within four feet of me. I worked as parachute instructor, which paratroopers refer to as "black hats." I went to Europe, had ski training, marched in parades in Boston, served as instructor for ROTC cadets, and numerous other ceremonies. The parades in Boston have always been special. I remember the good-looking girls from the colleges hanging out the windows and calling to us to "come on up!" That was quite tempting! I even went to Arizona to jump in for the weekend and then returned to Fort Bragg, North Carolina and jumped back again. To round off the year, I had special training in the desert near Las Vegas, Nevada for nearly thirty days. I got to see the strip, saw a cousin at Caesar's Palace and saw Frank Sinatra.

Chapter Twenty Four

Operation Bright Star

In 1983 I was assigned to Operational Detachment A team #573, A Company 3rd Battalion, 5th Special Forces Group at Fort Bragg, North Carolina. I was entering a new and much better phase in my life. There was finally light at the end of the tunnel for me. I was approaching completion of all financial disasters from the past and now I could date if I wanted to and go out more often and be a person again. I found a few friends very soon after arriving at Fort Bragg; I had a new unit to be part of, new friends, starting to get more money with a promotion to Sergeant and a fresh beginning that I absolutely knew I deserved.

My first day at the reception point, I met Rudy Wilson. He and I became instant friends. We had the chemistry of being fellow long-time soldiers and shared a paratrooper brotherhood. Rudy was assigned to Signal Company, because he was a wireman, and I was assigned to Operational Detachment 573 Detachment, 5th Special Forces Group. I was interviewed by the Command Sergeant, a part of in-processing, and after a week Rudy and I became regulars at Hardies Restaurant to go over our day, talk army, and share our experiences prior to the military.

Shortly after a week or so, Rudy introduced me to John Murphy. Now we had a solid threesome, and became inseparable friends. The most unique part of our relationship was the fact that we were all prior service veterans. John was in the Marine Corps, Rudy spent his time in the army before, and I also had a long hitch before. We were all divorced and had ex wives bugging us, and of course, child support problems. Rudy used to do body work on cars, John used to be a paramedic, and I had been in construction.

The three of us shared our coffee time at Hardies every morning and evening. We all had limited funds so only one night a week we would really go out. On the weekends we would go to the 82nd Airborne Enlisted Club. They had a band there and the place was wall to wall young bucks. There weren't many ladies and they would fight over the girls. Rudy, John and I would get a table up in the balcony and watch the young enlisted fight. It seemed that every ten minutes there would be a fight. There were tables flying, beer bottles crashing and lots of excitement. I think it was most exciting when the girls fought over the guys. That was great. We were in a safe spot up on the balcony.

We would share a cab to and from the barracks to the club or to a pizza joint on Bragg Boulevard or something. There was not a lot of excitement for a while because we had no car, limited funds, and a busy army schedule. There were not many places to meet women, at least the type of women to bring home to mom.

I was jumping constantly, trying to add up my jumps to obtain my master parachute wings. John was starting HALO school (high altitude low opening). Rudy was quiet about things for a while, but because we were all so tight, he opened up with a story that we could write another book about. Rudy was a character. He was in charge of twins in his unit. They were on his signal company wire team. They were depressed about finances and problems at home, so Rudy, being a cool sergeant, decided to take them down town and treat them to some young ladies of the night. Their work habits and moods changed rapidly the very next day. He was unbelievable! He would make you laugh all the time. I guess the three of us were a unique combination with a variety of personalities to go around and keep the party going.

One time Rudy said to John and I, "Guys, I have a problem!" It took what seemed like forever for him to spit it out and finally Rudy said, "I'm deathly afraid of heights and I don't think I can do another jump. I think I have to drop out."

We didn't know what to say. There he was in 5th Special Forces Group and they were looking for paperwork so he could get orders to jump and get paid for it. But Rudy really didn't think he could make another jump. He was also afraid of what the other soldiers would think if they found out how much he hated flying and jumping. And he hated the idea of quitting.

THE EASTSIDE KID

John and I put our heads together and came up with a scheme. I was a jumpmaster and John was experienced as well. We tutored Rudy several times during the week and Rudy was a good student. We managed to convince him to be put on the manifest.

Now John and I were both on this parachute jump with Rudy. We gave him all the instruction we could. After the jumpmaster checked, we loaded the aircraft. I will never forget this jump. I sat across from Rudy and watched every move he was to make. I could not help but wonder how frightened he was or how he must have felt. The jump commands came and we were hooked up, the green light was on and moments later our feet and knees were in the wind. Rudy needed four more jumps as part of our agreement to help him. Rudy went on to complete another two jumps and his guts and determination were unbelievable. I was very proud of him. We saved a soldier, and aided in the rebirth of a paratrooper.

I could go on and on about this guy. You could always count on Rudy. He always came through and was the type of guy who would give you the shirt off his back. In fact all three of us were like that. We had so much in common. I talked about my baseball but didn't get too involved. Maybe I should have, but that was not the right time for me. John played hockey and did well and enjoyed that, just as I enjoyed baseball.

John eventually got a little Honda motorcycle. He wore this German headgear and we made fun of it but we were happy for him as well. Rudy was next to buy a car. He bought this big Buick pimp mobile, with dice on the mirror, fuzz on the steering wheel and white interior. We started going to more clubs and meeting the ladies in Fayetteville. We seem to never stop laughing. We hit all the GI Joe stores by day and the strip bars at night. Rudy had the hots for this waitress at one restaurant. Rudy brought me there relatively close to Easter Sunday. We grabbed a table, I ordered ice tea for us and Rudy told us he'd be right back. I had no idea what he was up to so I patiently waited. A moment later I looked up, dumbfounded, and could not believe my eyes. He rented a bunny suit and went to his car to put it on. He came hopping into the restaurant and down the isle to where his favorite waitress was and confronted her to ask her out. Unbelievable! The whole place busted up with laughter. My stomach hurt I had laughed so hard. He did get a date with her, so I guess it was worth it.

Our entire group was on alert for a training operation in the Middle East. I was going to Jordan, Rudy to Saudi Arabia, and John to Tunisia. We sure would have a lot to catch up on after this trip to the Middle East.

Our trips were as usual—stop over in the Azores, isolation in England, or in my case, we went straight to Jordan. When we arrived in Jordan, it was unlike any other trip. We were treated much differently and the scenery was different, as well as the culture there.

We were completely examined in customs; they really checked our names on our passports carefully to see if there were any Jewish folks. It was quite uncomfortable. We then boarded a smelly bus and were rerouted to King Hussein's Palace Guard complex. Don't get excited, this was nothing special. We were there to teach basic tactics to the Ranger Special Forces elite guards for the King. They were not so elite at all, but thought they were. We met our counterparts the next day, exchanged souvenir clothing, like berets and jump wings, and had very limited communication. We were told not to out-do them in physical activity or games because we were guests. We were told not to wear shorts and to grow mustaches and learn a little Arabic.

The next evening we were invited to the officer headquarters for dinner. There were large community bowls full of rice, lamb and something that resembled vegetables. It was horrible and there was no silverware. Everyone was grabbing with their hands into the bowls. It made us sick. I made up my mind I would not eat any more Middle East food. I then bought a case of c-rations. At least I knew what I was eating. I knew I made the right decision the next day when I saw a soldier cleaning the tables with the same squeegee he used in the latrine. They would dump tea on the barracks floor routinely and squeegee it into the latrine which was just a hole in the floor with foot prints and a water faucet. They did not believe in toilet paper and laughed at us when it was presented.

We had a fun parachute jump as we were awarded Jordanian Parachute wings, and their soldiers were awarded American Parachute wings. It was truly amazing—they had brand new Hercules C-130 aircrafts, new M1 rifles, new rucksacks, while we on the other hand had all old, beat-up equipment. This was a beautiful, sunny day with clear skies, no wind, and after loading up with new parachutes (*where did they come from?*), the aircraft soon was off the ground. We would be jumping from the tail gate instead of the side doors. I was a safety but jumping as well. I checked the jumpers and one man was not hooked up. I tried to fix and reattach his static line but he and his captain nodded me off. I told my captain and I wanted to make sure I would not be in any International charge. The soldier said, "Allah will take care of me." I said, "I don't think so! Not if you're not hooked up at less than eight-hundred feet!"

We survived our parachute jump and were awarded our foreign parachute wings and the next day I would prepare to assist my team into a desert parachute jump. I was on the area study team and a master parachute jumpmaster for this jump.

The next evening we loaded up and I believe it was about 2200 hours, or ten p.m. and we were flying very low and fast. The red light came on and I started the jump commands, gesturing with my hands: "Twenty minutes," then "ten minutes,"then "six minutes." After this the Air Force pilot opened the rear tailgate and after it was secure in its down position, I went out with a cable. This time I was not jumping. I had stretched out on my belly and was looking into the wind, searching for the indicator on the ground with lighted pots in a configuration of "F," as in foxtrot. When I found the spot for the drop zone I led the teams to the edge of the aircraft door and on the green light pushed the first jumper out, and moments later they were all out. I pulled in the d-bags from the parachutes, and the pilot closed the hatch. The aircraft picked up speed, banked and we were off and away.

We later received word that the soldiers had landed safely and went on with their mission. Two days later, the Captain and I would load a bundle onto the aircraft for an air drop of supplies to the teams. We had all day to kill, so we flew all over the country, the aircraft shooting its radar dust and flying low. The pilot opened the tailgate and we were hooked up with a harness and sat on the edge of the tailgate as the aircraft flew about four-hundred feet off the ground. That was so cool. I was nervous at first but adapted quickly. We could see the farmers, camels, donkeys, and the ugly desert. They were waving to us and it was definitely cool to sit on the tailgate and view all of this.

We made a stop somewhere in the desert and when we were flying again, the country side was pointed out as we could see the bunkers in Israel along the banks of the Dead Sea. Our bundle drop went well, and the days went by slowly until the teams returned. When they did return, I managed to get them cold Pepsi. That was a treat for them. We had some down time and arrangements were made to see downtown Amman, Jordan. That was not really a treat. I'm surprised we were not attacked, as the look of hatred was upon us at all times.

We did tour some Temples, ruins, and unfortunately I bought a few souvenirs. I immediately threw it all away after 9/11. We also visited the embassy in Jordan and met up with some Marines stationed there. They had no ammunition so we gave them some for their personal survival, just in case.

We left the barracks and went to an airport where there wasn't a soul. There was evidence of mortar bursts and we waited for what seemed like hours. There was communication that if anything should break out, like war, we would be on our own. I immediately looked at my map, got my compass out and started thinking where I would go and how I would survive. I was looking at going to Israel. The aircraft soon landed and those thoughts were erased.

Our aircraft stopped in Tunisia, and Morocco, to pack up other paratroopers and off we went to England for a long journey back to Fort Bragg, North Carolina. After the briefings were completed we were released and went back to our normal routines. Rudy, John and I all had a variety of stories, so a lot of cups of coffee later all stories were told. We used to run on the matte mile down there at Fort Bragg.

Shortly after our return from Operation Bright Star, I must comment on my Company Commander Capt. Bill Davis. He was a great Commander as I knew him as First Lieutenant, up at Fort Devens, Massachusetts some five years earlier at the 10th Special Forces Group. His leadership and personal guidance for me on my career in the Military has always been respected and appreciated.

During his time as a Commander, I will never ever forget the unexpected treat he gave his soldiers. I remember it was payday, and usually on payday we gather information about on coming projects, awards, promotions, and a safety talk. We had all that on this particular day but we met at the Main (Non Commission Officers Club) at Fort Bragg, N.C. and we had a real special breakfast with tablecloths, nice silverware, waitresses and a full breakfast. The amazing part was, we had a Champagne Toast this is not at all common for enlisted soldiers and we wondered if he, our commander, would get in trouble for it. He did not and he toasted to the honor of serving us. I was so touched, as I will always treasure that memory.

In fact one day some soldiers stole a five-ton truck, ran over some deer, threw them in the back and must have taken the deer home. They did, however, leave one deer in the driver's seat, with hoofs tied to the steering wheel and a beret on its head. This is how the Military Police found their stolen truck. This was in the newspaper down there in Fayetteville at the time I was there.

When we were not at the Green Beret Club, or the 82nd Enlisted Club, or the army/navy stores, we were always doing something as a group. But, inevitably, the three amigos were finally broken up when I was transferred to Fort Devens, Massachusetts, John to Fort Lewis, Washington and Rudy, up to his usual tricks, remained in Fayetteville.

I saw John and spent some time with him at Fort Lewis, Washington while I was out there. My heart problems forced me out of the military and sent me back east here. While on my way back I stopped to see Rudy and had a brief visit. I talked to him once after that and tried so very hard to find him later, but failed. John was hard to locate as well, and then suddenly, I was notified in the Special Forces magazine that he had died. That was a heart breaker. They were treasures, my friendships with both John and Rudy, as they became so close to me. I'm sorry we were separated. You just never know what life has in store for you or if you'll see someone again. They were friends I had enjoyed so much. I only hope Rudy is doing well and happy with a family.

Chapter Twenty Five

My Passion Within

My personal devotion in this game of baseball feels so right all the time. I have ten thousand games more in my tank. I'm exaggerating, but that's how I feel. My health will dictate exactly how many more games there are, so until I can't play any more I will give one-hundred percent in all games. I will play each game as if it's my last. After all, any one game could be my last.

I would never be on the mound ever at this stage in my life if I were not ready, if I put the team in jeopardy, or if I wasn't physically playing to my potential. Then it would be time for me to consider becoming a coach, or finding another way to stay close to the game.

I am truly thankful that I am able to compete, at the age of sixty, with thirty-year-olds. I have no explanation; I was away from the game for thirty-six years. But I have continually worked very hard, and trained every off-season…as a matter of fact, I train year round. I seem to get better with my skills, in batting, pitching and especially defense, on the mound and on third base. I am so pleased and I feel so great after making a tough play, double play balls, or a diving catch. After completion of a great play it really feels as good as hitting a long double. I get the same positive rush or charge from that. This had been a productive career for me. I ended up batting four-hundred and ten for my final batting average. I was third in the league with an error of 1.93, had the least amount of walks, and defensively, I don't think I made any errors on the field at all. I had no home runs but hit the ball sharply and moved up to batting second in the batting order.

I started a new plan of attack this year. I decided to look on the internet to see who we are playing. If I was pitching, I would close my eyes and do my pre warm-ups, and begin the game in my head. I would think about who I was pitching to, what the count may be and then try something to keep them guessing. I played my game before I went to the ballpark. If I was to face a tough pitcher, I would concentrate and decide how I was to hit them. My plan did not have me thinking at the plate. When I approached the plate, my thoughts were, *see the ball, hit the ball.*

These are what I see as "tools." Many ballplayers are just plain gifted. Some see the gift they were born with, and others have incredible talent but either don't use it, or have no interest. They also change the moods on teams with attitudes that share a low desire. I guess you could say, one error leads to many errors in a game. Getting a hit to start things off is contagious and sets the tone and others continue to hit as well. This is where poor sportsmanship and attitudes smother any possible chemistry on a team. I wonder why some people even decide to play. The same guys strike out three times a game, make critical errors, and to them I guess it's ok. How on earth can that be fun? Some poor players bring their kids to team practices, and their little kids are better than they are. That's very embarrassing.

Many times during a game or in the dugout I go back in time and remember the old days with wood bats taped up because they were broken, taped baseballs, and very poor equipment. When we arrived at a field we would do "choosing up," hand over hand on the bat to choose sides. I can visualize riding my beat-up bicycle, bat through the glove over the handlebars and my dog Ginger following behind me to the game or sandlot baseball.

The fire in my belly, infatuation with the game, the emotions and standards I set for myself are an extraordinary experience. If you come to a game, you may as well play hard and try to win right. I mean, you're there, why not do your very best? I do try to set the example and be all I can be for the team, as well as reach my personal goals that I have from season to season.

Baseball is full of superstitions, luck, hard work, chance, and talent. I read Derek Jeter's story and enjoyed it so much. The Boston area folks don't like to hear my thoughts about the great Yankee ballplayers but, let's face it—they always seem to know how to play baseball. When I was in Arizona, I played short stop and did real well. In one particular game I made about twelve plays in a row. I looked like Derek Jeter at that point. Then late in the eighth inning, the sun made a turn and then there was a pop up, I lost the ball in the sun, and missed it. The very next play, a ball went through the wickets. I immediately said to myself, *remember what Derek said!* I slammed my fist into my glove, erased all that had happened, and then I wanted the ball. Sure enough, the next ball was hit very hard up the middle. I ran almost in a diving motion, snow coned the ball, stepped on second and fired the ball to first for the double play, ending the chances of a score and also ended the inning. I was so relieved and jubilant, for I was back on top of things.

The term "riding the pine" hits a nerve with me. It means someone is spending most of the time sitting on the bench and not participating. They may think the coach is bad, or unfair, they have many questions for the coach but are afraid to ask. The problem is not the coach but them. They have no enthusiasm, they're not a regular at practice, they don't give one-hundred percent and they're always complaining.

You need to dig down deep and give full effort and concentration and force yourself to beat the other guy for his job at second base or left field or whatever position it is. Why be lonesome, wasting time on the bench when you could be playing and making a difference on the team?

There are responsibilities being a teammate. They are not written on the wall or anything, but there are things that are expected as a team member. For example, run to the coach's box instead of waiting for someone else to go there. Pick up the score book or learn how to score if you don't know. Chase after the foul balls, maybe pick up the bats away from the front of the dugout instead of making the umpire upset. Those are just a few things but you get the idea. You could challenge yourself, set goals and standards and be involved in the game or practice.

When a team member can keep a team focused, and tries to set a good example, and is also a leader, this leadership spreads. It is contagious and allows a team to be stronger and more competitive. This is where champions are found. Only a few share the experience of being a champion. Some share the honors singularly in a sport like tennis or golf. Yes, there are a lot of individual feats in baseball too, but collectively, all is for the team. The moment of becoming a champion is your moment in time. Some people experience that numerous times. Some never have that experience ever in their lifetime.

I feel that there is also a special way to carry you into victory. It's not necessary to rub your opponent's face in defeat. He knows he's lost the game – why not have some respect for the game, honor to opposing players and demonstrate respect and dignity? I think it will go a long way.

I hear parents and adults teaching young kids things like, "Yankees suck." This really bothers me. The little kid does not know what he is reciting but repeats it anyway. Why not teach the kid fundamentals of the game? Children don't know what a base is, nor what a put out is, yet the parents think this is cute. Correct me if I'm wrong, but the Yankees seem to always be on top, either winning or very close to it. They have such superiority and such history in their organization. It's ok to have a favorite team, but how about protecting the sport of baseball and its values? I have to agree with Bill: Astro Turf, designated hitters, and metal bats have to go. Make pitchers bat, use wood bats and play the game as it was meant to be played.

I was in an elevator the other day wearing a baseball t-shirt from Cooperstown. A little boy with his mother in the elevator looked up to me and said, "Baseball." I said, "That's right. And if you play baseball you will always have fun and be happy." He walked away smiling.

When the winter slowly makes its turn to fade away, the thoughts of baseball, spring training, and the crack of the bat echo in my dreams. Not everyone can feel or see the game as clearly as the passion within this ballplayer. It's like magic, as the dreams come closer and get louder to opening day.

The smells of the ballpark change sporadically with cigar smoke, a few tobacco pipes, concession stands, and freshly cut grass. The maintenance landscapers are working frantically, grooming the field with fresh white lines leading to the foul poles. Spraying of water darkens the infield momentarily as the reflection of rainbows glisten across the baseball sky...but wait! We haven't gotten to spring training yet. See how the dreams and thoughts can carry you away? It's quite amazing but so very true. If you dream and believe, soon the time will pass and you will be there. Timeless baseball is where we are – we drift away and absorb thoughts of baseball even though we look out the window and see a snow storm in February.

I believe keeping the game close to your heart brings the best out of you. To further explain, listen to sports radio talk shows, talking baseball with friends, planning tournaments for off season, being involved in batting cages, working on your mechanics, whether it's pitching, hitting, or throwing. Work on your fundamentals like defense and improving your techniques. Maybe try holding a bat, or a ball and glove, while you're watching television. If your mind is glued to baseball there's less room for error. They say practice makes perfect. Well, that might not be entirely true, but practice and more practice improves your skill level no matter what age you are.

My training is constant, year round. There's no way I could play or compete if I didn't want to train consistently. To start, like many others, two weeks before the season starts and expect to be competitive – that just doesn't work. You must tune your body just like a car and prepare it for effective training and playing for this game of baseball. In amateur baseball it's truly fun to compete. To play the game you have loved your whole life; to watch your fellow ballplayers improving as you are, is special. To witness your friends hitting home runs and getting a walk-off hit to win a game for your team – that's special too.

Your age doesn't matter. Most adult baseball leagues are over thirty years old, and the challenge is still there – the other players are cocky and want to demolish you. They especially work harder at it when you are older and the opposing pitcher, like I am. That's ok. Put your game face on and bring it on. Are you ready to play now?

The passion I have within my mind and body has always been there my entire life. I had a period when my life had many changes but that's ok. I'm back and baseball is very much alive within me. I train in throwing the baseball, for example, three times a week. I throw about twenty-five to thirty pitches in each workout. I use blue painter's tape and make little one-inch spots depicting a strike zone, but a small strike zone. I do this in a gym or racquetball court. I sometimes use the incredible balls that little kids use. These balls are a little lighter but are the same size as a regular baseball and good for training indoors. I throw to the strike zone and do a series of low left, low right, high left, high right, and then dead center. Then, as I said, I throw about twenty balls. Some days I train with weighted balls, and throw them at a heavy pad. The weighted balls are from five to twelve ounces. When opening day comes, my arm is ready.

I also have great expectations of myself to have above-average sportsmanship towards any opponent at all times. I demonstrate that with umpires as well. If I think they did a good fair job, I shake their hand after the game and tell them so. If they were bad, I say nothing.

Some of my favorite ballplayers are Sadaharu Oh, Derek Jeter, Alex Rodriguez, Mickey Mantle and Lou Gehrig. I respect the way Ty Cobb played but did not like his sportsmanship. I love to see great plays, hard gritty baseball, and I have no specific favorite baseball team. I enjoy watching talent.

Because of the operation on my right wrist at the age of twelve, a critical time in my life, and poor baseball coaches, I drifted away from baseball. Then, after thirty-five years, I came back with the fire in my belly, and an attitude to appreciate.

I am having fun now. Despite the fact that I have heart disabilities, and was away from the game for so long, I can't explain it but, with all my training and hard work, I am improving my skills each year. It's not that I want to brag at all, it's the fact that I feel so surprised. I never thought I would reach the level of play where I am at right now. I do look younger and I'm treated with so much respect from players on my team as well as opponents. That's a great feeling.

My passion will continue as long as I can play effectively and compete to my high expectations without hurting my team. So I will continue as long as I can breathe, swing a bat, field a ball, and pitch until my arm drops.

Chapter Twenty Six

Guardian Angel

When I think of a Guardian Angel, immediately I think of unique episodes in my life when there were no reasonable answers for the conclusions. Mysteriously there has always been a sense of protection, or the presence of someone looking out for me. On television, there are movies and shows depicting angels that appear and help people with problems, many times involving religion, good deeds, or someone going down a dark road and being saved. You may view this as nonsense, but there are many who see this topic as very real. I will share my experiences and thoughts and see how close we agree. There are angels among us and it could possibly be someone you have known sometime in your life who is now gone.

If I were to recap my life, go into my memory bank and open the many thoughts of spectacular experiences and situations, I would have to question why these things have happened and who was really looking out for me. There have been choices and mistakes I've made, challenges, poor decisions, and yet I've always had hope in my heart.

Visions I have of my early days are very positive. I had a strong role model in my life without realizing it, only to find later in life how much I really do appreciate that roll model now. As I look back, I realize my mom was my roll model, and she guided me in the right direction as best as she was able to. At that point it was up to me to demonstrate to myself and the world what I had to offer. She really set the tone, set the example for my sister, my brothers, and myself, to leave the nest and face the world. She asked nothing in return, and sacrificed much of her life for us. I came to realize why I believe she had been my silent guardian angel throughout my life.

I have made a lot of wrong turns in my life; I slipped and fell, went aimlessly in directions unknown to me now, and I feel late in my life I have made a full circle and I am back at the beginning. I ask myself quite frequently why on earth I have traveled in so many foolish directions. I guess I forgot to listen. I was in too much of a hurry to grow up and experience things I knew nothing about. One important decision process I failed drastically on was the choices I made in relationships and friends, which ultimately cost me the life I really wanted. I should have been more particular, more cautious, as I'm sure I would have enjoyed with no doubt a better career, better relationships, and the opportunity I desired so much playing baseball. At this point in my life I recognize this difference, and appreciate what life presently offers.

Previously there were moments from the past when multiple negative things would happen. It seemed that bad luck came in bunches. Just like in baseball when a team makes an error, they become contagious and they multiply. But there are positive things that multiply in a bunch as well. There is no explanation for this but when it happens, suck it up and drive on. If it's positive, enjoy it while it lasts.

There are many superstitions in baseball. I used to cross the plate when I got in the batting box. Sometimes I got a hit, sometimes I didn't. Almost all baseball players have some sort of strategy. At present I go to the ball fields and look behind the backstop or in the woods where foul balls would go. I try to find a few before every game. Whenever I find one I feel I will have a great game. It's all in my head, but again—sometimes it works and sometimes it doesn't.

In my youth I would take chances hitchhiking and I was lucky I didn't get picked up by some nut. I rode in speeding cars with friends, and got in car accidents. I got a new Chevrolet after the military. My dad loved to work on carburetors. He would tune it up, I would go out Friday and Saturday nights, and drag-race and beat the car silly. Sunday, with beer cans in the back seat and the car filthy, I would say to my dad, "What's wrong with this new car?" He would fix it and in no time I would be leaving rubber around the corner or downtown. I had little fear at the time, as I always took chances, and later I regretted it.

One day I was traveling home, very relaxed and driving at a steady rate of speed. I was obeying the speed limit and as I approached an intersection, I had the green light. I continued my speed but instantly the car coming towards me turned left in front of me with no directional. At the same time, a car from the right also snuck by and turned left between the other car and my own. I was narrowly missed by both cars! I drifted across the street and came to a stop. I was all shaken up and could not believe I was not hit or hurt. It took a while for me to collect my thoughts.

I drove a jeep for a while and on two separate occasions, for no apparent reason, the gas pedal went to the floor and it was all I could do to avoid hitting other cars or people. There was no apparent reason for the incidents. On one more occasion I was coming home from work and traveling at high rate of speed and, after realizing there was some sort of problem with the wheel, I pulled into a car dealership. The moment I turned into the car lot, the wheel broke off…but I was not hurt.

I have had five heart attacks and five stints in my heart. There were many close calls, and death was knocking on my door. I have been air lifted by chopper to hospitals, ambulance emergencies, and more than my share of medical awareness. I even drove myself to the hospital and don't know how on earth I was able to get there. I have had a few close calls parachuting as well as with construction accidents. I truly believe I am blessed with my mom being my guardian angel. I feel touched by her presence whenever I am in danger or experience questionable episodes. Sometimes I feel she is on my shoulder when I'm pitching or at the plate. I will say to myself, *Mom, I really need to strike this guy out right now*, or *I need to hit a line drive for a hit*. Sometimes this works in my favor and sometimes it doesn't .I am never let down when it doesn't work. I am just so pleased that she is close when I need her.

I very much appreciate Mom's teachings, her philosophy on work ethics, and honesty. I do however feel cheated so very much because she is gone and I'll never catch up on conversations with her, but I will always continue to dream.

I was twenty-one years old when I lost her and twenty-three years old when I lost my dad. They are not far from me, for they are there in my thoughts daily.

Angels are very real and very much with us. Maybe you have one yourself. I feel fortunate that I remain close to my mom, knowing she is my comfort and support system. Hopefully I will always be blessed with knowing that.

Chapter Twenty Seven

2007 Challenge

Hibernation? I don't think so. That wouldn't be for me, but in late October, November, and during the holidays, with snow on its way and a long winter ahead...this is a depressing time for me. My team lost in the playoffs, so my season was over earlier than anticipated. I had financial disappointments so I was unable to attend the Las Vegas or Phoenix tournaments. My birthday is approaching, and yes, I will be turning that magical age of sixty. Our other home has just sold and freedom is around the corner. My wife Beth will be able to continue her passion for riding horses and I will be able to play more baseball. That in itself is quite uplifting.

The current plans after the holidays are very positive. I will be returning with the Long Island Mets to Terry Park in Fort Myers, Florida for Bob Wagner's Wood Bat Classic in January, 2007. I am looking forward to that tournament. I have such a strong electric team there. My confidence is sky high knowing I have strong defense and a real good hitting team. My sidekick Brian Cole, my Red Sox catcher, will be coming with me. Wait until my teammates see him play! He is an awesome player. Last year there were sixteen teams in the tournament. They say that possibly twenty teams will be there this year. That means more and better talent. That tells me to be really ready, for every game is so important to win. I can't wait. This will happen the last week in January.

The batting cage that I organized will be starting in early November and will be every Tuesday through the winter, right up to opening day in the spring. I have my winter tournaments to give me hopefully a winning edge.

My contact has been super, as I'm hitting the ball well. I'm so confident that when I walk to the plate, I know I'm getting a hit, I just know it. When I'm in the field, I want the ball, I'm looking to make a great defensive play, and when I pitch, I have the confidence that I will either strike them out or make them hit poorly. I've worked hard to get to this point and I hope it lasts and lasts. I'm very sad that I missed so many years where I could have had so much fun, but for now I'll cash in on all these spectacular moments.

I will still play in my Sunday Over 30 leagues this season, but I will pass up on the night league baseball. I'm having trouble seeing the action, with poor lighting and bad fields. Not to mention getting home at midnight. There are holiday tournaments, over the fourth of July, Labor Day, and then the playoffs. The fall brings several tournaments and which one to attend is quite the dilemma. I know there's a lot of baseball in my future, so I need to be ready.

I need to get cracking on my acupuncture appointments, as I'm having trouble with my shoulder and neck. This usually happens off season and I don't have a lot of time, since January baseball is *so* close.

● ● ●

My Over 30 team took me to Hooter's for my sixtieth birthday bash. We had a lot of laughs, lots of food, and I even had my picture taken with the pretty Hooter's girls. That was fun. My team then gave me a picture of the 1918 World Series Red Sox in a nice frame. That was great. It was hung quickly on the wall in my study the next morning.

Just prior to my turning sixty years old, I had received a birthday card from my brother. There were disturbing newspaper articles that he had included in the card. I guess his mind was somewhere else, as this news was devastating to me. The news was as follows: The Eastside Improvement Association was in the process of selling the ball fields, and they were planning on building condos on the baseball field property. The reason I was devastated was because, as I stated in Chapter Two, Organized Baseball, I had mentioned that when I was awarded the Most Valuable Player award, they made a plaque in my honor and it had hung ever so proudly for over forty-eight years on the walls of the club on that property. From 1957 until 2006, the Most Valuable Players' plaques had hung there with pictures to correspond with each year. I always felt it was safe. My award represented to me, work ethic, challenge, dedication, and proof that I was the best baseball player in that league in 1959.

This also was the only time in my life that both my mom and dad were present together at a special moment in my life before they died. This was the beginning of my baseball journey and also the most important, emotional and perfect monumental moment in my entire life. I think about being presented this award even now as I write about it, and I still find emotion uncontrollable to this day.

Upon hearing this news of closure of the property, I immediately went into a frenzy and asked my sister to check with the president of the association to retrieve my plaque. She had been unsuccessful and someone had taken it. I contacted a radio announcer, and wrote a letter to him asking for his support. I called a dear friend to use his political clout to find my plaque as well. The problem was, they had a memorabilia day, which was announced in the newspaper, and unfortunately I live sixty miles from there and had no knowledge of when that would take place. The news I received was two weeks late. The public had stormed the building on this memorabilia day, stripped the walls of plaques and trophies, and little was left. I had contacted the other award recipients but there was still no news of my plaque. I lost a lot of weight, and lost a lot of sleep, as my heart was torn for the loss of my earned award.

I'm thinking my special award is probably sitting in some baseball player's house or office, who knows it isn't theirs and they didn't earn it. It's Christmas Eve and I still can't shake this loss and my only way to survive is to think about baseball the night after Christmas with my teammates at the Lowell batting cage training.

There was a time in the military when I was supposed to be promoted to sergeant and my promotion was sent back because of a personality clash with an officer. I earned that and deserved the promotion very much. I would come to earn it once again at a later date. Later in my baseball experience, I was in a Las Vegas Over 50 baseball tournament and pitched a perfect game, up to five innings complete. At the end of the game the opposing team picked me for the Most Valuable Player of the game. The manager turned around and gave it to a guy who made a good catch, thus I lost what I had earned once again. This time my history of this award goes back forty-eight years. This plaque was hung on the walls of that association for forty-eight years for all to see and honor my achievement. At that time there was no doubt I was the winner and the MVP; I was the best and work ethics were such a strong part of this accomplishment. To hear someone had taken it only for memorabilia, at my expense, tears my heart out. I feel I am beaten within, and somehow I will get through this terrible negative period and turn things around. It will be hard but I am a professional, a paratrooper and I have heart.

In my search for the plaque, I also requested help from friends like Roy, who I was friends with many years back in Brockton, and his political contacts. I additionally wrote and called other John DeCostas to see if anyone was looking to find me, yet I found no positive answers. I wrote a letter over the internet and some stranger told me to write to a radio announcer in Brockton, for he was on the subject and could possibly help. That's what I did, and when I least expected it, he emailed me and invited me onto his radio show!

I called the radio station, spoke to the producer, and then after a short wait, I was live on the radio. I was a tad nervous at first but got over it quickly. The talk show host, Bill Fulcher, spoke of my writing a baseball story, gave a brief history of me and the organization, and then introduced me to the audience. I responded and told my story – how I started baseball, my work ethics, and the challenge set before me upon entering this league many years ago.

I quickly went through my accomplishments, my love for baseball and how and why this baseball plaque had meant so much to me. We talked and I explained how baseball used to be, back in the 1950s and 1960s. That was fun, as Bill had guided me perfectly through the story. At the end, I gave a final plea for anyone with knowledge of the whereabouts of this award to contact the radio station to help me. I at least felt I had made a strong effort to locate it. I even wrote other baseball players and called others from that time frame, but got no results. I made a last-ditch effort and wrote to a player that was also mentioned on my award. I figured if he didn't know about my plaque then the probability of its whereabouts was lost, and I could forget about 2006 and move on. I was depressed over Christmas and New Year's, and decided to move on.

On January 1, 2007, I woke up with a slight cold. I took care of the dogs, and then I checked to see if there were any responses to my emails. My very first 2007 email was quite disappointing, as a disgruntled player from my Over 30 baseball team was complaining about how I wrote to team members to attend practice. My answer to him was "Happy New Year to you to." He had made two practices in five years so as far as I was concerned he had no grounds to complain about anything.

I recovered from the nasty email and looked through some old pictures. Then I got a phone call. It was Bill, my friend from Little League. He was the 1960 MVP and I was the 1959 MVP.

He opened up with "Happy New Year, John!" I said the same. He then apologized for not returning my calls. He then said, "I have your plaque and you may come and get it whenever you like, even today." I was immediately blown away. I checked with my wife to see if she needed me, and then jumped in the car and made the long journey in terrible icy weather to go to North Easton, Massachusetts to meet Bill at the Police department where he worked.

I waited for a few minutes, and then Bill came out of a room with two plaques. One was his and the other, of course, was mine. I brought a camera and had another officer take a picture of us holding our respective plaques. We talked baseball, and compared our baseball experiences with each other and spoke about old baseball friends and how things were on the eastside so many years ago.

While I was riding home with the plaque, it was very strange as I touched it all the way, just to make sure it was really there. I placed a loving and emotional touch to it and said, "You'll be home safe with me where you belong." I called Beth during my trip home, to let her know we would be home soon. When I arrived, Beth cleaned the plaque and we placed it in my baseball case where it is forever safe. I look at it so many times during the day and smile. The guardian angel I spoke of in Chapter Twenty-six had come to help me once again. I'm sure my guardian angel was beside me, directing this miracle right along, and again I felt truly blessed and grateful. This renewed my baseball spirit for 2007.

The next day I got the pictures developed, bought a frame and delivered a picture to Bill. I shared the story with Bill, the man who had interviewed me on the radio, and he wished to do another segment the following Friday on the radio again. The Brockton Enterprise newspaper wanted to do a story as well, so this was truly a great way to start off 2007!

I have a new practice set up in my home in the cellar: I have a pop-up target with a catcher's face and pocket. Now I can train as often as I find time. I'll just have to step it up and make sure I am far above any opponents so no one will take what I have earned ever again. I guess you could call this a temporary baseball clot in my veins, and a little baseball "extra training" will clear the way to my heart and soul.

My philosophy on baseball comes from many pros that I admire, like Lou Gehrig, Tyrus Cobb, Derek Jeter and Mickey Mantle, to name a few. I admire their attitude, work ethic, training, and mental aggression. In regards to batting, I feel that when you're on deck or in the dugout, try this (it works for me): say to yourself, *I will get a hit, I will be on base, I will make contact.* Your attitude and demeanor will work like gears in a clock and you will be more successful than your previous attempt at the same thing. Also, when fielding, say to yourself, *what will I do if I get the ball? Keep it in control, I want the ball,* and you'll be ready for it. If you're pitching or playing any position, this will work most of the time, or a high percentage of the time. I do love this game.

The blues of January have settled in. I am relieved and extremely pleased to have found my plaque and to have received so much attention in the newspaper and radio, but something about winter just gets to me. I need to be positive for Terry Park in Fort Myers, Florida. It is just fifteen days away. I hope to be rid of my winter flu so I can enjoy the smell of pine tar and freshly cut grass, and hear the crack of the bat echoing through the park.

Tomorrow is another segment on the radio show with Bill at WXBR in Brockton, to complete the east side improvement association happenings and the final chapter of my missing plaque troubles to his listening audience. I don't feel nervous at all. I don't feel like a celebrity. I feel like I am adding experiences and sharing with more people who hopefully will enjoy such a story. We'll see how it goes...

Bill leads me through the interview just as the last one, very professional and upbeat. The demeanor of our conversation is also positive as I retell my story, and explain how I recovered my plaque. In both interviews I had generated listeners to call in, but because of my home being so far away, I was unable to pick up the radio station. I have sent Bill, the man who returned my plaque, a thank you card, and I brought the photos to the radio station for the newspaper-write up. Now this chapter is closed. I have my plaque in my special case and I am so pleased and enriched. I will have such a positive feeling hovering over me for the tournament. I am excited and in shape as well as ready to play baseball. I had my big stress test and pre-season cardiac check up and now I have the green light. So, wood bat tournament at Terry Park, here I come!

The tournament atmosphere was immediately felt during our practice session Sunday, an hour after getting off the plane. We didn't get too many swings in, but there was a lot of infield practice. I did well and felt I would have a good tournament. I love infield practice. I could do that all day long. I guess hitting is the same way, as I could do that all day as well. We played on the great fields of Terry Park and also in The Player Development Complex. The Boston Red Sox play there. We played six games, losing three and winning three. We did not get into the playoffs. I could not believe it, as we had by far the best offensive and defensive team there, out of sixteen teams. The problem was simply luck. Errors are contagious as well as hitting. Our team just was not clicking at all. We had our team dinners, banquet, watched the New England Patriots lose to the Colts, and I went home feeling very disappointed about the week. I had some good games–four straight hits and a few real good defensive plays, but in general it was a disappointing week of baseball. I did see Bill while I was down there, and he asked me to play in a North and South baseball game. Who knows if that will ever happen–you know Bill "The Spaceman."

I met another gentleman, Al. He's writing a book about amateur baseball and gave me some advice. He also said I was in his book!

My Over 30 league is still a few months away, and there will be numerous practices to come before opening day. After the summer and playoffs, I believe I'll be making another trip to Cooperstown to play in that tournament. The home of baseball is so reviving and great for a long season reward. The unique uniform for the tournament is purchased ahead. You have your choice of either the Legends of Baseball or the Cooperstown uniform. This helps you to really enjoy being there in rare form. I'll be playing once again on the field of dreams, Doubleday field, and the village of Cooperstown.

In March 2007, I was given the opportunity to have my own baseball column in the town newspaper. It came out well, as I have numerous articles prepared nine weeks in advance. This should be fun. I plan to share sportsmanship, baseball tips, nostalgic baseball memories, and the passion to enjoy baseball and softball for everyone.

My baseball column had been successful and allowed me to grow as a writer. In the last two years I had more than 35 articles published. This is all about sharing what I feel about sportsmanship, teamwork, and leadership as well as tips of the game. I had the intention for younger players to be excited and challenge themselves in baseball but, I got more adults reading than the younger adults. It seems older guys in their thirties and up are more nostalgic than one realizes. It did feel good seeing my articles in a real newspaper and especially when I went to a ballpark and when people had no knowledge of who I was, and then talked about my articles in a positive manner. That was truly a nice accomplishment and extra boost of confidence for me.

The newspaper is cutting back because of cost, economy and whatever other reasons are floating around so I will have to search for a new paper or magazine in my future. I will look into other avenues to extend my articles to something new in the horizons soon. That's the plan anyway.

My involvement with so many age groups becomes a problem at times. Maybe you as a reader can identify with this as well. My point, if I can explain it properly, is this…. I play baseball with over thirty year old guys, and many in their forties, and fifties and god forbid someone close to my age at times. Well every ten years is quite different. It doesn't sound like much but we are all different. Take a listen for a moment. The thirty year olds; they have no understanding of any type of discipline, the military or music as our culture has changed so much. The forty year olds are not much different either. Once again their music, education process is similar with the electronics world but their way of thinking about things is so far from mine.

They are referred to, by me as the gadget generation. They all have cell phones, now iphones, computers, blackberry's and all sorts of things with ear phones etc. I'm lucky I can turn something on and off. I broke down and got a cell phone which I unfortunately have to admit do use a lot, but I'm so foreign with that little gadget I can't even retrieve missed phone calls. I am lost, I keep getting asked; did you get my message? I say please, how will I be able to check that out? as they shake their heads. When I speak to them about sand lot baseball, or wood bats, they look at me like I came out of the corn stalks from field of dreams.

The over forty guys are a little understanding because for the most part they have older relatives still alive and well and have listened to their stories from long ago. The over 50 guys are close so are to be much easier to deal with. I am too laid back for the younger guys when it comes to arguments and making decisions. They seem to have road rage even when they play baseball. I say relax and be thankful and appreciate the fact, you're healthy and able to play this game we all love. If they were in another foreign country maybe they would be carrying a rifle.

The thinking of each generation is very different when it comes to how they get along, their outlook on life, with family and the career decisions. I decided we can be like the Army was; Hurry up and wait! Maybe all generations have to give in a little so we can have quality of life.

I really enjoy setting the example with these younger guys. How on earth can I be faster than they are? I think 30% are athletes and the other 70% can't get away from the couch or computer. They say I amaze them but maybe they could challenge themselves a little more. When I am competing, I want their best because it makes me play a higher level. If I lose I gave them a fight and I can keep my head high.

The Eastside Kid 2007 has experienced many baseball experiences that to not mention would be a sin. This continuation of more baseball and tender moments is at its best. In March and April 2007 I had just returned from Fort Myers, Florida from the Bob Wagner's Wood Bat Classic at Terry Park. Yes, it's still early for the 2007 season to start right now but the heavy duty planning for baseball 2007 season was underway.

What better place to do that than my time spent at the athletic facility during my training or at the batting cages in Lowell, Massachusetts? I have been working very hard and felt I was getting even better with my mechanics pitching and hitting. I was chosen by my new team the Philly's in the over 30 baseball draft. That was good for me and once again I had to prove my worth at the cage practices with my new teammates. I still had another cage night with my old team the Red Sox to include other players from other teams so a lot of off season baseball. I could not attend any other away tournaments but I was fine with that.

I had experienced shoulder problems too often so I had myself checked out by my doctor and found there was no problem physically accept I had pursued the questions with athletic and sports trainers. I drilled these folks with constant questions about throwing, soreness, stretching etc. What I found was I had been not working my muscles correctly. Yes I was stretching but not using the hand weights correctly. I developed exercises with 15# dumb bells and set up a routine with 10 new exercises pulling these weights in all directions and making the workout very effective.

Besides the exercise with dumb bells, I found through other pitchers such as my friend Brian that I should ice more. I took his advice as I hadn't ever iced. I bought myself new ice bags and iced my arm before and after throwing and before you know it, I had success and almost immediately my throwing had improved and I think my speed had as well. The aches and pains had gone and I felt strong and healthy as a horse. I did well pitching in the cages with my new team and soon outside experiencing positive results. The wait for the new season was slow, as I was anxious and the weather was not cooperating at all. Cold wet winter and extreme wet spring was demoralizing to me.

I was given an opportunity to share my baseball thoughts in a column in my small town newspaper. I actually had a column, called "The Baseball Corner". I will share some of the columns here from time to time. So here I am thinking about my new season to come, looking at the weather situation wanting to get outside and feel my thought to be improvement and plans for selection of leagues to play in. I signed up and made plans for Legends of Baseball at Cooperstown, New York for September 8 through September 15th 2007 for starters. That's confirmed; I even purchased a Legends uniform to go in style.

Then as I said earlier, I once again signed up for over 30 baseball in Lowell, Ma for the 2007 season and was picked up by the Philly's.

Then I signed up for The Night over 30 League in Lowell, Ma on the Devil Rays team. Yes, not enough for me, I then signed up for another night league in Boston called the Men's Amateur Baseball League in Boston, Ma, this is over 40 baseball, I am on the Astro's team there. We are looking at three leagues at present, playing four games each week. I was asked to play in my town for another over 40 baseball league. This team is also called the Astro's but I just couldn't fit another league in my plan. It was closer in travel but I was already committed so I just practice with the team once in a while for plans in the future.

Boston-MABL Men's Amateur Baseball League, The Astro's, I'll cover those experiences now. My first time going to a game with this team, like most all of my experiences, I fit in early like a new glove. Things didn't make me happy in one department: Hitting; the manager said he didn't have pitchers hit. I pitched well and won the game. After I got home, I wrote him via email.

I said I will not travel all over hell's kitchen to play baseball and not bat. I continued that I was a .400 hitter and that would be a waste for both of us. He said next game for sure I would hit.

I was a little set back now but also my usual gamer self, I came to the next game and now I was not only pitching but on the batting list as well. I got two hits, one run batted in and one score for the hitting side of things. I pitched another gem against a pretty good club. I had 7 k's and 1 walk. This was an average outing for me, with amateur baseball. I did however find it hard to make these games for one game would be up in the north shore 60 miles away from my home, and other games 55 to 60 miles in another direction to the south. The games were all over the city and after the 8 pm games I would not roll into my driveway until 12:30 to 1:00 AM. This became tiresome dangerous driving, and as soon as the games were over I had to book on home.

Most of the guys are whipping out the coolers opening a cold one in honor of winning or losing the game. Sometimes I would join in but most of the time I had to hit the road because of my obligation to take care of my dogs who were patiently waiting all of this time. I played 10 possibly 11 games with this group and we were a .500 ball club. I believe I got at least one hit every game and three or four games had multiple hits. I pitched very well as I had 5 wins and almost 6 wins as I came out of a game against a top team with the lead and the next pitcher gave up too many runs as we lost that game.

In the playoffs, I pitched against a team I beat twice before. This time, they had a real ace for a pitcher. He had a lot of strikeouts and threw very hard. The game was close back and fourth as each inning was exciting. I pitched the whole 7 innings and had 8 strikeouts. I pitched very well but lost 7-6 with only 2 earned runs. I do like those exciting nail biting games. It was especially nice when the opposing team acknowledges your effort as they had after the game. The umpires even went out of their way to extend their thoughts as well.

In this league which was wood bat and real baseball as one can imagine I batted only about 300. But my error was low as I had pitched very well. The guys were a good bunch but the travel to the games was very far and difficult for me to handle in the future.

My Night over Thirty Baseball league was not as exciting and only had 3 wood bat games in the schedule. The travel was much easier and all the teams had a great bunch of guys. I played for three different teams from year to year but this year no matter if we won or lost a game I had fun playing. That is not the case for many teams so this was a real fun baseball time for me. We had a .500 season but lost in the playoffs and could not continue.

I have mentioned earlier in the book one that I go to the games early, stretch, work out, look for lost baseballs, and mingle with opponents and other early teammates. This was a different night. Yes I experienced the same things I had just mentioned but this time after the game I searched every where for the keys to my car. Fortunately I had not locked the car but the search went on. Then I had teammates and opponents helping me search. I remembered that while looking for baseballs I dropped my baseball bag along with the keys and I knew the general direction and area but now this was late at night, no lights and no flashlight. My friends and I looked moved leaves and sticks around and finally my friend Frank my lifesaver found the keys. I may have slept out there till morning if he hadn't found the keys. I felt very stupid but this was not my first experience losing keys, wallets, or anything like that. I am just fortunate that the outcome was positive.

The last few games we played, the lighting had affected me immensely. I had played second base which was just the opposite for me being traditionally a third baseman or shortstop. I miss played a ball and my finger was so swollen. I had iced it and it was quite sore for the next few days. I knew I had to pitch Sunday in an important game for my over 30 team, the Phillies; this had turned out to be a fantastic year pitching. My batting was suspect and which batter would show up this week, I would ask myself. My pitching, I had enough confidence for the whole league. I had so many super tight games through the season. I stayed ahead of the league. I lost the very first game by one of the best teams in the league the Yankee's but after that- I won, I kept winning and did not look back. I led both leagues with 9 wins and one loss. When all was said and done I had 42 Strikeouts, with an era of .317 it was my year.

Late in the season, as my record had been progressing and getting noticed by the league, I had the big game coming up against my old Red Sox Team. I played for the Red Sox for five seasons and I played well. It was sad to leave friends as I said before but the Red Sox were a .500 ball club and I wanted more. Not that I was any better but I needed a change of scenery and the adjustment helped the Red Sox get new players and for me to re- establish myself. That's just what I did.

The game was set for August 12th. I was ready and for some reason the Red Sox acquired a new group of players and were in the top two teams of the 16 team league. Yes, I had a challenge set before me, I also would have to face the new ball players, prove to the Red Sox I still had it and they lost a gem. I also had to prove to the Phillies that I was their guy now and their ace. So there was a lot to prove. I got there early in the morning shooting hoops by the basketball court nearby, getting loose. It was time now to go over and get ready to play third base. I would not start this game but would come in later in the game. I could tell that the older regular players were telling their new players there he is Johnny D over there on third. I sized them up as well. I said to myself, I just want to see who I will strike out. I told the guys early on in the season I would beat them well, now here is the day. The old guy, the mascot, was at the game, as he follows the Red Sox. His name is," pickles". I said to Pickles, I'm going to win today, watch me. He laughed.

I made a few defensive plays, was heavily involved with the game. It was now about the 6th inning and now I was called in the game. We were losing by one run and now I had to prove I still had it. Every pitch was critical and also my teams defensive ability. This was the turning point of the season. My rival and friend was at bat , Brian. He caught for me for five years and tournaments and the batting cage so I wasn't going to fool him very much.

My first pitch was a changeup low on the corner and he hit it out for a homerun. I struck out two and my team came back with more runs and now I had to protect. Yes, another crucial tense game I held them back and made the final strike out in the ninth to get the win and topple the first place Red Sox and move us up in a better position.

During that week in a night game, I broke my finger fielding a ball with poor lighting but played anyway. I played again in Boston and made my finger worse.

The last few games as I mentioned I had broken my finger. Well the swelling got worse therefore, I was forced to immediately get an x-ray and see the doctor. I did that and found my finger was officially broken. Yes, my middle finger of my throwing hand. I had a portable cast and told the doctor I would be good but as soon as Sunday came, I had an important playoff game. My team was counting on me as I had such a winning season that if the team was to continue I had to make sure we won. I had put orajel ointment on my finger which is used for toothaches and put on my finger to numb the pain. I also used "tiger balm" and ibuprofen to allow me to play in this game. I tore a tendon in my left ankle area, along with bruises from a line drive earlier that week. I pitched, and every single pitch hurt so badly but I pitched well despite the injury. I was a bit slower but I was effective as we won the game. I even contributed two hits while being injured in that game.

The next game, I would not be there as I had plans before the season started to play in Cooperstown New York for a team called Washington Nationals. I was excited to play in Cooperstown once again as I was packed for a week. I knew of a few on my team and only hoped my finger would be ready. Some of those teammates were following my performances in over 30 baseball on the internet so again, my services were needed on the mound.

I had cell numbers an email list so while I was in Cooperstown, I could check to see how my Phillies were doing the following Sunday. I would be playing the very same time in Cooperstown. During this game I had pitched a gem and won 3-2 at Milford field in Cooperstown and on my way back to the hotel in Cooperstown village my friend and teammate Rob had called me to tell me the Phillies won in a dramatic fashion and I would be pitching against the Giants upon my return which was the most important game in the over thirty league playoffs.

Chapter Twenty Eight

Cooperstown 2007

The time has finally come for my Cooperstown trip. I had planned all year long right down to every little detail. The only thing I had not counted on was missing a playoff game. I had miscalculated the dates. We were packed and made our journey west to Cooperstown, New York. It's truly a great scenic drive but not pleasant when it rains off and on during the trip and getting lost due to not paying attention doesn't help the journey at all. After the bumps and turns, wrong directions, and eventually taking the long way to Cooperstown we finally got there before dark. Our top notch suite, as advertised on the internet in an old hotel off Main Street in Cooperstown, was not a happy moment. We soon left the hotel and went to a nationally known hotel which made the week one hundred percent better.

I had gone with my wife shopping in Cooperstown village and my first stop was to purchase a wood bat. I had "The Eastside Kid" engraved on the barrel of the bat. This was great and another piece of memorabilia to take home. I did not use this bat in the games but it sure felt good in my hands.

Rain reports would be an issue all week long. I was worried about if we would play our game and also had in the back of my mind my over thirty team playing their second playoff game. I pitched the last three innings and won the game 3-2 at Milford Field. I had a good outing and established myself with my new team the Washington Nationals. When the game was over, we went to Beaver Valley "The Field of Dreams" but the rain came and we were done for the day. Game cancelled and that's a bad way to start a tournament.

The problem with the hotel finally was resolved and the new hotel sure was relaxing. I got my gear ready for the two games on Monday at Doubleday field so there was a lot to be excited about. Yep, I'm up bright and early and ready to play baseball. I brought breakfast back to the room for my wife, had a quick coffee and set out for Doubleday.

Parking was not a problem because I was early. I admired the field again. I studied the mound and had my pre- game jitters but that was good. I was excited and ready to do this.

We were home team as I walked with a fast pace to the mound as I was starting the game. I pitched my usual self, had a few struggles with some of the batters but we came out on top 3-2. I was on my way back from Milford field to play another game but we were rained out.

While I was on my way back, I got a call on my cell phone from Rob my teammate back home. My Phillies team had won and now when I return, I had the call to start in the final playoff game to get us into the National League Championship game. That was great news and powered me up for the next day.

The tournament continued with close games. We lost the next game 4-3 but still doing well in the tournament. The next day was poor weather but we managed to get ahead and stay ahead and won 6-4. I collected a few hits and rushed after the game to go to the village next to Doubleday for a deep tissue massage. After that I was renewed and rushed back for the double header and just made it on time. I think the coach was mad because I was 10 minutes late so I sat on the bench for two innings. We were losing the game and finally I got the nod to come in the game.

I came in with a Johnny D attitude and struck out the sides. I pitched the rest of the game and had 7 strikeouts as we won another game. The next morning, we had a game against the defending winners in this tournament against the Red Sox who were from the Boston area. We had another pitcher come in and start for us. He did ok, but it just wasn't our day.

I came in a little too late. We were down by five runs. There were two women on this team. One was Jenny Mills a New England native and already in the Hall of Fame because she was on the U.S. Olympic team, a college super star in softball and better than half of the guys. The other girl was a solid player competitive with many male baseball players and when she sat on the bench she "spit" as good as or better than most.

I came in the game when the game was really lost because of the run differential. I struck out this girl that spits and the umpire made a comment to her about my curve ball. He said to her "that would be curveball miss" and she flew off the handle and threw her bat like a spear at the dugout wall as the bat splintered. The umpire threw her out of the game. She then threw her helmet and said something of a four letter quality and was then tossed out of the tournament. Too much negative excitement, as we finished the game with another loss. If the game is close and competitive, I enjoy the challenge but when it's lost and poor sportsmanship enters the game, I'd rather be in the batting cage.

After this, our final chance at the semi- finals would be at Doubleday to see who goes to the finals against the Red Sox team that we previously lost to the day before. We were warming up and I knew this was a critical game. There was even a crowd here. This team that we previously beat had four new additions to their lineup. Some had to leave the tournament and therefore the tournament officials put four solid players on their team. I thought it was unfair but those things happen and this was another baseball game but more importantly a final game at Doubleday Field in Cooperstown New York.

This was my game, as I was strong and definitely respected by this team. The game was close 1-1, then 2-2, like that for 7 innings. In-between innings, one of the umpires was talking with me. He would throw a knuckleball at me or something and as we talked he said that he instructed kids between 18 to 21 years old. He said I have more movement on the ball than his students. I was flattered but I have no idea how it is on the receiving end of my pitchers, I just enjoyed the positive remarks. The other umpire behind the plate was fierce and takes no prisoners. He was a retired Police Chief. I tried not to encourage any conversation with him. He had a postage type strike zone, but I knew that and now I have to make my pitches.

The game was on edge from start to finish but this was no stranger to me as I have had a bundle of those games this year. The game was supposed to go 7 innings but we had a tie 4-4 so now it was extra innings. I had no walks and struck out 8 bad guys. Every pitch of this game was a nail biter, as the tension level was way up there. The crowd was getting into it in a big way, as this game was so exciting. Being the one on the mound with all this stress is where I love to be. This is what I live for, now I have there homerun hitter up. I made him whiff on two sliders and he was not happy. I finally threw him a changeup and he hit a ground ball for the second out. Then the other big hitter gets up same thing. I then bust him outside slider, got him to foul a ball off and now a changeup low inside and he golf's the pitch high and deep. The question was "did the ball curve before or after the foul pole" for the homerun. They called it fair as I went to the third base line to greet him, great hit I said.

The crowd did not like the call but as you know once a call is made in baseball they do not change it. I struck the last guy out and now we had our final chance to either go down in defeat or win on a walk off. There was our first man who got a single, the next walked, and then 1 guy struck out, then there was a pop up.

Now with two outs, game on the line, last of extra innings and the tournament at risk I was up. I had pitched well enough for the win and all the accolades but now was when it counts. I ran up the count with watching the strike zone carefully but now it was a full count. I saw the ball well and hit a hard line drive up the middle but the short stop made a great play and stepped on second base for the final out and the win. So I didn't come through, lost the game but gave a hard fight on behalf of my team. It was a tough way to lose at Doubleday   but a fun week of baseball and as I was greeted by the opposing team I got a lot of praise and "man hugs" from the other team along with a hand shake and they were so genuine to me with their positive compliments to my pitching ability and the kind words they said to me, made the hurt of losing filter away.

Our team had said their goodbye's as well with hopes and dreams for other upcoming amateur baseball tournaments in the near future.

The slow journey back to West Townsend, Ma was underway. The check out of the hotel, packing stopped for a sandwich at the 'Bean" and headed home. I was relieved that it was over, pleased my team back home had pulled off a victory for our Phillies and now my emotional second wind would kick in for the upcoming game on Sunday. Three days rest no problem;   I   just racked up 20 innings this week followed by 22 innings the week before so this was a piece of cake.

My arm and body had been in bad shape once I had time to relax, look into the mirror and see the wear and tear. My arm had pitched over 50 innings at this point and after the season was over, my innings had grown to 154 not counting practice games ,batting practice and the cage and sand lot, so I was sore. I have come so far and many other good teams would be eliminated during the tournament and I'm still hanging in there. I could not let my team down either in my Boston over 40 leagues as I was pitching well there too. The Lowell over 30 needed me now but despite any pain after I took ibuprofen and my other remedies to keep going; the moment I got on the mound all pain was forgotten.

Its amazing the heart, desire and determination you can see all around you in amateur baseball whether it's a tournament or local league. It also doesn't matter the age, as I see people with the same if not worse disabilities than I have and still keep going like an energizer bunny.

I remember a gentleman that was 75 years old and you only knew this when someone alerted you to that information. He would play 12,- 7 inning games in a week at the Las Vegas tournament. He would catch behind the plate most games and jog a few miles between the double headers. Sometimes he would catch one game and pitch the whole next game. I remember him well as he had a new joke each time you saw him. What a nice man he was.

Chapter Twenty Nine

Lowell over Thirty Baseball Tournament

The next game as I had returned was the important game that would either end the season or go to the National leagues Championship game. We were playing against the Cardinals. We had beaten them early in the season. They were on a long winning streak and beating everyone, but so were we. This is the big game. I am on the mound as I'm the leader in wins in the league now. The game is close, they're ahead, and then we are ahead, but we edged in front to maintain the lead. Finally we make the brake for a few more insurance runs in the fifth inning as I contributed a few hits as well for the boost. Our other pitcher Mike takes us to the finish for the save of the game. Mike was our Manager and a good one and where I had such a positive year, Mike also had a lot of save's with my pitching. There were some close moments but we managed the victory and now we are the National League Champs. This felt very good, finally being the best and not hanging your head low as I also have experienced before.

The last season this team, my Phillies came in last place and this year we came in first place. This is the first time I have ever been on a championship baseball team. I was on a basketball Junior High School championship team in 1960 but this is real special now.

The plans are in effect and we will play the next weekend at LeLacheur Stadium in Lowell, Mass where the "Spinners" play baseball a minor league baseball team, great stadium. The day before is a homerun derby/hitting contest at the same stadium yes I will be there for that.

There will be a hitting contest for up to age 47 years and another after age 48 years. Yes I qualify for over age 48, I am 60 very close to age 61. They have markers in different places on the field to score points. I hit a few in the warning track and was consistent enough to get enough points to come in second place for the small trophy for that category. The fun part was also watching the younger group as there were three guys consistently hitting homeruns out of the park. One guy was a number one draft pick for the Florida Marlins baseball team.

His name was Jeff Allison, the declared winner. I would meet up with him later. This was a fun day, a lot of picture taking and great to be on the stadium field. The only thing I didn't like was the pitching for this hitting contest was very short less than little league distance so your swing was faster and mechanics a bit off for everyone.

This was also a good preparation for the Championship game tomorrow between My Phillies the National League Champions vs. the White Sox the American league Champions. I was ready now for I was hitting very well and ready for the big game.

I hadn't slept very well all week long thinking about this game. In my mind I had planned my pitching performance and would wake up in the middle of the night wondering "what inning is it"? I was so absorbed with wanting to win this game. I told many friends and relatives to come, for the crowds doesn't bother me these days, I look forward to an audience. I think it encourages me to do well. Even though the fans are there yelling and making noise I know they are there but I don't hear a thing because my mind is on the game.

My mental thoughts leading up to this game were as such. I would envision in my mind the different batters, the excitement, the fans from other teams and families and in between these thoughts I would catch up on how much work and effort to get to this present position; I would not experience what Sadaharu Oh had experienced in his last heroic game but I would go back in history to my triumphs and exciting games. I would also go back to my childhood, my pets and my old house at 22 Massasoit Avenue in Brockton, Massachusetts where it all began for me. I visited the home on numerous occasions through the years as, with so many memories I would enter the driveway or just ride by and the tears would dribble out of my eyes and down my cheeks as so many family memories would fill my heart and soul. There were so many opportunities to re-purchase the home but that never worked out and buying an old home filled with emotion was just sending me too far in the rear view mirror. This would happen for many years. Finally , as I neared the end of this book I visited once again. I met the new owners and they were gracious and I made arrangements to come another time to see the home. I did so, and shared many of my old memories with them.

I told them so many things about the home that no one could ever know unless it came from me or my family. I chased this ghost of love and emotion of my family roots and upon the completion of this visit I finally was able to really let go of this home. It was not as big as I had dreamed and was not decorated or had any of my family feelings. I finally was able to let go, but I still walk away with strength, loyalty, work ethics, honor and my love and passions of my family character.

The many thoughts had also given me closure and the ability to focus. I know I would give my best and I was not afraid of the competition or how big the games were. In my early days , I would be afraid of a crowd but now I encourage the crowd and play to it. This is just another type of challenge, determination and my passion.

I told my friends that my wife would be there; I said she will be the one well dressed, with a book. My wife didn't like that comment but on the other hand they all knew how to find her. I was thinking all week that I would start the game but was disappointed when the White Sox were chosen to be home team based on their record. I would still start the game but only after we batted.

I entered the stadium and got my wife settled near our dug out. The whole team started warming up, stretching, joking and getting ready for the showdown. We were all friends with the White Sox so we exchanged good words with each other, shook hands and tried to get the jitters out.

We had infield practice but I did not participate. I needed to relive my pitching performance and plan my attack on their tough lineup. I walked around the field and then after I was ready, found a few teammates to warm up with. I usually throw a lot of balls to get myself ready. I mean a lot. I'll throw a hundred balls to warm up then I am fine.

There were four umpires at this game. I thought, gee they better get things right, and sure enough later I would be disappointed in their performance. Then the loud speaker came on. There were a few announcements. Then they would introduce the National League Champions first, my team. Then, they would introduce the American League Champions the White Sox. When I was introduced I felt rewarded for my hard work getting there to the finals.

We slapped hands after being introduced and lined up on the third base line. Then, there was a first pitch by a person in the league followed by a young lady name Amy (a relative of a player on the other team) would sing the National anthem. She sang so beautifully and graciously that I felt like I was at a ceremony back in the Army on a parade field at Fort Bragg, North Carolina or Fort Devens, Massachusetts. That was very special.

Now the game was on and the pitcher from the White Sox was around the plate nothing special and our Phillies were hungry and anxious. We went down first three batters. Now it's me; my manager thought he was funny. He came to me and said John; this is your game you earned it. Just remember the distance is 60'6" the same as any other field. I thought wow he saw the movie "Indiana Hoosiers" too.

I went to work; I bounced the ball off the rubber and catch it for good luck. I do this most all the time before I pitch. I threw my warm ups and I was ready. I knew because they have a strong hitting lineup that they would hit me and my strikeouts would be down so I had to have a good defense to win this game.

My first pitch was a strike, the game was on. I provided a ground out, a pop up and now the best hitter is up. He lets the first ball come in for a strike, and then he hits a long foul ball. Then on a change up, he cracks the hardest line drive I ever saw up the middle directly to my center fielder and it bounces out of his glove. He gets a stand up double. The next batter hits a ball very catch-able left center field, and the same thing happens. This is with two outs and then a blooper. Then finally, I get a ground ball and get the third out. We now will bat losing 2-0.

We start off with a single, a walk then another single, and then I am up. I hit a line drive up just away from the short stop for a single and a run scores. Now its 2-1 then there's an out and we are back out in the field. We get three outs and we are at bat again. We have a rally and go ahead 8-2. Then we have a long inning and its now 9-3. The 4th inning we go down quickly and then the damage starts.

The white sox hit the ball to people but the errors start multiplying and now the score is 9-7. We get another run and after the fifth inning is complete we are winning 10- 9. This will be my 10th win if we continue to win this game. I come out of the game and my manager Mike, comes in to pitch. He also had a good year pitching. He gets 6 strikeouts and we are hoping he gets the save but with errors, hitting the ball where we were not gave them the lead again.

I came into the game and played third base my usual position. I was ready for everything. Then there's a ball hit hard with a high bounce, I jumped as high as I possibly could and was able to catch the ball in my web of my glove. When I placed my feet comfortably I set and threw the ball to first base. I could hear my guys in the dug out." Scoop it Billy" but it didn't happen. I made a great play but end result the guy was safe. I hit another ground ball moved the runner but I was out at first. We ended up loosing this game and the Championship by a final score of 13-11.

We shook hands, packed our gear and greeted the winners. Before we were to leave the dug out, I said to all, "in two weeks I have a slot at the batting cage for the entire winter". They all laughed but I was serious. My brother came to the game and made a comment to me before the game. I did not recognize him at the time, as I had many thoughts running through my mind and did not pay attention to the crowd or fans. I thought he was another player in the league because he had a baseball hat on, which was not his usual choice of attire. My wife and I took him to lunch on the way home to celebrate our losing cause.

It did not take very long at all before I started getting cranky, reliving the ball game and missing baseball. I then found a weekend tournament locally three games to play so that fired me up. I had known players on most of the other teams but the team I played on did not know of my history or talent. I first started batting 7th, and by the third game I was batting second as I had pitched a total of three innings and pitched well. I had a very weak baseball team but it was more baseball, so who's complaining.

I played short stop and did pretty well but as I said, I had a weak team. When the three games were over, a woman came to me as I was getting into my car and said to me, "I just want you to know that my husband said you are an inspiration to him and I think you played very well." I was so touched by her pleasant thoughts that losing all of a sudden was not so bad at all.

Chapter Thirty

Sand lot Baseball once again!

Once again I fell to being depressed with baseball being all over. I then got a brain storm and decided to write, call, beg, and try to have a sand lot baseball game on Sunday's because the weather was so good and why not take advantage of playing more baseball. The idea attracted many other players as well. We met at a High School in Chelmsford and 18 guys showed up. We played innings and had a good competitive baseball game. Can you believe 1-0 game there were no errors, and at least four pitchers from each team and good solid baseball.

The highlight of the day was Jeff Allison, the number one draft picks from North of Boston who was picked up by the Florida Marlins. He won the homerun derby and was playing short stop for the opposing team. I pitched the first three innings of shut out ball and had 5 strikeouts. Then Brian went in for three with the same results and then another guy would pitch the last inning for us.

Jeff pitched for the other team and what an experience facing him was! He is known for throwing 97 mph but when I faced him after he struck out the last three guys; I was determined to get a hit. I fouled off the first one. Then a ball, then the next pitch a little inside but as I swung the bat I was hit on the hand, There was a time out as everyone was looking at my black and blue knuckles and finger. I said foul ball strike two; let's finish this at bat before the pain comes.

The ball went off my knuckles and landed near the dug out. Jeff was back on the mound and I was hurt and in pain but ready. The next pitch was right down the middle and I grounded the ball up the middle for a base hit. I was just pleased that I was the only one to make contact with him.

When it was Jeff's turn to bat, he hit a homerun that was the longest homerun I had ever witnessed in a game that I was in. He hit the ball minimum of 430 feet and high and deep. He hit the ball so easily with such great mechanics. He rounded the bases like he had done that so many times. I wish we had a replay of that when I was pitching to him; I got him to swing and miss at a slider. That's my claim to fame against him; he then hit a hard ground ball to third that was tough to handle by the third baseman.

I now can only wish for more good weather to bail my emotions until the cold weather sets in. Hopefully there will be a good turn out for the next sand lot game. We decided that this will be our after season sand lot group, were fortunate to play most of the month of November on Sundays. The heavy sweatshirts, stocking hats and batting gloves were the way to travel.

Our team the Philly's won the National League Championship as well as edging out a team for the best season as well. So at our banquet, we went home with some extra hardware. More trophy's for my baseball room. This will add more memories to look back on. I initiated a cage rental at the Connector batting cage and have a list of potential off season ballplayers to participate. There are also managers looking into the 2008 season to see who's in and who's out come spring.

I have new ailments to add to my bag of tricks; I have a sore tendon injury on my left ankle and arthritis in most all my joints. My right shoulder is the worse, as it is my throwing arm. I have gone through the doctors, x-rays, which led to physical therapy. The doctor wants to operate. He said, as he looked into my eyes; I see the glow in your eyes for playing baseball. Get the thought out of your mind, for a while. I chose to finish the physical therapy appointments and I also started acupuncture twice a week and in addition I started "body pump classes" and "Turbo kick" classes which are similar to cardio kick. I am getting stronger already and feel improvement. I am usually the only man in the classes as there are about 25 women trying to look good for their soul mates. Most are friendly and forget that I'm there at all. I still go to the batting cage each Tuesday evening with my group but I can't throw the ball at all. I can bat with no pain but absolutely no throwing for a while.

I told my team the Philly's I would not return this next season. I will not be the same pitcher and now they will have the chance to get another pitcher in the draft. I will play however in the night league and possibly in the over 48 division in Boston. I will go back to the over 30 division next season when I am more in my game. This is only my dream sequence; who really knows what will happen but it is positive thinking to plan and dream.

My arthritis disease is also a progressive disease as also my heart? Now I have two progressive diseases trying to stop my baseball but I'll be a fighter and stay ahead of this.

The body pump classes are truly remarkable as I feel the strength increase already. I was losing my touch from the three point line a few months ago and now it's come back to me. I was shooting baskets at the athletic facility as I do regularly and I shot the ball very smooth and accurate with no pain.

My end of baseball season had other significant notable things to mention; I wrote a company commander I served with in the 5th Special Forces Group, Fort Bragg, North Carolina. I saw his picture in the Special Forces Drop magazine and wrote him a personal letter in which was forwarded to him. He responded very quickly with such a positive letter to me. I was totally amazed that he remembered me but more taken back by the very high opinion he had of me. I have not spoken to or seen him in twenty five years but our conversation was like yesterday. I sent him a copy of my book as I signed it for him. We had talked on the phone for an hour or so on a few occasions. The conversation went from our experiences down at Fort Bragg to the Middle East (Jordan), but hovered about our physical conditions, our medical outlook and most enjoyable baseball experiences our preferred models of bats, the positions on the field, and the feelings we both had with experiences in big major league stadiums. He has quite the interesting and remarkable life and background.

I told him about Louisville slugger bats, he would respond with Hickory or Adirondack bats. Then model numbers and weight of bats. The old major league players and again because of my physical status what my outlook and reality towards playing in the near future would be like. He was very understanding and carefully chose his words because he could feel the adrenalin and passion that I was not willing to give up without a fight. Having a friend like this is so valuable to me, one who understands your love and passion but is also right there with honesty and carefully soothing your heart guiding you with constant feelings for your emotional goals.

His name is Col Bill Davis. His career in Special Forces was unbelievable as he has done it all. He went from a detachment commander to Company Commander, to Instructor at the War College as well as numerous operational security positions. I was truly honored to serve under him. I had mentioned some of his experiences with me in Jordan in a previous chapter. He was truly a remarkable soldier serving our country.

I will say this once again; just as Berge Avadanian, Jim Costa, Buck O'Brien and others I have mentioned in the past, again and again Paratroopers and baseball are side by side and within each story. Once again, I won't disappoint you. Bill Davis was no exception.

During active duty, while I was stationed with him, the conversations were much different than present,. As enlisted approaching officers on many occasions were not very easy but now things are different with retired soldiers as we are.

Col. Davis did such a memorable act while being Company Commander while I was at Fort Bragg, North Carolina. I believe we just returned from the Middle East on training. This day was the first of the month and the military had what was a termed payday activity. Col Davis had our entire company stand in front of the old Special Forces museum in front of the "Bronze Bruce" statue's we took a Company picture which is in this book. When picture taking was completed, we went to the NCO Club... Non Commissioned Officers Club for a company breakfast.

There we are enjoying a fantastic catered breakfast but this time we had a champagne toast by Col. Davis to his unit. I never forgot that, as that was a very passionate and high moment in the military for me.

I found a better relationship with Bill late in 2007. I mentioned how I tracked him down from a picture and article and how he responded; Well the important part of all this was the fact that both of our lives at different levels have been similar. While I was serving under him, it was not easy to have routine conversations in the military with officers let alone commanders. Now our relationship is pure, genuine care for one another and he will always be my friend. We share the bond of Parachuting, Military, Special Forces experience and our baseball passion.

He also has a passion for surf boarding and he was very good at it. It's amazing how turns of events not only re-unite and changes but are emotional and caring relationships.

He has shared his pictures when he was young as a bat boy for an old timer's game with Joe DiMaggio and his numerous other major league personalities he has met. It just seems like most people I have come in contact with either are baseball players, paratroopers or both. I guess I have a way of attracting such people which makes me happy.

Hickory, Rawlings and Louisville wooden baseball bats have been engraved with "The Eastside Kid" for model description. They definitely should be easily identified at the ball field now. My wife Beth bought these for me for Christmas. They feel great and a small part of me is worrying if I'll have the chance to use them this coming year.

I try to use wood while at the batting cage, for it defines you as a hitter. Therefore I use wood as often as possible. The metal bats deceive your capabilities. During the off season is the time you need to spend on injuries, maintenance of your equipment, improving on your deficiencies from the season, and plotting your next season's strategy. I do this and try to help others follow my lead.

To speculate and continue dreams of playing more seasons, more games have been my motivation right along. It seems as I stated a long while ago that "Luck" is not just a word but affects our every day life. I have caved in to what the doctors have suggested. My own workouts, acupuncture, turbo kick, palates and body pump are just not the present answer for me. The results came back from the MRI I had done a week ago and the news is not good.

It seems that I have several cysts in my shoulder pocket; the upper arm is rubbing against bone in the socket, numerous long medical explanations in the file just discourage me more. The pain that I routinely under go, says it all. So, I gave in and will have surgery the end of this month. The rotator cuff is not damaged but has some damage. If I load up with medications, icy hot, Ben gay, tiger balm and Motrin etc., I will only mask the pain and my problem will get worse and "no baseball". Yes, I gave in and my hopes are that my physical therapy work out after surgery and my determination will help me play baseball in the fall of this year. I will cover the rest of this story as it unfolds.

I had always thought that throwing a lot was good for me or any ball player. I think if I had not had previous injury in my neck and back from parachuting, I would have been ok. Who knows after surgery, maybe I'll be throwing 80 mph at age 61, you think? Great thought anyway.

This past year I had many big nail biter type games where I was pitching and everything mattered. I won many of those games as I felt wonderful about my confidence to do so well in those games. The biggest thing that stays with me in thought is this; I lost two of the biggest games this season. I had mentioned about the semi final game at Doubleday in Cooperstown and how the guy hit a homerun.

Many had said it was foul, but never the less the umpire had ruled it fair. That was a very tough loss. Then the big championship back here at LeLacheur Stadium in Lowell, Ma. The longest game on record I think, and who knows a few balls caught here and there, an extra base hit, a stolen base and; well it doesn't matter now; we lost the big game but I carry that with me. I need one more real big game. I don't care if it's a local league championship game or a tournament in Las Vegas or Fort Myers at Terry Park. I just want to win one big game. I have it in my mind and hopefully I will physically be able to do this sometime within a few years before I can't do it.

Each off season is evaluating, correcting, improving, calculating and developing new personal challenges for myself or for any ballplayer I would think. I'm sure you as a reader think the same way. This particular year will be difficult being in the background not on the weekly computer statistics of the league. Reading my friends results and being in the shadows, I will find myself cranky, bored, and aggravated and my temperament which is usually uplifting, serious, with lots of smiles but competitive nature flowing about the field. I am hyper at times and full of faults as we all have but as soon as I can work out and feel self improvement I will be ok. The time is creeping forward to slow for me.

There had been a January thaw for a week or so. That's ok but you know you're being teased as the snow and cold are not over yet. To mix things up a bit, I was lurking out into the woods from my study as it is high and overlooks the brook and woods. I noticed a goat of all things away from a farm and lost. I made contact with police and the farmer but they couldn't catch the little guy. He ran from his captors and gave them a work out. I am not sure if he was ever captured or if he was committed to being a run-away, which would not be good for a goat with little defenses in the forest. I worried about him for a few weeks and hoped he was ok.

Some thoughts about young people had come to surprise me. I had distributed some of my books and one teammate gave his son a copy of my book as he was eleven years old. He came to many of our games. Little Rob, I would call him. I would say something like; did you see the ball I hit for you? Or did you see the guy I struck out? He read my book and did a book report in his New York school, in the Bronx. His Dad would see him on weekends. I was impressed and a nice feeling came about me as I felt my example to strangers has been a positive thing for me.

I have completed surgery and with the Patriot's Super Bowl with the Giants on Sunday, I will see my doctor Monday, start rehabilitation on Tuesday and see what will be in my current outlook for baseball for this season and my future.

Most of my friends and other ballplayers are in the midst of planning new teams, draft strategy and getting players acquainted with one another for the 2008 season. Others are planning on tournaments and recruiting to capture the best players and chemistry of a team for the tournaments throughout the year.

I am looking to play in the fall out in Las Vegas for two teams over 50 year old and over 60 year old teams. to compete out there in the fall tournament.

I have quite a while to get myself ready for that. I will also manage a team for a local tournament here in Leominster, Massachusetts as a tune-up for Las Vegas. I have plenty of time to train as recovery playing in low key night leagues are a tool to get myself in shape for this season. There are tournaments all over the country surely a great tease for me. I want to participate in all of them but don't have the money and possibly health could be an issue as well as my health is restricted with heart, arthritis, and my throwing arm. They tell me I will need a replacement shoulder at some point. I am not in the market for that nor wanting to consider that right now. Yes, that's the official word as of today.

My Doctor tells me good news and some not so good news; I have progressive arthritis in all of my joints, some are worse than other areas. The important thing to do is stay active, do a lot of work, aerobics, and sports. So, that's right up my alley as the older I get the choices are slim. I am starting my physical therapy tomorrow bright and early tomorrow. I am anxious to start my comeback; Did I say, "comeback" yes I did; How many comebacks do I have to date, now? - well I lost count but I will point my heart and thoughts on that right now and the rest of this year with hopes of being like I was this past season. In the back of my mind I do have this little voice telling me the best has come and gone. Go fly some pigeons, or go coach some little league baseball or organize some sand-lot games. There are many thoughts but my burning desire to compete in amateur baseball is so dear to my heart and soul. Maybe I can get even better than before. That will shake things up -right? Let's just go see what's left in the tank and give my opponents a good fight.

I have progressed, so much in rehab it's unbelievable. My Doctor tells me that most people with the same surgery as I are at 16 weeks and now it's only been four weeks for me right now. I started swinging a metal practice bat in my study and it feels good. I know I am months away from pitching but I can hit and play a different position like second base. I started hitting balls off at and it felt good so maybe I am on my way.

I have a busy weekend coming up. Snow is falling tonight but Sunday an old friend of mine my first little girlfriend at 10 years old, her name is Donna Duval and truly has become a wonderful woman through the years. She has offered to provide a book signing combined with a reunion of old eastside friends from Brockton where I grew up.

I am very excited to do this as I have also made arrangements for a deceased friends Mother and her son Robert to join us. She is now in her eighties Mrs. Ginny Perry a wonderful woman. I had her son's picture taken with me at seven or eight years old and we are in Cub Scout uniforms holding hands. I had the picture blown up for her and put into a frame. There is also a young boy of twelve years old dealing with personal problems, so I had a baseball study guide that I made and gave to young baseball players who love and appreciate baseball. Sunday had arrived and I made the long journey to Lakeville, Massachusetts.

When I arrived and entered Donna's home, here was a girl I have not seen since 1959 as I instantly was drawn to her and shared a wonderful hug. Donna's Mom was there as I had not seen her in all that time either. She must have thought, there's the little skinny kid that bothered my daughter! She was wonderful as well. Meeting old friends from 50 years was so rewarding I was so honored to share my story with them and know their stories as well. Friendships seem to be different in the previous decades as our culture had been so honorable; Mrs. Perry came into the room as many eyes were on us immediately. There was a special feeling being in her presence as we picked up where we left off. The young boy Cameron, I had signed a baseball for him along with the baseball study guide I made as this became a special occasion. My friend Bobby Butler as I mentioned in chapter #3 was the pitcher who I hit my first little league homerun off of. So he was there along with his wonderful sister Patty. There were many friends there from my early days Paul, Fred, Tom and family. It turned out to not only be a successful book signing but reunion of nostalgia and special friends from so long ago. My challenges seem to grow constantly for me. This coming year will be no different as my passion continually grows.

With my shoulder recovery and rehabilitation as an on going problem and especially as opening day comes close I start to worry now as my Sunday league I was late signing up due to my recovery. I will be able to hit but not pitch for a few months. It's very difficult for me to consider watching and not playing. I have many other league possibilities to play but I also have to consider playing in the fall tournament in Las Vegas.

I will continue playing baseball as long as my health will allow me to do so. I will attend all of the tournaments, and play the local leagues and be as active as possible, enjoying this game of baseball and sharing my friendship and enthusiasm wherever I go.

My goal in writing this story was to inspire others, maybe like yourself, who had a distant memory of Little League baseball and to encourage them to take a slice of their life and bring back those wonderful glory days. I hope I can help them remember how they really enjoyed the game of baseball, to bring back the sounds of the crack of the bat, the smells of grass, cigar smoke and to watch the big boys chew tobacco and bubble gum, full of excitement, putting their old fashioned dusty skills to the best of their abilities. Maybe the passion they have missed will soon fill their heart and soul and more memories can be made.

If you can't run very fast or hit the ball very far or the ball bounces out of your glove, have no fear-the next game you may be better. It doesn't matter if you are the best player as long as you are a team player. Your skills may surprise you, as it's like riding a bike and it comes back so easily, like you never stopped playing. In most cases the skills are better at an older age and the more you play, the more you will surprise yourself.

Chapter Thirty One

My Passion Moves on

Many readers have read The Eastside Kid, original story of me John F DeCosta; In the course of time after publication of this book, way too many important, exciting and interesting things have happened in my life that to not share all of these things would be a shame. Hang on for another ride around many back roads and visiting more baseball diamonds.

During the time The Eastside Kid was published many things have taken place. I have re-united with numerous old friends from Brockton's eastside from school, and my baseball life. It's been great! I also met up with and currently share communication with an old friend that was my mentor at the Downey little League from back in 1957. He, Herby Jones, and I share our love for the baseball game as well as our accomplishments which has been fun.

There have been baseball players I once played with in Little League that surfaced as well, like Al Fararra, Fred Barnard and Bobby Butler to mention a few. Many people had known one or more of my friends and the time frame has brought attention to detail in their memory banks as well. I have touched many, in a warm way and I never, ever thought that my writing could be so powerful and generate such positive feelings.

From that, I had a radio interview from a St Louis radio station www. showmetalkradio.com that even provided more interest to me the rookie writer from Brockton, Ma- now living in Metro-west, Ma-USA. There were other radio interviews from Brockton, Ma as well, but not as powerful as show me talk radio or the popular web sites either like face book and classmates. The word got out and I was also able to have a book signing, and communication with people from Alaska, all over America as well as Italy and other countries. It has been so much fun and my last two years have been so magnificent I felt I needed to share even more.

So, sit back, get comfy in your home, turn the lights down, grab your favorite beverage and listen to my heartbeat once again!

Late February here in New England 2008, I am on the mend from shoulder surgery. I had a small tumor, pieces of floating bone and a lot of arthritis. The surgery went well as he the doctor went in from three directions and I was very sore for a while. The basic news I had received from my doctor was this; Dr Blute said John I see the love and passion in your eyes but I think you are done! I think best scenario is you will only have 60 to possibly 80 % of your previous ability. I will help you with rehab- and see where this goes. I thought to myself- your having a bad dream Doc and I walked out of his office with my arm in a sling.

I began my rehab- along with my personal rehab. Stretch bands, weird exercises, organizing my comeback etc; I knew what I was working for, a" comeback". To make a long story short! I was late signing up for the draft for over 30 baseball. I didn't want to hurt my team the Phillies so I waited and waited too long. I then became an extra and had to wait for a player to be hurt on any team in order to play baseball. I got picked up by the Cubs three weeks later and that was a solid team but I was a new "old guy" I played pretty well but because they had already a large list of pitchers I saw little action. I then concentrated on rehab, hitting and plans for the next season. I also had no baseball tournaments out of town to plan on so it was back to basics for me.

I basically came to complete realization that I needed to make myself better than ever and work extremely hard on my comeback. My main team at this point the Cubs was temporary for this year but I had my night league the D-Rays. I consciously made it a point to coach myself carefully and practiced, practiced and more practiced. I worked out with other teams, gone to the batting cages and I played in Boston as well. On the Watertown Nationals, an over 40 league (wood bat).

While playing for the Watertown Nationals, I had known the coach as his name was Ace and Ace was 81 years old. He had been asking me to play for 4 years so finally I agreed. It was an off year for me so why not. I went to several mid winter practices at the Watertown batting cages and introduced to several players on the team. Finally after a so so winter training my pitching abilities were not there yet. I was starting to throw the ball but nothing serious at this time. I would play second base and bat, focus and go easy.

I was not happy with the Cubs at my over thirty league because there really was no room for me .I therefore played in the Night Over Thirty League and to increase my rehab and training abilities I played extra here in Boston with the Watertown Nationals. We had a pre-season game that many looked forward to.

We played two games back to back Thursday evenings. We played against a team called "The Knights" When I got there I looked to see if there was anyone I knew from some other year I played in this league. Nothing familiar so back to the stretching and pre-game warm ups. We were home team and after listening to the lineup I took the field and played second base. We had a good pitcher but I wanted to be there but for now I was concerned about reaching first base with my throws as this was my first real game.

Our opponents were scrambling around and fans came out of nowhere. I asked what's going on. It was said that the three Flutie brothers were on this team along with Charlie Moore (The Mad Fisherman) a TV program. So we have Doug Flutie, Daren and I forget the other brothers name but popular to many there. Surprisingly they all played well. I was really impressed with Charlie Moore as he went 4 for 4 at bat and played a good outfield. When I got to bat I faced Daren Flutie Doug's brother and he sure was cocky. I then said to myself, ok sore arm come thru now. I hit a long line drive in the gap left field, so that's my claim to fame off of Daren big mouth Flutie. He complained after every pitch to the umpire and was such a baby. Doug Flutie was just calm as a cucumber and was serious but knew, Hey he already has accomplished everything with nothing to prove so he just played baseball and did very well, just another experience for me, in my baseball life.

I finished out my season in the three leagues and batted a low .300 and not myself as usual. I pitched the second half of the season with low visibility and filling in but more of a practice for me as my eyes were looking for the next season and a positive draft. When the season was over I got together my die hard ball players and played sand lot baseball on Sundays and because I was not ready or my normal self, I had turned down several tournaments opportunities. When November rolled around it was time for the batting cage again. I got invited by several teams to practice as well as my friends from my old Red Sox Team. My normal groups of die hards were always willing and able to come inside or outside even when the weather was not so great. Just one more day we would say.

Then I was approached by The White Sox. This is the team I pitched against at the stadium two years ago and lost a hard battle at LeLacheur Stadium in Lowell, Ma. Mike and Billy had called me independently as they were the manager and coach of the White Sox. We talked for hours about philosophy of baseball and the team and they really wanted me. I told them it was a done deal.

I was very happy because they really wanted me a lot. This was an over 30 baseball league and they used their #1 draft pick to get me on their team. Others had told them they made a mistake.

My new manager Mike and Coach Billy were very confident and believed in me and my abilities. The draft opened and closed and now, I was officially a White Sox teammate, and that was really great news for me. Billy jokingly said I went to another team, just to get my reaction but I blew that off.

I started going to regular practices mid winter 2009 with my new White Sox team. I was also getting offers to play in Boston in the MSBL and New Hampshire-Granite State Baseball, Mike Levine league as well. New Hampshire was an acquaintance I met through the league's internet site. He wrote and called me and checks my previous leagues stats and needed a pitcher and wanted me very much.

I went to some practices with his newly recruited team and something was off but I could not figure it out at that time. I later played a pre-season game against the Tigers. We were the Nashua Dodgers! I got there early up in Merrimac New Hampshire at the field. I did my usual routine of shooting baskets at a nearby court by the field and soon all of the players showed up. I began to mingle with the team and I was to start pitching the game. They thought I was there ace! The first catcher I had got hurt by the middle of the first inning. The replacement happens to be a catcher from the other team, Ronnie Perrin.

Ronnie and I was a combo a few years back so I was really excited to have him catch for me. I pitched three innings, no walks and 7 k; s and felt really strong. I thought wow! This is a great start for me. This was now late April and most all of the leagues had just started. I was trying to fit three leagues into my life but that was quite difficult. I played for the White Sox on Sunday morning.

I pitched and got a few hits and won the game with 5 k; s.1 earned runs a few hits to go with my win. This was a game against a team, Red Sox that I played for 5 years. I was just in control and not going to get beat that day. I was so dominant and having a day as one would say that this was a very good win against my old teammates and very good powerful team.

I quickly left the field, got my GPS on the phone and dialed in a field up in New Hampshire. On the way, I grabbed a soda stopped at a Mc Donald's restaurant changed into my new Dodger uniform and continued to the field. I barely had my spikes on when it was time for me to bat. I was still tucking in my shirt as I approached the plate and shortly there after hit a line drive to the right fielder. I played third base for a few innings then I came into the game pitched the last few innings and got the save.

I decided at that point, yes- this was fun but too much rushing and driving around to get in a double header, although it was a fun day! My arm was feeling great, I was seeing the ball great but I could not push things as the season was long and pitchers like me middle ages or maybe older like me needed to be extra vigilant when it came to injuries, surgery's, recovery, rehab and training. So just like my heart history I had to be very careful training and trying too hard to fit in.

My team was great and I never felt like a rookie because I play on a night league with some of the players and the others knew me from other teams I played for. I still had to come through and prove my worth because, I was their first draft pick at age 62 when they could have gotten a much younger player like 30 ish or even 40 ish but they stuck with me. There were some that thought they were taking a chance but after all each year I had been in the top ten statistics in most categories of this 16 team, 15 man roster for the last ten years. The fact was I wasn't going away and I of course, was a chance!

The off season was at the extra innings training facility in Tewksbury, Ma and I was still going to the Connector Batting facility and getting instruction from Adam McCusker my batting instructor and for pitching I had John Cahill as he spent time in AA ball and also a few years with the Anaheim Angels; So before my new season started I had instruction weekly as well as team cage time and serious training on my own at the health club. I was determined to have a successful season with the White Sox.

My batting lessons were relatively easy for me as I am a good student and progressed very well with Adam. I just felt like I could stay in the cage and hit all day long. I just love to hit. When I was with John, I was anxious to show him what I had but we started with basics as I had a college catcher that was surprised with my control and speed for my age. There were some interest of people watching me throw but my concentration was with John as I wanted to correct anything I was not aware of.

I quickly adapted to John's teaching techniques and had a mental list I needed to work on. I guess you could call it, Johnny D's homework until next lesson. I began to bolster my confidence and improved quickly with his help.

Chapter Thirty Two

Pigeons gone wild

My first and biggest hurdle was to keep my balance point, knee high pointing towards third base and follow through to my target behind the plate. Inside training ,to guide my knee I place a baseball in that direction to help me with that hint and outside I usually draw a line deep on the right side of the mound that I can see for direction but sometimes either the umpire or opposing pitcher will erase my line just to aggravate me but that's not a problem to me at all.

My training, rehab, meeting my White Sox teammates and gearing up for my 2009 season was right on track although it was still early but I was on the right track.

I was going through boxes, pictures and I came across pictures of my old pigeon coop, pigeon books and sitting there thinking that I gave them up because of my involvement and dedication with baseball. Since then I had often thought of getting back to this hobby and now being retired with both military as well as my contracting years behind me, was a great thought for me to once again think about getting back to this bobby.

I had some free time so I had this extra large dog house sitting there in my fenced in back yard. My dogs were so spoiled they found no use in going in it. I started making plans and doing repairs and I converted this shed into a very fancy pigeon coop. It was fun to craft it and I do love building things and soon it took shape and really, I needed to now make a decision to either just get the birds, research my old resources and gather as much useful information before I go any further.

I looked up some older gentlemen, that were retired from racing pigeons and I was given books, pigeon clocks, magazines, phone numbers and contacts. One gentleman Harold Shanklin was very kind to me and shared some pigeon stories but came down very sick with multiple problems. He was hospitalized in a nursing home and soon after died. I was given some gifts from him as his family and dear friends said he wanted me to have. There was a pair of ceramic pigeons that I shall explain a little later. One other gift I was presented was a pigeon book prior to the church service they had for the friends and relatives I had not known him long or real well but I was proud to be there for him with respect. He was a Veteran as well. Listened to a nice service and many got up and shared their remembrance of Harold and drew some chuckles and some had cried but being a very hot and stuffy evening there I was glad it was over.

I drove an old timer to the service as he was also someone who raised racing pigeons for 60 years and a great one to know. He won more races than anyone, he was Lee Landry.

Lee Landry was also a War Veteran from Korean Conflict so he shared stories of his unit there; we both shared being very cold and miserable there.

After calculation my experience, background ,research prospects, supplies problems from town and neighbors I was now ready to do the paper work shuffle in regards to covering myself legally and do the right thing. I knew I would have negative complaints and resistance from a few neighbors next to me so I knew I had to be very prepared.

I gathered my research, documents necessary to file a permit to raise, train, and house and perform my American Pleasure of enjoying an innocent hobby in my back yard on my 5 acre's of property. I felt I was an American citizen, and Veteran and I must ad that I was pursuing "My pursuit of Happiness" and I meant to follow this all of the way to the highest court if necessary.

The City Hall had several departments for me to visit, talk to folks, gather papers to sign and go forward with my request. They had a problem finding a set price because no one ever made this attempt ever before, so (I was number one filing for a pigeon permit.

I filled out the many papers, paid the $190.00 to the Town and was on notice waiting for a town hearing to allow or disallow my request to raise and train pigeons. This had taken place early December 2008. So, in a matter of a few days-sure enough there is resistance and a lot of it but mostly from one big advocate to wage war against me. She, my neighbor had recruited all of her friends and neighbors, as she drove the neighborhood, passed out flyers, and grabbed an told as many people to support her fight against my wanting this hobby. As she could find her support she also typed out a 4 page report and filed it with the City hall. This act created a public document making this newsworthy.

I started getting phone calls from the Sentinel Enterprise Newspaper and the Lowell Sun; they started questioning me about my permit and I was not clearly thinking and asked them. Are you inquiring about my book, The Eastside Kid? They said no and continued asking about the pigeon permit. They asked if they could see my pigeon coops. Then they arrive and start taking pictures of my pigeon coop. I still did not understand the attention then Walla! The next day my picture is plastered all over the newspapers in several towns. Man wants to raise pigeons and neighbor is giving him a fight!

So, many phone calls, and interviews and surprise visits by officials in town to see what I am doing in my back yard. I simply stated that I have the "Pursuit of Happiness going on" Meaning, I have 5 acres of land, a simple hobby of racing pigeons, not bothering anyone and this is a country setting.

My neighbor rounded up many of her friends and some neighbors to complain about my future with pigeons. It was a fact of them not knowing anything about pigeons and being nosey and wanting to complain. My neighbor was adamant on destroying any thoughts of me doing anything. If I wanted to raise butterflies, have a worm farm or rock collection she would plan on finding something to complain about. The fact that she had pages of written documents with numerous complaints, fighting my wishes for a hobby and pleasure of raising pigeons, was now in print and a legal document, because she sent it to the City Hall for a formal hearing on the matter. What that did was alerted the newspapers in several towns, and radio stations as they had a field day and when they took pictures, I was plastered all over the front page newspaper. My defense was simply; I have 5 acres of land, we are in the USA. I am a Veteran, I have had this hobby for years prior, and this is according to the constitution and my right of "Pursuit of Happiness". They wanted to know the flight path, if they were to bombard their swimming pool which was a child's pool 3'x4'. Oh there was a whole bunch of nonsense and I followed my plan and built my coops and turned in the proper paperwork and finally received a date from the town for a hearing. I had to supply, pictures, diagrams, measurements and explain everything about the hobby in my defense. I did so and finally have a date for a hearing at the city hall.

Then all of a sudden I had a serious problem with my heart and had to go to Mass General Hospital in Boston for a "cath" Therefore I had more serious things to handle before the pigeon problem and requested another date.

MGH. Mass General Hospital in Boston was my next stop after pre- testing with my Primary care Doctor Thomas Goodman and my Cardiologist Dr Anjum Butte, you know the whole battery of test like EKG, echo cardiogram, Nuclear stress test and a few others that escape my mind at present but indicators showed there may be a problem and the possibility of either another stent or by-pass surgery. Naturally I thought the worse! My first thought was "baseball". I am on top of my game now, as this is not the time for these medical issues. So, the pigeon problem could wait for now as I have more present realistic life threatening problems to deal with.

The drive was mindless to me as my wife Elizabeth drove me to Boston as my mind was cluttered with numerous thoughts about my present and my future. We parked and walked through the maze of people through the cluttered corridors as Beth was use to it as she worked there and this was common and natural for her. This walk for me was much different as I thought," Is this my last stop"? "Is this the end of my baseball"? Then before I had realized it, we were in line in the cath-administration desk and shuttled like a prisoner to a bed, prep work bounced around and rolled down the corridor to a large room, I mean large as there were about 24 beds waiting for Cath's surgery, by pass, heart transplants, valve problems and numerous cardiac care people walking a fast pace in all directions as I soon got a head ache from all of this.

The emotional trauma, yet once again dealing with heart problems is besides emotional, physical as well with my entire body. I usually bounce right back after any medical procedure depending on the degree of damage. Most people will think about what I just explained and say" wow" and then the thought is gone for them. The thought process for me is continuous; I do think to myself, how long before the next episode or will I have warning at all. With that thought alone, I try to make things count that are real in life, my hobbies, love for animals, family values, and my love for baseball. Every pitch, every inning, every at bat and every game I try to do my very best always.

I was now officially on the roster, I didn't know what position I would play but I knew I was not pitching or batting. I waited and waited for hours. It was just a bad time as numerous emergencies kept coming in the hospital and they go from most serious to not so serious. The problem is! No one officially knows how serious you are till they put the line up your groin into your heart and have a look see; We'll hang in there I am on deck! Just wheeled in to the cath lab and positioned ever so carefully. I waited and waited and suddenly all systems were off. Bring John back we have more emergencies coming in. Now I was back and a long wait! I was starved as I had not eaten all day and this line up just made me tired and more hungry.

The waiting continued for a few hours and now I was getting very uneasy! Then all of a sudden I was re-called to the cath room and wheeled quickly there and, this time all systems go! My Dr Anjum Butte re assured me all would be fine. I talked baseball to the techs there as I am sure they thought to themselves," Who is this guy kidding?" Baseball, he is far too old for that. I just suspected that was their real thoughts. I sent my wife home as she was exhausted and the doctor would call her after the procedure.

The procedure had started and all systems go! All the techs had their positions as I was awake watching the TV monitor and watching every moment and every movement of the entire procedure. Fortunately the pain meds were working well! Dr Butte checked all of my older stents from years before and all was ok. She checked for any new problems and my arteries were just fine. That was super good news for me. That meant baseball was still on for the 2009 season for me.

I finally went to my room, and begged for food. I didn't even care if it was hospital food or not I was hungry. The nurse I had was strictly by the book as many are and she brought me a few sandwiches and I was thrilled. She said to me, you look like the new guy playing James Bond! I said thank you, I think. Wish I had his lute; my wife came early the next morning and I was free at last and on my way home. I took in the sites and fresh air and now I was relieved that at least for this season, I was good to go.

In two more weeks I would finally have my pigeon meeting to obtain a permit from the town at the City Hall. I prepared my defense, complete folders full of all types of documents. My orderly fashion and experience from the Military and contracting business helped me organize and give a precise avenue of my intensions at the hearing.

I was alone and had not known what to expect. There were a lot of people there my wonderful neighbors were all lined up behind me. I was in the front row. They had previously sent out flyers to discredit me but also at the meeting were 3 different pigeon racers, and keepers that I didn't know had showed up to support me as well as some other Veterans.

They raddled off their nonsense and the board had previously come to my home to see my set up and they were 100% on board with me. I had a lot of popular township supporters in writing, as they prepared statements on my behalf and on the board. It was stated by a board member that if you left the city to come out to the country and change the rules of country living then maybe your city life was a better place for you. That got many chuckles and I was victorious after the voting and a certificate was awarded to me the following week.

I went on to raise the pigeons and enjoy the hobby for over a year and not one person from the neighborhood ever asked; Hey John, can I see what you are doing with pigeons? Can you show me or share so I understand! No, no one at all they just had no knowledge about the hobby and did not wish to ask or learn they just stuck together like a pack of wolves and created an unhappy neighborhood but that's how people can be!

I was very glad that was over and now I can resume my pitching and batting as I await the draft results from my over 30 baseball league. I had been being recruited by the White Sox as that was the team I pitched against in the finals at the minor league stadium two years ago. They liked my style of play and my age and heart problems were not a factor. The whole team wanted me so they gave up their number one pick to get me.

I was very happy that I would be going to a team that wanted me, a team I would be able to pitch and get a lot of innings and when not pitching I would play third base.

I went to the batting cages and met my teammates and all was well. This was also like any team I had been on. You must prove yourself to these guys each and every one of them. That never changes especially for John DeCosta the pitcher, the guy with heart problems, the old guy and "can he still compete" like the previous years and will he stay with the club etc. It was clearly up to me at this point and because they fought so hard to get me on the White Sox, I then will provide loyalty, character, and baseball skills to be accepted on this over thirty baseball team.

Chapter Thirty Three

Show me talk radio Interview!

I met Donna Linn back in September of 2008 and I met her from a classmate's baseball site and communicated with her back and fourth with several emails and then she caught me off guard! She then revealed to me her background and present position. She reveals that her strong background was Public Relations from a large Corporation from California and numerous marketing analysis's, radio and Television projects. That was for starters then she shares with me her present ownership of show me talk radio, a talk radio station in St Louis, Mo. Now I am all ears and then I clicked on her radio station and I was overwhelmed with the extent of her radio station, the people interviewed and the professionalism she possessed handling these interviews.

We continued to write back and fourth and then she wanted to see my book so I mailed her a copy. She read it and immediately said John, how would you like to be interviewed on my radio talk show? I was maybe out of breath for a moment and then I replied that, yes, I would like that. We talked and planned and I was wondering, is this really going to happen? The thing was, it's a long, very long intricate process and her whole staff is quite busy, exciting and professional gadget athletes! It was amazing to think of the process of planning involved.

Finally, late January 2009 we taped a show, then we fine tuned it and I can't even remember all the steps taken from her staff putting all of this together. We talked about my book, my family values, baseball from the 1950's and covered each and every topic throughout my book as well as my take on baseball, athletes as I formed my baseball career around. MLB athletes , I adored and respected and even talked about steroids use. I did this over the telephone from my sports room/ office at home. It turned out to be fun and exciting, to say the least. I guess talking about hitting a home run and actually hitting one is completely different. When I first started writing, I thought nothing of it until I saw it in print in the newspaper, my first article published that is. That's when reality had set in for me.

I think about late February or March 2009 my interview was officially on line on her radio web site! It was amazing how great she made me sound. Most people give me the credit but when you listen you can see her professionalism leading me like a puppy dog on a leash. She was great and I am forever thankful for finding her trusting her and proud I was able to do well with the finished product. I did as much marketing on my own as I could think of and emailed all of my baseball friends and attacked the free web sites to help me along this very new road for me. I think it was two hours after my interview a pigeon associate and dear friend I met on line from Italy listened to my interview and wanted my book. I mailed him a copy and he replied with such a wonderful reviews of my book and that felt great.

Although his reading ability was with Italian/English differences he loved my story. He could not figure a way of sending me money for the book, so I said to him; forget it (Gian Pietro Boschiroli) from Derovere Cremora Italy. That puzzled him and for months after that he felt so much guilt that he had to find a way as he put it to clear his debt to me. He felt he must do something nice for me and I didn't know what to say, so I continued to not be concerned about money.

Then a few months later he wrote to me and said, John-I sent you a gift from me to you. Please tell me when you receive it. It took about 25 days but a package arrived in the mail to my home. I opened it up and there it was a miniature violin; I read on and saw that this was a model, an antique gift in a small violin case about 9 " long x 3" wide ¾" thick case. It looked like a real large one but a miniature.. Antonio Stradivari the great Violin maker from Cremora, Italy- This was a fantastic piece of work and such a wonderful gift. The history is unbelievable!

He made intricate precise unique Violins as they were called (Stradivarius Violins) originally he had made 1,100 precise violins for special purchase through the years but it is said that only 650 presently exist today. You know that this gift is on my special shelf in my sports room to reflect on good friends. Gian Pietro Boschiroli will always be in my heart.

Gian Pietro also sent me pictures and videos of his roller pigeons as they were beautiful and his coops were made with precision as although we have many cultures people are people and respectful in many parts of our world but I am very touched but people like Gian Pietro as for sure, he is also from the greatest generation like our people here from the greatest generation. I am thankful and honored I had met him and carry a life long friendship.

The marketing and sharing my interview has been a lot of work but also fun because of the finished product of this interview has leaped over the rainbow much more than I ever expected and the thoughts of hosting a show and future interviews are in the works for my future.

The experience of sharing my story, and being proud of it has broadened my horizons and I have linked up with old friends from many years ago and touched so many people in a positive manor that feels so good I do not have the words to describe.

Chapter Thirty Four

Baseball 2009 plans!

You have heard this before from me about making everything count, my work ethic etc, that is still true but this particular year, I have much to prove and gain. Several people in my league thought that John is an ok guy, a gamer, but he is getting older , maybe lost a step and in the trade talk certain Managers voiced their opinions on this and the loudest person to voice his opinion was my old Phillies team's manager Bill ! He wanted to go young which was ok with me, I can handle that but he tried to make sure all of the quality teams would not choose me. "I took this as a personal attack."

I had an answer for him as I will tell shortly. Incidentally, when I was with the Phillies, as I had an incredible year and brought the team to the finals at LeLacheur stadium. They never would have gone there with out me. The chemistry, friendships and my heart felt gamer personality was forgotten. Therefore, John F DeCosta has much to prove and stick it to many in this league.

With my dead year last season recovering from the loss at the finals the season before, my shoulder surgery, rehab, late start and thrown to the wolves to just play on a team as an extra. It was a wasted year in many ways but now being discarded by my old team, gives me so much to prove and deal with the positive abilities I know I have. I am hungry!

The world of baseball is before me. I am finally very happy with my new teammates on the White Sox as I am the first one as always at the batting cage. I can't wait to bat or pitch and the sounds of baseball around the cage allow me to concentrate and build my confidence. I am now stronger and pitching well with no pain and I am on my mark as far as control, hitting my spots and when I need to make that pitch. My batting is coming along fine as I see the ball so well. I also go to another batting cage for instruction on hitting and pitching just so I will remain on top of my game, not pick up any bad habits and continue with my good mechanics. I need to be better than good that's why I train so much. Practicing bad mechanics is like practicing mistakes.

In addition, I go to the athletic facility as I described to you before and I throw the soft baseball in the racquetball court. I use the blue painters tape and mark spots for the strike zone and separate from that I place blue tape, small spots two feet a part and go left, go right, up down continually hitting my spots. I throw three times a week total. I would say about 200 to 250 balls each time so now my arm is strong as an ox.

I say to myself," is spring ever going to get here"? I am ready. Now the recruitments have started from other leagues. GSBL, New Hampshire the Nashua Dodgers are looking and wanting me on their pitching staff! I went to several work outs with the manager. He wanted me to pitch so I did and cracked his thumb the first day. I easily struck out his teammates but the practices and games were quite the travel distance .I went to a pre-season game with this Dodger team. I pitched three innings and had 5 K; s and no walks. Our catcher was not there so a catcher from the other team caught for me .It happen to be Ronny Perron from my old team several years ago. He was a minor league player and made me look so good on the mound. That was so much fun as that really boosted my confidence.

Continuation of my workouts at the athletic facility, meeting at the batting cage with my New White Sox team, personal catching and hitting lessons, a little bit of New Hampshire baseball and at the same time I am making plans to go to West palm beach, Florida to play at "Play at the Plate" baseball tournament at Roger Dean Stadium! So this is a great pre-season for me.

I let my White Sox Team know all what's going on as they are my number one choice for any baseball, which I attempt. There is a lot going on in my life, and at present- not even mentioning my home and personal life. Its seems everyone wants something. The Military organizations want me to participate in numerous activities constantly. Most of them do not play sports nor have a part in animals they way I do so they can't understand my commitment with pigeons, baseball, practicing etc; That is fine I will do what I can do when it fits my life style. Right now its baseball!

Looking ahead I have pre-season games, over thirty baseball schedule, then night league baseball, playoffs, sandlot baseball and Phoenix, Arizona once again

Chapter Thirty Five

Play at the Plate Baseball

West palm Beach, Florida

The excitement for me had grown as West Palm Beach baseball or "Play at the Plate" baseball tournament very near. I concentrated heavily on my batting and pitching mechanics because I was anxious to play and I wanted to do well to see where I was at in my pre-season plan for the 2009 season.

Making plans for these tournaments are a lot of fun. You find out about what hotels the team is staying at, and many times you will share with one or two players to a suite to save on your expenses. Then there is the transportation to the fields of practice, games and team dinners in which a select few always get cars and the others like me chip in with the expenses. I never get a car as I absolutely hate driving. I want to appear at the ball park and play baseball and not think about anything else. Getting lost, stuck in traffic is not in the cards for me.

In my case I have to plan on a limo guy to take me to the airport! No, I am not a big shot it's just easier and worth the money because on how much the airport parking charges and location of where I live.   The airlines is not the way it was for traveling many years ago but even though with today's threats and horrible air quality on the plane you always worry about ;who is seated next to you? Is there a fat guy overflowing into your seat? a person with poor hygiene, or someone sick.? It's never the gorgeous model sitting next to you, not yet anyway!

The registration fee and being recruited to a team are the first and primary things done a few months out. The players like me who absolutely alive just for baseball start packing soon. Even though it is early, you know, the right bats to take, your baseball bag with spikes, uniforms, batting gloves, your own helmet(using someone else's helmet may lead to lice or bugs) then off course your glove needs oiling maybe a lace tightened. Besides registration like everything else in life these days you must download a waiver form to protect the tournament founders and facility insurance folks.

In my case because of my sensitive heart problems I must get a real strong check up by my cardiologist, a whole battery of test to assure my safety especially when the tournament is so far away. Then there are my medications, see if there's a hospital near where I am going on map quest or check with AAA and pack for sure a medication list.

With all systems go! I am ready with my bags in my garage waiting for the ride to airport. The limo approaches my street and backs up to me and I say right place, let's go! Then of course the conversation is like are you playing golf? Are you vacationing? I say baseball. Then he thinks oh, your going to watch some games? I say no, I am playing baseball. Then there's silence as usual because of my age no one ever takes you serious playing baseball unless you are on the field playing your position.

Off to the airport a short 40 minute ride and I can't wait to get started and get on out of there. After security and sitting in the waiting area, you naturally look for other ballplayers but there are none here. Load up time, no this is not a parachute jump just a friendly little ride to sunshine and warmer weather. Then I am looking for wheels up and hit the gas I am playing baseball. I am always cautious in and around the airports because of our world situation. If you remember back in my original book The Eastside Kid, there was a chapter about Terrorist Training.

My training and mind set of that training immediately makes me aware of my mental state of safety. I always get the aisle seat and preferably left side so my throwing arm is by the aisle. I carry a baseball in my carry on and available to me. They never question it whenever I fly. My thought is if there is a terrorist on the plane; with my pitching velocity, accuracy and ability, I will throw the ball between his eyes as hard as I can. That is my plan anyway.

Fortunately we are safe and I land and look for my baseball equipment at baggage claim. I grab it and go outside to catch a free shuttle to the avis car center to meet with a teammate I never met before; He will be my team mate. I meet up with Bill and off we go to the hotel to get our suite, get our baseball gear and go to practice field complex attached to Roger Dean Stadium. Before these tournaments there are always field practicing the day before to acclimatize ball players who have traveled, for the beginning of the tournament and to meet there other teammates as well. Some players are newly recruited and the teams would like to view their abilities ahead of time prior to playing it's just a fact of life.

The ball fields are MLB quality, such a beautiful site as the fields are so near perfect you can't believe your eyes. The crack of the bat , the sun, balls flying around and chit chat about baseball is always within hearing distance. You either take a field position or get in line to hit.

At this point many of the players there have met in other tournaments, so an opportunity to catch up with old gamer friends. The ones you don't know are trying to impress the large group with their hitting skills even though its practice and it doesn't count and I guess we are all guilty of that. It seems the older you get there are more challenges and more to prove as fitting in is important, just like when you were a teenager.

At the end of practice back to the hotel to get organized, uniform laid out for the double header in the morning so there no fumbling around from the start. Breakfast at the hotel

Started the day off and off to the stadium locker rooms. There, the locker rooms with large, carpeted nicely and large lockers with our team logo and our names on the locker. That was a nice gesture. These were the stadium locker rooms and attached were fantastic batting cages, small perfect infields for the minor leaguers and major leaguers. Outside of that were 16 ball fields. The Marlins and Cardinals split the whole complex and shared all facilities. We were not allowed to interfere with the professionals that were there.

We were introduced to our teammates and then the long walk to field number 4 for our first game of the double header. It was hot, bright sun and pure baseball before us. The fields were constantly groomed and finally lined and hosed down and moments later we took the field and then the umpire said" Play Ball"!

This was one of my first tests with my arm, from previous surgery a year ago. I felt great and each game I was hitting, making my plays at third base and pitching well. I had pitched about 17 innings for the week. Not as much as I usually pitch at tournaments but I was playing a lot of baseball. Middle of the tournament we had our stadium game!

I didn't pitch here as others were in line but I hit well as I went 2 for 3 at bat. It always feels great getting those hits at a stadium game. Especially when you go to bat and they announce your number and name for example; "Now batting, playing 3rd base # 22 John DeCosta" So this is it the stadium games draw a little crowd and everything echo's and you are on the big stage and getting your hits mean so much more. People cheering for you and you have no idea who they are but it feels good. Did I mention that, yes of course I did my usual course of events. I collected a small bottle of dirt from Roger Dean Stadium for my souvenir for my sports room at home.

The last game I pitched I had a catcher that was age 68 and he was Tony Cabrera who was better than most 40 year old catchers that I have had in the past he was great and we worked well together. He just knew my thought process and known how to get the best pitching from me. I went on to have about 8 k; s and no walks that game. It was fun.

Our team was close to.500 baseball. Not a championship team but we had a great time playing baseball on the MLB ball fields in April just a classy primer for me as a strong pre-season training.

Between games I would roam around and watch these minor league baseball players working out! I was amazed. It seemed that every player was between 6'2" and 6'5" tall lean and mean. Unbelievable, they would have about 200 ballplayers trying out and spread about in numerous ability groups, for training. They would be in the batting cages hitting baseballs at 6 am working very hard all day until 5 pm and then after two months of intense training they would maybe keep two or three players. That should make you appreciate the real talent we have in the Major League Baseball.

Another time while I was roaming after the double header they always have beer on ice for the players after the games and you really need one at that point. Well, I was waiting for my ride back to the hotel. I had my bat bag over my shoulder, in uniform all beat up from the day with beer in my hand. I walked into the wrong hallway and locker room and there was this big huge guy, bald head that had looked like Mr. Clean. He was the instructor for these baseball recruit training and similar to Military Drill Sergeants. He looked at me and I thought he was going to yell at me for being in the wrong area, he simply looked at me up and down, saw the beer and gave me the thumbs up with a smile and said how it go today. I said I had a great time. When I walked away I thought I should have said where's my contract? Just joking but the great comebacks and things to say always come late, isn't that true?

We played 8 games in four days and that was great! Fred Schwartz and Tony Cabrera took me aside and said John we would really like to have you come to Phoenix World Series and pitch for our team. I was quite pleased and said I will try but no promises as it's a financial matter. They said don't worry we will call you. I thought, Gee they are great guys, great chemistry but they will not call me, they are just being nice. You know how it is, many people say a lot of things but seldom come through with real intentions.

September rolled around and I get an email from Fred Schwartz. Fred left a long message and asked if I could call him back. I did so and reached a Law Office. His secretary got him and apparently he was a District Judge, wow I thought. !!He always takes baseball calls

We talked and he gave me an intense run down on how he would run the team and how he would use me and I was sold. He even offered to help me with transportation, hotel expenses etc. I arranged to get my own Braves Uniform complete and I was on this team and excited to play. This off course was for Nov 2 thru Nov 6th 2009.

In my story I shall continue with events and finally get to the Phoenix Arizona trip of all trips. You will fall out of your chair with excitement in that series.

With out going too fast and leaving anything out of order I am now going back to Boston with another Tournament under my belt or more experience added to my resume. I was anxious to share my fun I experienced with my White Sox team next week at the batting cage. I can only say this; Until you go to a baseball tournament and physically play the full tournament, 8 games and a Stadium game, the banquets and team dinners you have no idea what you are missing.

You could probably equate this with any interest or any passion for people starting to age. I think it's a matter of regrets in people's lives, the need for self improvement, finding or defining their lives as they grow older. I also find that people I meet in baseball or any sporting activity they have a different sense of competitive edge. In most all cases you can see the talent they once had, or ability and training in the past but what is different now is they are smarter, confident and have a desire to improve as young people have little of that and just go along.

Even women that are over thirty years old take up- golf, swimming, ice hockey , running races, aerobics' I know one woman who happens to be a hairdresser over 40+ years old and plays ice hockey on a co ed hockey team, another team she plays for is women adult hockey league and deck hockey as well. There are also women adult baseball leagues in New York and other cities around the country.

Basically what I am saying is" you are never too old to pursue any desires in any sport. If you check on line these days you can find a team, any age group in any sports and then it's up to you to find a team or opportunity in the area near where you live.

Chapter Thirty Six

Just more training

I am a regular of course at the batting cages; I go with my team the White Sox to a facility called "Extra Innings" In Tewksbury, Ma. We meet once a week there and only about 7 players come to that because many just don't have the time during the winter for extra baseball. So training is important and what you do in training is what you will do in a game.   There's plenty of batting and plenty of throwing. I just love that live pitching at the cages. I can still get into a zone and enjoy my training there but it's not enough for me. My teammates are great and very supportive. I don't always know what is said about me but I feel they have enormous confidence in me.

Twice a week sometimes three times a week I will go to my athletic facility not far from my home and work out with the nautilus machines, shot some hoops and do my pitching there in the racquetball court and throw about 150 to 225 pitches on an average workout.

My other training facility is of course The Connector batting cage in Lowell, Ma- My batting instructor Adam McCusker really makes me work and helps me so much. I love to bat and I think I could bat for hours as I just love to hit. So, after my batting lesson I see Jon Cahill my pitching instructor who spent time with the California Angels system and he has really stepped up my pitching ability. Adam and Jon give me homework exercises which are great and I also take notes.

If all bets are off or if I am just strolling around the house, you may find me in the cellar hitting balls off the "T" or throwing the ball into the screen

I made. If anyone calls me I just simply say, Hay I have a new pitch! That usually draws a smile and laugh;

I have a ton of work around our home to do routinely as there's never enough time

To" get er done" hah   the pigeons are here in the coop as I have my racing pigeons and the roller pigeons so plenty of care for this hobby as well. To include Maintenance, breeding, banding, and training etc.

The night over thirty baseball registration is coming soon, opening day for my over thirty Sunday baseball, is coming right up as well;

Chapter Thirty Seven

Over Thirty Baseball

Opening Day 2009

Opening day is so special no matter what team, sport or league you are in; it's the point in time when you try to get the cob webs out early and have a great efficient start. That was true for me! This year will be different as I feel it in my bones.   We won big as everyone contributed and it was special for me because I need to fit in quickly with my new teammates and get on the board. I did so with three hits, an RBI and a score to start things off.

I have been on top of my game thus far but I did notice recently as in West Palm Beach Tournament that I was starting to have problems picking up the ball. I have always been a very good fielder and had my quickness to handle the ball but now I feel a problem with my eyes. I do not delay as I went to the eye doctor and had a compete test and naturally they look at a 62 year old as if you are in dream land or something when you share anything about actually playing baseball. At any rate after the test was completed the news was my eyes had changed with perception.

I ordered very expensive sports glasses to wear while I am playing baseball. The glasses would not be ready for me for three weeks or so. This was a set back as I was forces to use my (reading glasses) in place until my magic glasses arrive. I tough it out and now I am more conscious of my problem than before. I do not have a problem with pitching at all. When I bat, I am seeing the ball well but its on defense playing third base that is my problem. Opening day against the Dodgers, I went three for four at bat and continued despite my eye problems on a steady pace. The first 6 games go by and I am hitting and pitching up a storm with a low era and plenty of hits as I am in the top ten batting in the league. Finally, my new glasses arrive and I am excited.

They give me a new look and a lot of remarks but who cares I can see now and I am not receiving any baseballs in the chest, face or legs so this is good. I can't seem to use them pitching nor hitting because of the bar that separate each eye is greatly a problem distorting my vision. Now ,I know my situation and only use glasses on defense so mentally this problem is gone.

I am starting to grab attention from a few fans," The Eastside Kid" called out to me, teammates and I am earning my worth ,on and off the field. My chemistry with my team seems to be improving by the minute. Usually, your first year with a new team, you hear words like "rookie" but not said to me, as I was accepted immediately and that is all positive. My team already has some very good pitching and great fielders as well. Our hitting and scoring runs/runs against are in the top statistics of our 16 team league but we are losing a few games that we should have won. My thought is, we have a strong team but need to be very hungry. I'll have to work harder I think!

These over 30/over 40 baseball leagues in general, have family guys and only a few singles guys. Therefore responsibility is for work and family. Most players do not put baseball first, as I do. It's hard to accept this at times, but I truly understand the other side of the coin too. Usually the family guys are the ones who bring wives and families for our fans! The single guys occasionally bring different girlfriends to our games. Many times, "distractions", if they are real pretty.

It's funny, when you are the pitcher in a game. All eyes are on you. There is an incredible amount of pressure because, you are in charge. Good things happen and everyone on your team is happy. If you strike them out, make them hit ground balls or have short innings you are wonderful. If you give up too many hits, walk batters, your players make errors or wild pitches then you are looking bad because you have had a long inning.

The reason why I say," it's funny", is because I just explained the pressure and responsibility of your pitcher as in me! The thing is, being on the mound you notice sounds, movement and distractions between 3rd base coaches area to 1st base coaching area. That would also include behind backstop when a pretty girl watching the game in a revealing outfit. It sounds funny but, yes the pitchers do notice this stuff. You wonder if the opposing team sets this up on purpose to distract you. I did hear a guy say this at one time as he did place his girlfriend in a strategic location (it worked).

This all means that you must be disciplined to play your game and not be taken out of your mind set. Yes, you notice joggers, fans, and screams, things being said to and about you. My all time favorite is; when I strike someone out, on their way to the dugout they are swearing, slamming there helmet or tossing their bat against the dug out or fence." I absolutely love it." I usually look towards center field and have my private smile and laugh in that direction being careful not to intimidate the opposing team.

They apply statistics for every game on the internet with numerous categories such as batting average, homeruns, runs batted in, pitching wins, strikeouts, walks, wins and losses. Then they have team statistics as everyone says they don't look at it but trust me an hour after the game they have their laptops out and they are checking for correct write-ups about themselves, there team stats and popular players about the league, I use it like others especially to see what player I will face the next game so for that, this is a great tool. Who will try to be stealing bases, which players are the best hitters etc?

As I stated I could not ask for a better start for this season. I am batting like .550, boosting up my wins pitching, and in the top ten with statistics in the leader's board. I know many say, hey there is no "I" in team. I have heard that but think of this; why do they keep records and stats of individuals who rank the highest in every league everywhere? Its because, individuals make the team what they are, therefore you can try very hard to improve your statistics which means that you are helping your team to a higher and winning percentage and level. That's what I think!

My Night over thirty league has just started as well and my positive playing continues. I am hitting and pitching and my new glasses are really helping out. Hey I can see the ball, ground balls that are. I always have trouble with high pop ups. I don't know what I is but I have the hardest time judging those balls. I can't pick them up or they move and my eyes just have enormous difficulty seeing them. So, I tell my short stop; Hey buddy need your help here; in the daytime not to much of a problem. On the mound is definitely my best defensive position.

I love the hard hit balls and the line drives. My favorite is a ball heading toward short stop as I can be quicker going to my left and make an on the run scoop and fire to 2nd for a double play or just to first base firing the ball hard. There have been many games rained out this year both night league and Sunday league as you look so forward to playing baseball then it's cancelled. One Sunday game, the players arrived and wanted to play but the conditions became worse and continued to stay that way. One teammate another pitcher John Marlin and I felt we came, let's throw the ball so we did as we got drenched throwing to each other as there was no game and the rest of the teammates didn't want to be bothered but we ended up with a great work out.

That's what's great about these amateur leagues the players have so must pride in their improving their quality of play that conditions do not matter. Also, many play with injuries as in MLB if they have a small rash or minor problem they are on the (DL).Disabled List

We are having great games this season as many close exciting games; great comebacks and I just love my teams, great chemistry and even if we lose a game you knew your teammates tried their best and you went home smiling and happy because you had a great time with your teammates. Many teams are not like this at all.

I have been on my night league team now for about 4 years maybe 5 not sure, can't remember! Our team is so chemically sound that its fun each and every time I step on the field with these guys. We are first and second, right up there during the whole summer, we have some great games. I am in the top of statistics in this league also as this years is absolutely so great and I don't want it to end.

We had what we refer to as a "rain game" last year on the night league as it was the last game of the season. It rained and poured and we were all soaked. The entire infield was full of water and mud. I pitched the last inning and struck out the sides and now we were to bat in the last of the 7th with a tie game. One of our teammates Chad Kirby had a long at bat, the rain was pouring down from the dug out you could hardly see him and he had one of these at bats with about 15 foul balls. The game was tie, full count, bases loaded and he continued to hit foul balls down the third base line and finally, finally he hit a ground ball that died and we won the game.

The guys ran around and head first dived through the mud and water in jubilation. That was a game to remember as I thank the umpires for allowing us to play through. Our same team responded this year as well. We had heart you might say and we loved to come back in a game. It seemed someone would step up when it counted and our bench was a strong bench as far as cheerleading goes. The games started at 8;00 pm which was difficult but very laid back. There was a weekly concert a mile away as you could hear the music and loud Harleys echo over our ball park. There was a swamp on the other side of left field and third base line so you could hear the frogs, and beetles chirping away during the game. One night there were millions of moths's flying down from the sky just like a snow storm but went away in a short time with an explanation. The mosquitoes and black June flies were the most difficult especially at bat but it's all somehow worked out and we played through.

Chapter Thirty Eight

Our 25th Wedding Anniversary

Elizabeth and I share our 25th Wedding Anniversary 3, July 2009- The years really fly by before you realize it. When I first met Beth I was in the Army jumping out of airplanes and living the life of danger. That was back in 1984, so long ago. We managed to make it a go and it wasn't easy with the changes in my health, jobs, moving around the country and finally settling in the metro west, for now. This is a big anniversary and I felt that Beth has really supported me with baseball and earned her stripes as a baseball wife or sometimes she refers it to baseball widow. That's because, gone every Sundays and three nights a week for practices and games. So she has earned a treat.

Beth as her passion has been indicated loves horses and in particular Frisian Horses. So, I came up with an idea, or we both came up with an idea to go away to the Frisian farm up in vermont to ride horses for the weekend. I am not a rider, lets get that understood! Beth did not want to be embarrassed so she wanted me to see her friend and trainer Emily.

Beth thought, before we go to Townshend, Vermont, at "The Frisians of Majesty Farm" I should at least have a little lesson on basics to ride a horse "English style". I then meet up with Emily as she's full of smiles and I am dragging my way in. I actually like horses. I am fine with taking a horse on a lead, walking them and brushing them, give them a carrot or talk to them but "riding" just not sure about this riding at all. But, I will give it a shot. Emily gave me a quick lesson about cleaning, bushing and putting the saddle on for the great ride. We walk over to the indoor, I get up on the stepping block and on to Duke I go.

She walked me around and I thought this is not so bad but I never felt secure and it was not a smooth ride. Then she has me doing exercises with my legs and hands and balance now I have a lot to remember. She has me on a lunge line and going in circles and then from corner to corner but the horse even knows, there's something wrong here with this human. I was not jelling with the horse. I got through the lesson and really did not do as bad as I was describing but it seemed that was the best I will ever get.

I walked like a Texan back to my car as I am sure she had a good laugh about this silly old man trying to ride a horse. She is use to young people, women and people very interested in riding as opposed to a guy trying to please his wife for a weekend. I am now very, very sore. I said to Beth, I hope I recover, as my big game against the Phillies is this weekend; we planned this trip mid week so I wouldn't miss a baseball game.

Beth had her laugh as she was thrilled about my lesson and our weekend to come, for our anniversary at the farm. We pack up as Beth is constantly quizzing me about how to ride so, I throw at her that I mastered riding horses and it's easy, no big deal. She laughed as well as I had. It was a long drive up to Vermont and thank goodness to GPS to help us get there. Our drive was very nice and scenic along the way as I love Vermont and the country side. It's my kind of place. We stopped for gas and a quick lunch as we dodged rain drops from the car to diner and back to the car. Beth was getting anxious because this was her dream to ride real Frisian horses. They come from Holland and very elegant, mysterious, and intelligent. They are very calm and gentle with humans. I can see and understand the bonding that takes place, with her and other horse people. It also helps when horses have this super temperament that I had experienced.

We arrive through the long winding roads from this tiny town in the middle of nowhere and acres and acres of forest, trails and farms. We finally arrive at the Frisians of Majesty farm at Townshend, Vermont. It has enormous riding stables, and two barns very elaborate for these magnificent animals. The indoor arena where there are shows all of the time was breath taking as all I could think of was hitting baseballs inside this place that was more than 350 feel long by 200 feet wide and about 80 feet high, Great for baseball. They had a balcony to watch the horse shows and inside on the right a group of horses just hanging out staying out of the rain. We met the owner Robert labrie and we greeted and he was non stop chatting then we were directed to our small cottage where we would stay.

This quaint little cottage was rustic and fully equipped and more like a bunk house and surely not a five star facility but we adapted and no matter what window you gazed out of there were horses the entire place. There were 70horses total and 10 babies born earlier that month. It was exciting seeing them as often as we did and every time they were a new experience. This is a 650 acre farm with scenic views everywhere. Beth was excited as we both would have a lesson on one of these Frisians in the morning. Then Beth would have another lesson the following day.

We saw so many amazing things that weekend as we witnessed the entire breeding process as Robert Labrie had done an ultra sound and retrieved embryo's before our eyes with also a monitor and later saw the horse attack a phantom and retrieve the sperm to transfer to a mare across the country via transportation. Quite an interesting procedure, so besides the adventures of riding Frisians, for our weekend we were educated as well. This was all new and foreign to me, but my wife being a sophisticated higher level nurse, she easily captures all of this information so easily.

The big event has arrived and I get my lesson from "Isabella" She is an experienced attractive trainer and now managing this farm. I was impressed with her and how she coached me because, right off the bat I told her, I am a real, real, rookie; This is a one time thing for me as I further explained about our anniversary and sharing the weekend. She brought me through several sequences of events on a long line again and bouncing up and down, I thought, this is not good! The lesson could not get over soon enough!

After the lesson I was petting the other horses nearby and telling them of my ordeal. I actually thought they understood. Beth got her lesson as she is high as a kite as well as when I am in a MLB stadium, pitching from the mound and feeling that rush; well that's what Beth is feeling right now with her horse and the horse farm environment.

We went on a short tour around the farm and watched the baby horses cuddle with their Mom's in the stalls as that was a neat site. Robert sleeps off and on with these horses –in with the babies when they are fairly young and that makes quite the difference as they grow older as they become very gentle and take quite nicely to humans. I handle the young squabs shortly after hatching and every time I go into the coops I make an attempt to touch and handle them just for a few moments every day as that also makes a difference to their gentleness there after. So human bonding does work miracles with nature!

We started our drive home as we wrapped up the weekend. Beth was already making plans for the woman's weekend come fall as she would bring several women to the camp and also stay in cottage, have a few lessons and also drive a horse carriage so she is excited as It took her a few days to come down from her high but she was right at it again at the local farm riding her "Bravo" her half Frisian horse.

Meanwhile, preparation for me was already in my head, with a huge game this weekend. You might say this was the big show down between me and my old team Phillies for all the marbles of respect; Playing against an old team is always difficult but in this case my integrity was on the line.

Chapter Thirty Nine

Here Come the Phillies

I have been waiting for this game even before the season had started,. I tried not to make it personal but during the draft some of my old teammates from the Phillies had slammed me. They chose to pick and chose a younger player and that is fine with me but where is the love and integrity or loyalty come to play. Yes, they moved on with a plan to fit their needs but in the process they did what they could to demolish my baseball career in this over thirty baseball league.

They could have just moved on and that would be fine but what they did or what their manager had done! He told other teams that they were out of their minds to pick a guy with medical issues and age 62. He could have just left it alone but he did what he could to destroy my season before it started. So, when I was on the Phillies personally I brought them to the finals and without me that was impossibility. It happened to be against this very team I now belong to-the white sox as I was finally chosen by them for 2009 season.

My new managers Mike and Billy had showed respect and spent quality time demonstrating that they really want me on their team. I was sold completely but one last chance with the Phillies because of my team loyalty, and then once again I was turned down by their manager. This to me gave me such a passion to show them and the league how people could be so wrong about a person, and baseball player regardless of my disability with my heart, other medical issues and my age.

I trained even harder and I marked it on my calendar 28 July 2009, White Sox vs. Phillies at Hadley Field on the Chelmsford/Lowell line. I arrive early as usual. I go to the basketball hoop just like clockwork and shoot hoops to get loose. Then one of my teammates John Marlin joins me for the fun and exercise but he was not feeling what was in my heart in reference to the game before us. I notice a few Philly players arriving but I ignore that. I continue to hit some balls of the T and finish with my stretching. Then as time came close I started to warm up; Now I have the Phillies attention. They already know I have had a great start this season with batting and pitching so to this day they are undefeated and we have a few losses but I already know we are not losing today. Today is Johnny D's day and we will be victorious.

I gave 6 very strong innings as my White Sox team was too much for them and I was too much for them. Bill Keef stepped up to the plate and I said to myself" you are going down" I struck him out, In fact I struck him out twice and one time he popped up to the 1st baseman. I wanted to drill him when I first saw him at the plate but this was a better way to shut his mouth.

I went on to gather a bunch of Strikeouts and superb pitching and I collected 3 hits of 4 at bats, run batted in, stolen base and a score as well as made a few plays so I was very happy.

My White Sox team went on to smoke them"Phillies" like a cheap cigar. We did do our shaking of hands after the game but they knew they treated me badly with regrets I am sure from most of the teammates. I am done with that team and pay back was sooo sweet and now it's over and if we meet in the playoffs I will be victorious again. They will never beat me.

My manager Mick McNally immediately said out loud. How do you like the trade now, Bill? It's so great to have my team and Managers support as they believed in me, which was huge and as big as none could possibly envision the drive this produced for me. I held my head up high, I was not in anyone's' face, I was Johnny D and I kept my head up high as I found myself respected, new loyalty, and a great team to support me whether we win or lose together as a team.

I do not normally go on this type of attack towards another team but they did make it personal with me. Hopefully they have learned their lesson and finally learned what loyalty and respect mean!

Meanwhile my show me talk radio show is alive and well and going strong. I have had many people ask about it and others that have listened to it so that is all a plus because my book and my radio interview allows people to look back and feel what I am saying about my background that is similar to their experiences as well.

25 August 2009 is before us, what is this? It's the Night over Thirty Baseball Championship. We played well all season and here we are at the finals for our over 30 night league. Last year we made it to the finals and lost but our team is not worried at all. I mentioned before about how we have such great chemistry and come from behind! We'll, no one ever gets down because of lack of hitting, an error or mistake. We seem to just come back when we need to.

This team is so much fun to play with and even if we lose ,we go home with a smile because we all played hard, had fun and get along great. This season we were 9 wins 1 loss. The loss came from the team we are playing in the championship game. Most people are talking that we will get crushed and smoked and we come with our usual fun attitude and not let any talk bother us. Our thoughts are just play and have fun in this game. There are two pitchers feared from this team Diamondbacks. John Blaikie and Peter Farare.

We are cruising through this game crushing this team. Our defense is at its best. Catching everything and anything as the apposing team is making errors and dumb plays. They just are out of sink because they were so cocky and over confident. We continued to ,out bat, out pitch and just out play them for the entire game. Here we were supposed to get beat, everyone thought so and here we are beating this team badly. I am up at the plate bottom of the 4th and I am leadoff batter. John Blaikie is throwing pretty hard and I am like I said seeing the ball well. I let the first pitch go out side for a ball. The next pitch another fast ball and I clock it for a homerun into the twilight, over the fence into the trees. I made sure I touched every bag along the way and gracefully touched home plate as my teammates greeted me with a loud roar! It was fun.

Then they put in their ace, Peter Farare, who threw smoke! I believe he throws in the 80's and that's smoke for our league. He has a history of playing in the Boston Park League so he has credentials not to mention he is only 33 years old. Then the unbelievable happens, every guy on our team hits the ball and they continue to make errors. I am at bat one more time in the 7th my last time up in our night league and this championship game. I am facing Peter.

He is throwing hard and I foul a ball off then a ball. The next pitch I hit high left center and no one sees the ball as I raced down to first base for a single, Getting a hit off him was just as pleasurable as my homerun. I come into the game to close it out in the 7th and mow them down and force their top hitter to hit a ground ball for the final out and our D-Rays win the Championship 14-1.This truly was a great way to end the Night Over Thirty Baseball League in real fashion.

Chapter Forty

All Star Selection and Game & League Play offs

I continued to shine and lead my team as once again my sport glasses were working great so I got back to my normal defense. My hitting has continued as I led the team and it seemed, I was unstoppable. I got a hit every game the entire season! I was thrilled about that. I sported a high batting average, a high on base percentage and high slugging percentage. I was in the league leading top ten lists, in pitching. In many of the games, the game was on the line with incredible pressure that's the position and challenge I die for.

Our season kept moving along and our team collectively was hitting well. I kept up with the pace as I continued to see the ball well and my arm was full of endurance. My off season training surely accentuated that fact. I remain in the top of the list for leaders in the league and I am totally surprised but feel like, hey I am in the zone so go with the flow it all feels so right. We finish out the season on a high note as we romp them 21-5.I collected 4 more hits itched a strong 6 innings with a bunch of k;s and no walks. We are ready for the playoffs as we are in the middle of the pack as far as the brackets go and we are in great shape.

They do the voting for the all star selection as there are two selected from each team. I was voted in along with Mike Silvia. Labor Day weekend is the time for this all star game. The game is at Alumni Field and many of the league players and family's show up for this game as it's a time to reflect on the year and see your friends play under the lights.

The league champions' pitcher and league president Chris Augieri gets the nod to start the game on the mound. He got into trouble after the first inning and I am called to warm up and come in the game. I shut down the National league all stars and pitch very well as I went 3 innings and had no walks and 1 k no runs scored one hitter I believe. We, the American league all stars win in a blow out 17-8. I received MVP honors and winning pitcher as other pitchers only went two innings each. So, I was pretty honored winning that honor.

Our playoffs were not magical as I anticipated at all. Our first game started with a loud thunder. I was 6 wins 1 loss as pitching goes. I had a good game as I pitched 5 1/3 innings no walks 1 k, I hit a homerun had 2 rbi's and went 3 for 3 at bat, single, double and homerun. Our next game we won 16 -4 and lucky we were able to win. Then the last game that would have given us a free shot to the championship we all had a bad day. No one was hitting, didn't get the calls we deserved and the game just bounced away from us and ended our season on a sad ride home.

Our thoughts were ,we had a pretty good season but we came up short. The thoughts about, wait until next year was in the air but I was sad we had not gone all the way to become champs. I thought we had the team and I know next season we would be more confident as well.

Our White Sox Season was over; our year was productive and a time to rekindle our talents and play for many future games to share. My 2009 baseball was not over for me but I did have a remarkable year to look back on and be grateful I had my health and was able to be competitive and share accolades with my great teammates.

Chapter Forty One

Phoenix World Series Baseball

The Long Island Braves were from New York, while we were playing in the West Palm Beach Baseball Tournament. Fred Schwartz the team organizer/ Manager and his friend and now my friend Toni Cabrera had asked me to come to the Phoenix World Series! Well, this was back in April 2009. It sounded like so much fun and very well organized and something I would like very much. At the time I thought, We'll they are baseball players and just being polite ,I personally thought this is a very nice opportunity but will it ever come to be true? Soon I forgot all about it totally.

September rolls around, and I receive a phone call from Fred Schwartz from the Long Island Braves. I was lost for a few minutes as so much time had passed and I was having a mental block with my memory. Then Fred was nice enough, to realize all of this and reminded me completely of our old conversation. Then I was back to reality and completely understanding everything at present, Fred reassured me, the complete picture of this team and program as how it will be run , everyone's playing time, pitching time and where most people played their positions on the field. He then covered each person's capabilities in throwing, hitting, speed and fielding and then I was in awe because we had a very powerful team. He stated we would carry 14 players possibly 15 tops. He kept his word and especially wanted honesty about what I can contribute for pitching so he could sit and study and develop a strategy on who would start for what games, and who would come in middle of the games and would be closers.

My response is this. You have experience seeing everyone throw the ball, you know the teams we will facing and make your decision for me, I can give you 25 to 27 innings this week, that's what I can do physically. I do this and back it up in every tournament I can pitch all of that. So I know my limitations. I just need to go over things at home with my wife's work and time off, my animals to care for, two old English sheepdogs, and my pigeons to care for twice a day, so I am sure all of this can be met and dealt with.

The chemistry I shared with White Sox, D-Rays was super and now as this becomes my third super team. I am in, I repeated to Fred; then Fred continued to assure me, this was going to be great'

This is so key and so very important to feel this way about your team and teammate s as well; the positives seem to definitely be in place. I then, took care of my flight to Phoenix, limo to airport, and started packing baseball stuff. I organized bats to take, oiled my glove after a long season and spent a lot of time, which bat to bring, how many bats and sanded and cleaned the chosen ones for the trip. I purchased a new Braves uniform with my # 22 on it, hat belt, socks and pants ready to go. Now I have much to do to get ready for the big stage, for this tournament. This is the 55+ World Series Tournament MSBL. (Men's senior Baseball League).

I continued my work outs and self training as well as workouts at the athletic facility routinely. Then I gathered a few friends for sandlot baseball on Sundays (weather permitting). I usually went with a few ballplayers from other teams and my usual sandlot guy Jimmy Lyons. Jimmy was a south paw and always threw this slider and knuckleball and the pitches would always dive at my toes but as difficult as it was hitting off him, his pitching was great plate discipline for me and good workout.

This took place a few nights a week and on Sundays. The problem we had was day light savings time as it would get darker for us and less time to practice. We would usually meet up with ballplayers from another league so we had some positive baseball activity. I hadn't lost a step in reference to my hitting as I was once again seeing the ball well!

Chasing people to practice and always ready to play baseball alerts others to ask you to play baseball more! My teammate from the White Sox Miguel Walker, announced there would be a tournament at Lawrence High School complex the next weekend. I was excited because he put together some pretty awesome teams. The age group was 18 years and up! This was truly a challenge for me. There were three games to play in one day. The temperature was 36 degrees and a bit windy. It sure was cold as very few hit balls past the infield. The truth of the matter was that each player on all of the teams just wanted to play baseball and the cold elements were not stopping anyone. Every player was miserable but playing baseball in October here in the Boston area, was super!

The games were close, low scoring games, everyone bundles up and surely being affected by the cold weather. There were a few highlights for me! I did strike out a very good player about 20 years old. That was unexpected as most of these kids could hit the ball well. Then a game situation came up with a man on 2nd base. Everyone in the park knew I was going to bunt. I fouled off the first bunt attempt as it was close to the third base line. The third baseman was in so close and I surprised everyone as I bunted down the first base line, moved the runner to third base as I completed the important sacrifice play. We score on the next play.

It was great to play despite the weather as it was late October and not long before I head on out to Phoenix. I had many things to take care of around the house as far as getting ready for the winter because for sure when I return from Phoenix anything could happen in great New England. There could be snow, ice storm, cold or any type of miserable weather.

Most of my workouts now are inside at the athletic center with the nautilus machines, shooting hoops or get some throwing in. I also have my mini cage in the cellar so I can hit balls off a T. I did have a warmer day as I was able to go outside to the high school and get a work out. I threw about 125 balls off the mound into a screen by home plate. That felt great as my arm felt so well. This was exhilarating. Then I hit about 75 balls off a T into the back stop. There were some on lookers as I am sure they thought I was nuts!

Packing my bags and weighing them is fun as I know I am going soon. I carefully check my list and plan for any unknown circumstances like, torn lace on my glove, shoe string for my spikes, medications, and double checking my list. All is set now and I am up early like 3; 00 am. I have breakfast, get my bags on deck! The garage; I took the dogs out fed the pigeons and just before the limo came said good by to Beth.

The limo came down the street and backed in, Beth then went back to bed and I loaded up and off I went to Manchester, New Hampshire Airport. Security was quick and easy along with my check in; I was early so just eagerly waiting to load the plane as the morning light started to appear. I looked but didn't see any ballplayers from the area that might be on this flight but that's ok, I was going to play baseball!

This was a long direct flight to Phoenix. The weather reports close to Phoenix destination started an hour prior to landing. As the approach came near I was getting excited. Weather report 82 degrees clear skies! Great! I clutched my carry on and waited to deplane and go to baggage claim. I soon retrieved my bags, the baseball bag that is and off I went to grab a taxi and off to Legacy Golf Resort. Business was slow and the taxi driver was excited especially when I told him many ballplayers are coming in that weekend.

I arrived at the front desk and soon there after met up with Drew another teammate and soon after we entered our separate condos. Soon after more players arrived and then I said how about we throw the ball till other s get in! That's what we did and we were on the edge of the golf course throwing the ball and feeling the fresh western air and blinding sun.

The remainder of the team arrived as we were all introduced to one another and the decision was made to go to a nearby sports complex and grab a field and get some hits and a little infield practice. Everyone was on board and eager to check out each others talents and evaluate each other. No one says that but it happens. It seems no matter where you go, what ever league or team it is, you are constantly proving yourself over and over. This also happens from year to year as well. Hey, did he lose a step? Is he still hitting for power? How about his pitching? Is he as good as they said? All of these evaluations come out but after the ball gets passed around, a few hits at the plate and then everyone realizes, hey, we are a team!

The weather here in Phoenix is usually always very hot! I mean over 100 degrees and upwards to 110 degrees. The time we are there in late October first part of November is usually great weather about low 80's to 90 degrees, just my style. My manager Fred I road with in his car, with two other teammates. They seem to always know where they are going as I am lost out there! Lots of traffic and people/construction everywhere but the baseball fields are perfect. I think the baseball fields are the only places that have grass!

Then the manager, Fred wanted me to throw the ball with our catcher and another pitcher. I immediately developed a good connection with Joe our catcher and my friend Tony my previous catcher looked on and said, don't worry John you will be great!

We went to a super market and went shopping to stock our refrigerators and drinks for the week. Sunday tomorrow was our first organized long real practice at one of the training fields next to Tempe Diablo stadium. This was a huge field as we practiced for three hours. There were lots of hitting, and fielding and dealing with the hot sun. We had a long wait till our game Monday afternoon at the stadium. Yes, our first game would be at the Tempe Diablo Stadium. We all re- acquainted, at the outdoor hot tub by the outdoor pool. This became a regular hangout after practices and games. Hotel guest and of course the serious golfers also used the facility after all it was a golf course resort!

There was usually talk about what happened in practice, or a game, a quick fix and strategies for the next game plan.

Monday we are all in great emotional order. That is, we are rested, we had a great long productive practice Sunday and now we have the later stadium game at Tempe Diablo Stadium. We are all early just taking in the beautiful stadium that we will play in. There is a game going on so we have to wait for that to end and off course they will water and re-line the field for us. Meanwhile, there is a sports show going on inside the stadium undercover by bleachers all around. There are booths selling bats shirts, baseball memorabilia and training equipment.

The Hooter girls were in uniform selling stuff behind counters but don't you know it by time we arrive they are gone for the day! I did pick up a T shirt of Arizona baseball as I am familiar with Arizona State baseball for college World Series on TV as well as the girls ASU softball and yes there were absolutely no Jennie Finch sightings at all!

At a booth by the main entrance was Moose Skowron as he was in his 80's and mean as a junk yard dog! He was advertising for a Major League fantasy camp that would have Bucky Dent, Goose Gossage, Yogi Berra, Mickey Rivers, Don Larsen, Frank Howard, and many more. It was nice to see the old-timer and shake his hand; we got the signal as the game before us was over and we all filed down the walkways to the dugout entrance.

We only had a short time to stretch and throw the ball before our game would start.

I got my little jar out and started filling my jar with the red dirt from the stadium as that was my special little thing I started. While I was doing that a player said to me. "What on earth are you doing"? I said I am collecting sand as I have sand from all the major league ballparks and special places I have played baseball. He shook his head and walked away.

I do have quite the collection at home from Cooperstown to many fields and stadiums in Florida to a bunch of stadiums out here in Arizona.

It is now game time; the spectacular scoreboard all lit up with team logos and your name and number illuminated. When you are at bat, the loud speaker announces for example, The Pitcher #22 John F DeCosta, quite the nice touch. It started off as a close game but after 3 innings our pitcher was getting knocked around. I guess it was not his fault but the jitters from many of the players because, first game together. Learning about each other teammate and off course getting the right bounces and calls by the umpire usually sets the tone for the entire game.

I collected a few hits and some of my new friends also contributed as well; The third inning my friend Tony Cabrera, was playing second base as this game was late afternoon, 4; 00 pm game and the sun was going down and peered through the rafters of the stadium right dead in the fielders eyes on the right side of the field. Poor Tony got a line drive right into his chest and the glove had not absorbed it at all. He was sore and very tough and continued.

The inning was finished soon thereafter and then Tony happened to be the leadoff batter and hit a sharp ground ball up the middle and the short stop made a great play and threw the ball on the inside and high area of the first baseman and as Tony crossed the first base bag the big tall first baseman jumped up high to retrieve the ball as hi landed off balance with his knee high and slammed Tony to the ground as he crushed his chest with his weight.

It had looked like a very dirty play and Tony after seeing the Stadium EMT's he went to the hospital and did not return till the next morning. Tony had a broken rib and was out for the whole tournament. We definitely needed him as his bat was valuable to us. Now our team that was 14 is down to 11. Two had backed out just prior to tournament because of personal issues back home and now first day we lose Tony. Tough start but we are resilient as you will see!

The score is 3-1 as we are behind. I had warmed up and came into the game and was a little gun shy at first as nerves and finding my rhythm was a little misplaced but soon I would be on target. The problem now was our team was not hitting and we had a good hitting team, first game slump or jitters I guess.

Its getting late in the game and I am on the mound holding my own. Now like a dummy I hit a batter and put him on first base, I needed that like a hole in the head. Next batter hits a high bouncer down the third base line and I ran off the mound and caught the ball just before the foul line, caught the ball in my webbing, turned and fired a laser shot to 2nd base for what should have been a double play to end the inning. That did not happen as the ball was thrown perfectly and bounced out of the glove of my 2nd baseman and people safe all around. I then struck out the last batter and this gave us a chance to hit and possibly win this game. It did feel good making a great play even thought it was not successful.

We are now at bat and first batter strikes out and then its me,#22 John F DeCosta now batting. I have a good eye for my strike zone and I am feeling confident. In the middle of the count, I hit a real laser down the third base line just fair as I buzzed around the bases and glided in on a slide to 3rd base for a triple. We just need a base hit, with me to score to continue the game. This did not happen and we lined up to shake hands with the opposing team. We lost 4-3 after 9 innings.

We decided to go for lunch at "Gallagher's" this would become our routine stop after the games. The World Series games were on as New York Yankees playing against Philadelphia Phillies. TVs in all directions other sports programs on, and the loud pace of the sports bar and the many conversations going on was a new way to wind down. We were playing baseball and enjoying our team bonding time.

Because we lost players some of us were alone in our condos. I was one and loved it. I am a neat freak when it comes to hotels and being with groups so this was great. The alternate side of the large bed I would have my uniform all laid out for tomorrow's double header.

I would make sandwiches for lunch time and do laundry each night. It was all like clockwork but I was content. The news and weather stations were different in different areas of the country as it did not take long to get acquainted with. Things are different everywhere you travel.

The condo was a five star. I repeat a five star hotel condo! Entertainment centers, two each, a glass shower, a sauna and whirlpool, two baths, a complete kitchen to include stove, counter oven, dishwasher, refrigerator, micro wave, top and bottom laundry washer and dryer set up and small stuff like phones, safes, housekeepers, ironing board. You know, take down your bed covers with a piece of chocolate left on the pillow. I quickly got spoiled! There were things I am sure I forgot;

Tuesday would be a double header for us at Surprise complex. We were up bright and early, the quick fix breakfast toast, coffee etc and then meeting out in the parking lot ready for the convoy to head on out so we could stretch, throw the ball listen for the lineup and positions and prepare mentally for the next team challenge. I got some more pitching and we were really gelling now. We split games today but played hard and effective. I have been on a serious roll as I have been really hitting the ball well.

After the game, we are in the whirlpool back at Legacy Golf Resort. Everyone having a beer relaxing in the hot tub because Joe our catcher is also a chef and he is putting together a big Italian feast! Oh, I forgot to mention, I am Portuguese and the remainder of the team is Italian! I fit in just fine and with these guys for sure win or lose you always eat well. There's meatballs, lasagna, noodles, garlic bread deserts, pizza and it was all made in the condo! Unbelievable feast! This happened three times during the week.

Wednesday we are at Goodyear baseball complex for one game and we had a long close game with lots of action, we are playing well but lost by a thread. We had fun and now we know that tomorrow's game is real important. We have a double header at Red Mountain Complex. We are playing according to the records the two best teams in the tournament. So we have a challenge before us. I got the nod as I would be starting the game pitching. Today is my day. I pitched all 9 innings and shut them down. I won the game in fashion as no one reached third base. I had a bunch of strikeouts and I was just unhitable. I also collected a few hits at the plate and just a magnificent outing.

We had an hour break and then as the field were cleared and relined the next team came into the other dugout and I felt so good that, I started pitching the second game as well. I pitched 7 more innings, a few more hits; I shut this team down too. I then took a break and my friend Drew came in closed out the game.

While being on the bench for the last two innings was nerve ending; Drew pitched well but the other team just wanted to see another arm. Drew shut them down for the 7th and half of the 8th.Then they got a few hits and Rob our 3rd baseman made a great play to end the inning. Very nerve racking for me watching. Drew went out to close the game in the 9th inning. Then there's a ground ball, out number one. Then there were a couple of hits and a few runs now we have the winning run on first base. Drew got another strikeout and now we just need one run but we do have men on first and second base. The next batter hits a line drive through the hole up the middle and the ball went through the legs of the center fielder and right then and there I thought we would lose the game. Mike in center field ran after the ball and fired the ball to our short stop Ray Voorhees as he was in the correct position behind second base and fired a perfect throw to home plate as Joe Glorioso the catcher held on to tag the man out in a dust festival at home plate holding onto the ball as he raised the ball high to show the umpire and that was strike three, game over we won the game as that was my second win of the day. I collected two wins for the day after pitching 16 innings of shut out baseball with no walks and 9 k; s Great day for me to remember.

I guess during the lunch break having that Blue Bunny Ice Cream sandwich did the trick! It was great the biggest ice cream sandwich I ever had. They don't sell them in Boston like that. This was a great way for me to end the series; my team the Long Island Braves was able to get into the layoffs for the next days agenda. The problem I had was miscommunication with team schedule, and airfare.

That evening we were flying high as we had won a double header and important double header. My team voted me as team MVP and we went to our regular place "Gallagher's" and the dinner was a treat for me as our manager Fred Schwartz made a speech about my contributions to the team and tournament, as that was truly special.

Unfortunately, I was unable to change flight so I had to leave the next morning. I was very sad I had to leave my team as my other teammate and pitcher Rob had to leave as well. This left our team with 10 players! I was gone but they won the first game, and lost the second game by one run. If Rob and I were there I am sure we would have won. Keep in mind when Rob and I were there we had 12 players total; Almost every team that was in this tournament had 18 to 25 players on their teams for this competition. I thought that was unfair.

This was the over 55+ division of this World Series tournament; our team had 8 players over the age of 60 + years old. I think the oldest team. Many teams had all of their players between 55 and 60 years old. Knowing this statistic, we were the best defensively, strong with runs against, and a powerful hitting and pitching club so we have much to be proud of.

I was flying pretty high with my contributions and to think I could still play effective baseball after all these years was rewarding. In the world series according to scorebook.com My batting average was .571 with a .786 on base percentage, I pitched a total of 26.3 innings with 8 k;s and 7 walks with an era of 3.04 I had 2 wins and 1 loss and I played well defensively.

I barely made my flight in the morning back to Boston but I swore that next year, I would repeat and not have a flight problem. I will not lose site nor ever forget the chemistry I shared with this team as we played hard and played well and everyone seemed to be in step at all times. We also had the best defensive team in the tournament which is a real high praise. In all eight games played there were absolutely no errors at all from our team. That was an incredible feat!

Chapter Forty Two

OTB Banquet and Awards

This is an annual banquet, our Over Thirty Baseball league sponsors for all players and families connected to the league. There are many leagues around the Boston area but this one is by far the best of all because of their organizational activities and what they do for the community as well. Besides providing a baseball season, and play off schedule, in addition ,they offer a hitting contest as a charity for University of Massachusetts, a Golf Outing for another charity, an All-star game between the National and American league and their donations for many non-profit community needs like, ALS, Cancer and other good Samaritan areas.

The hall called lensies in Dracut; Ma is the site as it's a huge hall. There are normally large round tables which hold 10 people and each team has two tables so there is close to 400 people that come to this event and also our dear umpires with their families as well.

They acknowledge the loss of family members, families in need, a dedication to our Veterans within our league and the praise for the volunteers and management of the league in which keeps it afloat.

The presentations for manager's awards, MVP and team awards for championship are awarded which takes some time and it was a sit down five course dinner followed by dancing and pictures. Sometimes potential draft talk for the next season is in conversation as well as sharing a baseball friendship with teammates and other teams for this night is not for competition like on the field but for camaraderie and sharing this special time together.

I knew I would be presented with the MVP award from the all-star game and my first place award for the hitting contest at the minor league stadium in September but then more surprises were ahead for me. I was accompanied by my wife as she expects me to win everything all the time. I keep telling her that there is a lot of competition here and I am getting old! We'll, before I could say more it was announced that I was the teams MVP, White Sox and also the White Sox manager's award. As shortly after as they were taking pictures I had 4 trophies that I could hardly hold to pose for a photo! So that was very cool. I guess its sweeter when you don't expect it as part of me felt that, I guess this makes up for the times when I thought I was deserving and came up short.

When I had time to myself to reflect on my year and the awards, I felt that good things come back to you. Reason being, there were at least three other occasions when I really felt I deserved the MVP and did not receive one as this evening filled in a missing previous disappointment.

That finally I would be a winner among the other winners, Maybe they will look at me a little different when I am on the mound or at bat spring 2010.

Chapter Forty Three

Wicked Cool Year

I have much to be thankful for as number one, I had my health and family and so many positive memorable things to look back on and place in my special memory area of my heart for 2009. Besides my personal life with my wife Elizabeth, our home is in tack after a tough winter, ice storms and my heart alert back in January. I had my West Palm Beach baseball experience and Beth had her horseback riding with Bravo and the other horses she so much enjoyed. Then of course my winning battle with the town to have my pigeon hobby at my home. We shared birthdays and the start of my baseball league in Lowell as well as the night baseball league. Beth went on a twenty mile trail ride in New Hampshire and I gathered more friends from New Hampshire and tournament request.

Our 25th anniversary at the Friesian Horse farms in Towsend, Vermont another memorable experience and then of course my special baseball season that I well enjoyed. My radio interview was another accomplishment that opened many doors to friendship for me as well as the excitement there. Then there was the hitting contest at LeLacheur Stadium, the all-star game and playoffs. I then had a wonderful experience in Phoenix as I enjoyed my special friends from Long Island New York my teammates, so as a whole I had a great year.

Thinking all was over was difficult for me to accept until I saw an add about playing baseball in Boston called the Winter Baseball Freeze,(Toys for Tots charity) at Boston English High School and get this, on my birthday December 5,2009 .Now tell me, is this not a great way to close out the 2009 season or what! We met in Boston and entry fee was to give a gift for the charity and play baseball all day no matter what the weather would be. If it rained or snowed, nothing would be cancelled as this was a special event that must go on no matter what.

I showed up early as I always do. Today December 5th my birthday is already special but now there are thirty players on each team, the temperature is 36 degrees windy and cold as the weather report says snow and rain on its way mid day today. I swear it always snows on my birthday. We'll because today was my birthday a few players I met in an earlier tournament arranged so I could start off the game pitching to open the game. The mound was mud, cold and a catcher that did not know me and I had a good inning as I had one strikeout, no walks, one hitter and no runs scored. I was thrilled. I had one at bat and had a long at bat and (drew a walk) so not a bad day considering the weather situation.

While I was driving home I felt sad as my year was over, I was older and no more baseball for me. Most people do not even want to discuss baseball on the phone, on the internet or websites either. Its Christmas season and family matters are now the main concern. I can still look and plan on tournaments secretly and draw up a 2010 year to guide me ahead. It's like packing your bag for a tournament but a full scale plan for the year.

I was glad to see the New Year come, but as I wanted to move on to a fresh new year. I did not like the news reporters re-living the sad news and depressing news from our losses of people around the country nor our losses in combat from our Military. I do not wish to discuss politics in my writing at all; I will say this, I am a Patriot and a loyal American with Republican views and presently do not support our present administration.

I have a new positive feeling now as Scott Brown our newly elected Senator has just broken every barrier existing here in Massachusetts by beating the Democrats; He is truly a patriot, and honorable man and don't you know, he has served 30 years as a Lieutenant Colonel in the Military as an Army Reservists Paratrooper. He is truly, a breath of fresh air to our nation.

My wife had given me a series of lessons as she did the year before at Connector batting cage for pitching and hitting. I just love to hit and my pitching is my energy as well. I have Adam McCusker as my batting coach; he is currently a High School Coach and works with University of Massachusetts College players as well. Then, I have Jon Cahill as my Pitching coach. Jon is also a heavy duty instructor and was a top pick for the Anaheim Angels MLB system. So I am in good hands once again. I have 5 ½ hour pitching and 5 ½ hour hitting lessons as they are real valuable to me. I have been just constantly improving and my confidence is sky high. I look forward to the 2010 baseball as I am in rare form. I did have a negative emotional setback just for a few minutes. They used the radar gun on me and I averaged 62 to 65 mph on my fast ball and 49 mph on my change up. I was expecting somewhere in the 70's but I may have slowed a step or just had imagination within myself; Jon and Adam shook hands with me after my final lesson as I walked away feeling very confident.

Our teams are starting to gear up now for team practices and especially when you grab a break from a week of warmer weather like a January thaw you immediately get excited and want to train as I do. I am just in the mode of baseball 24/7 so I don't need a January thaw to excite me. I pretty much have my season carved out and formatted to suit me for the year. I just need to carefully plan my pitching as far as innings go so I will not have injury or over use and tire. Sometimes it's hard to say no but I have to be firm as this is my body and arm and if I break down with injury I am sure others will not be sad or feel the effects that will bother me. I am ready and physically capable of providing my best baseball ever!

Chapter Forty Four

Mid Winter Blues

I have been here before and most winters I repeat these emotions. I have been going to the batting cage and my personal training at the athletic club and just this week I completed all my lessons with pitching and hitting techniques and now I feel mechanic wise ,I am on top of my baseball world. Some of my league teams are getting together and some people struggle with their families and job situation that many are not sure if they will be playing this season or not so team training together is on hold. It's hard for me to not train with my guys as we developed our chemistry and I hope they all come back again this season.

I get asked to train with other teams often but more than just baseball friends they have spy motives in their request for my company. I compete against their teams all summer and most of the time I am winning the higher percentile of the games so they want to see me more on the mound which is for their benefit and not mine. I hate to say no but after all of my training and off course my great year, I think I'll just surprise them during the season. They really do not want to see me pitch now.

They all want to face me at the batting cage to se if I lost a step but I usually tell them, hey, I have a new pitch. Then, I say to them, listen to your catcher. Their catcher caught for me for five years Brian Cole and he would hear these guys come to the plate from other teams while he caught for me and their attitudes were, over confident saying I am glad he is pitching today (meaning me) and then they would get aggressive and have nerve enough to crowd my plate and I would brush them back, have them chasing ,then a slider or change up and now the cocky guy that could not wait to face me is now –is throwing his helmet and bat against the fence and swearing at anyone who will listen. I love it! I struck him out!

I do think I have the upper hand when I pitch and I am the guy on the mound representing my team. The fact is, I am supposed to be defeated, and I am looked at as the old guy that throws slower. They do know I have been a leader in the league for ten years with few walks, terrific control with passion and a lot of heart with a variety of pitches. I am respected but again I am supposed to be defeated by them. If they beat me, I will feel sad and try harder next time but its worse for them because they are younger and get fewer opportunities to face me in the future.

I definitely make them pay as often as I can and I give them my all. When they approach my home plate, I can see their demeanor and the look on their faces. I know it's me against them. They, in many cases have lost the battle with me before and I do remember whether they hit me or if I struck them out. I have to work harder each season because I have been in this league for 10 years now and it gets harder each year facing these guys in their 30's and 40's as they are use to me on the mound and at the plate. Therefore I have to work harder and be smarter to beat them again.

My friend now residing in Arlington, Texas-Herby Jones, has sent me a baseball video. It has music playing (John Fogerty's, "put me in coach") the video is about little league baseball with a young boy that has trouble hitting, throwing and fielding. As the music moves forward he grows older, with different uniforms and now his skills have improved as he is fielding the balls in every position, throwing lasers to home plate and hitting homeruns. It's an amazing video as it brings you back in time and gets those emotions within your heart pumping. It's the type of video that you want to view over and over.

I think of how I progressed in baseball and part of me has so many regrets for not playing the game I love for so many years but there again it was not my fault just fate but fate also brought me back .This time around ,I have a new appreciation for baseball. I am a great student with coaches and managers and teammates that have been around the block. I take a little information from each person and decide, does this make sense for John DeCosta? So, I evaluate all mechanical issues and see what fits and I have been fortunate to not only be confident but become dominant with my playing baseball.

The word is always out that I am available to practice, train, play extra games or go to a tournament. With that information available I do gather more opportunities to play baseball. I still have another week when my team will gather for our first training session and my last pitching and hitting session tomorrow. I will then be ready for sure for the season.

Teams and leagues from all over are carefully recruiting and designing their clubs. It is amateur but they take it serious just as the big dogs, in the "bigs". I continue to be asked to play in more leagues as three teams is enough for me! More than that and I am asking for trouble. I am continuing my lessons with Jon Cahill and Adam McCusker so that is fun and the one on one teaching you can't go wrong. This is absolutely great for me or anyone. My team is currently holding practice but some show up and many do not. I can't expect every player to be hungry like myself so I need to gear towards my own training and formulate a regular schedule.

The team batting cage sessions, are not as effective, as my own training. The only benefit I get out of it, is to be able to pitch harder than usual and see what works. Taking turns batting and pitching is not the same as my own training but its camaraderie if you look at it that way.

Friday rolls around and I thought! hey why don't I go to the athletic center and grab a racquetball court and do some throwing and hitting! Great idea, so I loaded up my back pack with soft baseballs, some whiffle balls, and batting Tee and some blue tape and off I go. I always get excited just like going to a game!

I have talked before about my "racquetball court training" you know, I put a single dot on the wall and focus on hitting the spot to warm up, then I have two spots with 18 " distance between spots and then left and then right! And then my strike zone, as I throw series of pitches! We'll when I arrived there were two guys finishing up playing racquet ball! While I was waiting, I stretched, gathered my thoughts and patiently waited till it was my turn to have the court! I started organizing my baseball equipment, placing the blue tape on the walls as I usually do and all of a sudden two guys enter the court and saw my balls and bats etc and went nuts! Hey this is a racquetball court, I said "really" Then they said you can't play baseball in here; I said do you have reservations? They said nothing. I said, I waited, it's my turn to have this court so "see ya "They went to complain about me but I already had permission and support from the club. This was mental disappointment as I had to readjust my mental training because of the potential upset! I quickly got into my training mood and continued.

I threw 165 balls just as usual and then I did one hand hitting drills, first the left arm and then the right arm and then full swing off the Tee as I hit about 50 balls. Then, I attack the nautilus machines. I felt good after that. It's all in the preparation! I am reading about Lou Brissie, The Corporal was a Pitcher, World War Two a Veteran who had been challenged by numerous wounds from combat nearly losing his leg as Connie Mack had believed in his capabilities even during his very tough dilemma. Its amazing the courage that many ball players have but I am not sure if that exist any longer in today's baseball.

It's that time again to organize bats and all of your baseball equipment, get uniforms ready, oil the gloves, and check the laces, spike and laces do your real maintenance. Many try to beat the rush when the sporting good stores stock up. The prices are not so great for new models but last years closed out items the good deals prevail. I have the American flag a small 2"x3" patch on the back of all my uniforms. My signature I guess you could say as there are few Military Veterans in my league.

Chapter Forty Five

Spring Baseball

The stage is set, yet another time for spring training for me. In just a few weeks I'll be attending play at the Plate Tournament in Jupiter, Florida. This is next to West Palm Beach at Roger Dean Stadium, the home of Florida Marlins and shared as well by another major league team Cardinals for the entire baseball complex. This is very exciting, to be here once again. The players will stay at Embassy Suites Hotel not far from the complex and share car rentals to travel to and from its complex. Its very exciting to be part of this, as the count down becomes very alive in your mind just thinking about spring baseball.

Like the other tournaments this is special once again. Your regular league opening days and season are special but a tournament is quite different as I will explain. You have heard from me my passion for baseball. In regular leagues around the country as there are many leagues in amateur baseball these days. We'll on an average team you have about 15 players in most leagues on an average team. These fifteen players you have absolutely 3 players that live and die baseball as little baseballs flow through the bloodstream. Then there are another 7 players that are good solid fundamental athletes. They have families and responsibilities but also have other avenues of interest as well. Then you have about 5 players that only come to play baseball so they can go to the water cooler on Monday to say "hey, I played baseball yesterday" That about sums that up!

In these tournaments you will see an incredible amount of teams that range on an average of 15 to 20 guys on a team and they have each and every player in the abnormal category I mentioned in the regular leagues. Yes, at the tournaments you will play double headers each day and in between games they devour their lunch and immediately hit the cages to get more swings at bat, hit off a Tee or do some fielding to stay loose. It's incredible and invigorating as most all of them are in the same mental zone as you are. I try to explain this when I return home to my Sunday leagues baseball friends but they have no comprehension to what I am saying. Every player in these tournaments lives and dies baseball. They could sure give the MLB a crash lesson on loyalty, dedication the purist of baseball attitudes and there's no money here. We all pay our way! For our love of the game.

These baseball acquaintances I speak of come from all nationalities, all parts of the country and all career fields. There're Doctors, Lawyers, Police, retired Military, Nurses, trades people or from all walks of life not to mention a few professional baseball players as well. Then the disabilities are another area to be concerned about. Much heart disease, transplants, cancer, recovery of all sorts of ailments, artificial limbs, loss of fingers, you name it and they are still taking their hacks and playing the game they love.

As I said, weeks to go and think about reservations for the hotel, airfare, tournament registration and the fun thing to do, think about what to pack for your stay and very importantly you particular baseball bats and equipment. Picking out the necessary bats to play in the tournament is an act of its own. No matter how many times I separate the bats, it's always a tough decision to leave a favorite behind! I guess I think they have feelings, ha and then there is the luck issue where some bats feel like the lucky bat! You know like in the Natural! Played by Robert Redford; I usually bring about 4 bats with me and I take turns with them depending on which ones provide the most hits! Yes, one more time the luck thing again.

I still raise pigeons and many times it is relaxing being involved with the birds and the training. Unfortunately because of how the hunting laws are now I am at a disadvantage with the prey that hurt the pigeon's sport .I should say prey kill the pigeons. I try to train them but have great difficulty with the massive amount of endangered hawks there are in the country area in which I live in. I let the birds out today and the hawks criss crossed through the yard and by the coop and killing 7 birds in a matter of a few minutes. I spent all of that time raising these birds and banding them and carefully taking great care of them and producing magnificent "athletes in the sky" so to speak and as fast as I organize these birds I am starting over. I guess I will not fly any for a long time now. I lost about 25 birds in the last few months! I'll continue but at a snail pace and carefully for now on.

The birds are a fun hobby and there are numerous fanciers around the country but that can stay in the back yard and I can focus on baseball like always. My slow packing has begun and finalizing my 2010 season is also carefully plotted too. At present I am on my White Sox Team in the over thirty baseball league in Lowell, Ma- and also on the Night over thirty baseball's D-Ray night league team. I have also linked up with Robert (Bob) Major (Manager of the Acton orioles) this is an over 40 baseball league and a competitive league as well. I played for this team for five years from 1995 thru 1999. I had a great time with this team and many memorable games. I left to try other teams and other leagues for more baseball. I went to a practice last week to feel things out and received a very warm reception from my old teammates.

Many of the players, had said to me, John, what happened to your muscles you once had? I said, I guess I got older! I was surprised but in some ways not surprised as my workouts now am much different than before because I am training for agility, being flexible, and mechanics. We are in the mix for much rain this late winter and early spring so it won't be long now before baseball begins.

I talked about some of those memories as in The Eastside Kid, original story. Bob Major is my manager here and a very good coach. Its amazing how he finds such a large group and keeps them all organized. I guess many years of managing will allow you to be successful like that. We have had our practices at a high speed place called Athletes Edge. They, the owners have special interest with up and coming baseball teams, the young guys and they also teach other sports as well. The technology they have in this batting facility is much different than I have seen in the past at other places.

This fits my schedule just great as I go here on Monday evening, my lessons on Wednesday and workout on my own Fridays and then I am ready for my over 30 team on Sundays.

My lesson program continues as its winding down now with only two lessons left! Adam McCusker, John Chill, and Mike Fahey continue to teach and give me pointers. They like my enthusiasm and how I am hungry to learn. I am a great student as I copy notes and practice what I learned as I am having so much fun playing baseball. Even this off season is fun especially with the one on one, training. When you go with a team to a batting cage is great to have the camaraderie and joke around but less real time training, unlike my training.

I have learned so many training techniques with batting and pitching that again when I am by myself I can self coach myself and improve constantly. People seem to just know that I am about baseball. My wife treated me to a spa day as I got the works, deep tissue massage, facial, pedicure and haircut to top things off. I felt pretty weak after that. The girls at the spa enjoy talking baseball as well, so I share with them all that's going on. The spa day surely gets you back ready for more baseball.

I am pleased to share that I have one more pitching/batting lesson lined up for Wed. I'll concentrate on my finer capabilities with my mechanics in pitching and for batting I will do bunting-sacrifice, drag bunting and bunt for a hit. That could help my batting average, I am sure!

Here it is 27 March 2010, just another day in New England with spring half way around the corner. The sun was in and out today as we played our first spring pre-season game today at Lawrence High School. It was fun and there were a few cold fans peeking through the blankets, as the temperature just doesn't want to go over 40 degrees. It is early baseball and you wonder when will spring ever get here?

Our game went pretty well today as we won 7-5 after 9 innings. This was a great outing for me .We pitchers had divided our duties. I started off pitching the first two innings and had 4 strikeouts and gave up two hits and two ground ball outs. So not bad for my first time on the mound. I got a long double, a walk and yes I hate to say this but struck out twice! Hold it! The catcher was making the calls so I was not happy about that. All and all, not a bad day. I played one more pre-season game before West Palm Beach Tournament as that was just a glorified practice for me but non the less more baseball.

The alarm goes off at 2; 30 am Wed morning and the limo will pick me up at 4; 00 am. I am quite excited as I go feed the pigeons I have in my coops and feed the dogs, final packing quick little breakfast, left my wife a note as she is working in Boston. I set the alarm, and wait patiently in front of the garage as I see the limo come around the corner with lights beaming through the darkness at "O Dark Thirty" as they say in the military. My little carry on, baseball bat bag filled with equipment and clothes and shaving gear. I kept a uniform spikes, and glove in my carry on bag just in case luggage is lost, then I can still play baseball if the worse happens. Running through security, a short wait and off I go on Jet Blue heading for West Palm Beach (direct flight).

The weather was nice and warm when I arrived and in fact was 80 to 85 degree's all week and absolutely great baseball weather. I quickly got a cab and not happy about paying $40.00 for a cab to the hotel but paid him anyway. When I arrived I got checked in, went to my room and prepared my small back pack to go to the stadium to have a planned batting practice and meet other baseball acquaintances.

They were all hitting balls from a pitching machine on one of the practice fields in the complex. I fielded some balls and took my turn at bat and hit my routine line drives and I felt real good hitting. This off course was my first time hitting off a pitching machine as opposed to the live pitching I was use to, but it was practice under the sun on a MLB baseball field so that was super. I looked around, took a deep breather as I was truly thankful for being alive and able to play baseball. Every day is a positive day in my life especially being 63 years old. Most of my team had not arrived as of yet just four of us as they arrived from the airport at all different times today. I only know half of the team from our Phoenix tournament as the others are new players, also from the New York area.

We have a pretty decent team here. I just think that if we play hard, play smart and play together we will be ok. Having fun and everything else should fall in place for us. After practice we went back to the hotel where we had "happy hour" and beer and munches provided along with many of the ballplayers that arrived late for the tournament. We received our schedule, do's and don'ts of the stadium complex and our team decided who was going to pitch and set the format for the rotation for our team.

I got the nod to start the first game Monday 9; 00 am. ! I was ready and pitched very well. I was throwing faster and harder than ever in my life and I loved it. No one could touch me at all. I pitched 4 innings of shut out ball and one of our relievers came into the game. I pitched 6 innings the next day with same results as I was on! My bat was not as I liked during this tournament as I was either hitting directly to positions for an out or the rookie umpires had called way outside pitches and took my bat away. I won two games and pitched as I said m best ever. It was fun to be so dominant. Then of course I was facing complete strangers and no one had seen me pitch before as back home in Massachusetts league baseball everyone has seen me before. So this was a treat!

We split every double header as we always seemed to be a morning team. We won all of our games in the morning and in the afternoon just didn't have it. We were all thankful for being there and able to play baseball so that was surely a plus. The second game that I pitched 6 innings and came out well, when I was scoring I slid into home plate and got spiked by the catcher a big guy. Then a week after the tournament, my toe was infected from being spiked. We shared MLB locker rooms, nice carpet and your name on lockers with a little chair and all the services as MLB players receive. We played double headers each day so in the middle of the day we had roast beef sandwiches, turkey, or peanut butter and jelly and water and soft drink that hit the spot then if we had time we would go to the vacant field and turn the machine on and hit some baseballs till the second game started.

After the second game as we returned back to the locker room there would be ice chest with cans and bottles of beer on ice. That was a great perk! The weather was like 85 degrees every day so the beer at the end of the day was super! The last day Sunday my arm was dragging and lots of aching in my bicep and shoulder. Surely a feeling I had not felt since before my shoulder surgery. We were not contenders in the tournament at this time so we played our final game as a consolation game, but it felt like a sandlot game, as I thought. Everyone was thinking about the wear and tear all week and catching a ride to the airport after the game.

I came into this game late and did my usual thing Struck out two and was in command but my arm was killing me and this has never happened before. I took myself out as I could not continue at all. It was a smart decision but a little late. Now that I was relaxed and making all sorts of plays the tournament was over. We raced to the showers to a final pack, shook hands and off to the airport! So now another tournament, completed for me. My arm was killing me and swollen and black and blue from my elbow to the top of my shoulder. My arm was so big that I looked like a body builder. I was in pain so that was not good.

I went to the doctor for my infected toe from being spiked and also had x-rays taken of my arm and shoulder as I had shoulder surgery 2 years before so I wanted every base covered and make sure I was ok. It's better to be safe than sorry. I had to cancel playing in my Boston league because there was no way I could continue with pitching on Sundays and then again on Mondays. So less baseball but more effective baseball providing I heal up. I am anxious to demonstrate my new pitching abilities at home in my over 30 league.

Complications for my toe being infected and swelling of my arm gone down some but opening day is this weekend and I will not be able to play completely. I may be DH Designated Hitter but no field, no running bases and absolutely no pitching. Wow, that will kill me! My Doctor for my shoulder had performed surgery on my shoulder about two years ago and now I have another appointment in which I am nervous but I want to get on with baseball and not lose any time if possible!

Great news from the doctor as no new damage since surgery two years ago! I am so happy now I can't explain. My toe is getting better but I am still on the mend. I had a great series pitching in Florida and now I am on hold at the beginning of the season. My arm is back to normal and my confidence sky high so I can't wait to show my new mechanics in the league play hopefully very soon. My team wanted to keep me on the shelf to be careful and to make sure I save my best for later in the season.

My team, the White Sox are in trouble right now. There are three brothers on my team. Mike, Chris and Steve McNally. They are such great ballplayer ,I can't explain. It feels good having them behind me on the field. We'll Steven the youngest McNally had brain surgery and it's complicated so his loss this season is devastating. Steve was an unbelievable short stop so his loss is tremendous especially the great person he is. Then Mike Walker our traveling super star wanted to try another league in Boston so he will only make a few games this season for us and with my temporary set back we are not having the season start we all wanted.

I had a severe mental scare with my arm as I thought maybe the doctor would talk about more surgery so with a green light I feel my confidence once again. I immediately cancelled my application and roster spot on the Boston league because I had not known the exact possible damage I had and not sure if I took on to much baseball. I am still in two leagues but three is another story. There is a possibility of a short tournament in September for the Ray Lammie Classic a friend of mine who died last year of cancer. That will be in September at a Long Island facility. That will be a real nice refresher before the World Series in Phoenix Fall 2010.

My 2010 regular season has started and wishes I had more time to recover. The infection from being spiked in my left toe has really disabled me with batting and pitching mechanics. I played the first game as a DH and the second game playing a few different positions and I actually pitched but absolutely nothing to advertise as I was so off! I got beat up and during the process I got smoked the first inning as placement of my left foot threw my mechanics way off! I gave a up a home run to what was a friend from the opposing team and when he rounded third base I shook his hand and my teammates did not like that at all! I felt he beat me, and that was good sportsmanship ,to do that. Maybe another time I will strike him out.

My slow beginning is besides a short rehab and psychological bearing on baseball, I am sure this will all turned around soon for me. I am starting to recognize that these baseball leagues at amateur level that are everywhere are not what I envision baseball to be. I have teammates that think totally different than I do. They come two minutes before game time, no stretch and ready to play. None of them want practice and when you ask them about off season training you would swear that I insulted their family or something.

When I go away to tournament play in many areas of the country I find so many ball players that are just like me Meaning, they eat, drink, and breathe baseball. They can't get enough practice and between ball games they are always willing to practice, play pepper, or hit in the available cages. Just what baseball is supposed to be like? I am thinking about next season and I think I will do this; I will play in the over 30 night league as its very relaxed and basically just extra at bats and get some pitching in as it's a glorified practice with uniforms.

Then I thought I would maybe go away and play in three baseball tournaments or more where people really care about playing baseball and the heck with the local leagues altogether. That will be my new plan, or dream! I am not sure what life has for me in the future, who knows.

I approached my third game with a relaxed attitude. My injuries were finally healed and although my confidence was a little under par, I ran through my re-game superstitions and practice. At 6; 00 am I was at the high school field near my home as the sky started to light up. I was there before the robins! I set up orange cones between short stop and second base positions, about 30 feet apart. I then stretched ,grabbed a few wooden bats and put my ball bag near home plate with my new batting T in position in front of the plate. I took my trusty bat and took a few practice swings and then began hitting balls as best I could placing line drives between the cones. I think out of 55 balls in my bag I hit 52 between the cones, so all in all a great little pre-game work out!

I then packed up and headed to the ball field in Westford, ma where the game will be. I first stopped at the basketball court and shot hoops for twenty minutes to warm up, relax and get into my comfort zone. Then, I still had time as our game starts at 8; 30 am but of course I am the first one there and early! I then grabbed my ball bag and went to softball field behind our baseball field to gather some privacy.

I began to throw balls at an easy pace to warm up. I had no idea that I would pitch at all because after my last horrible outing, I just did not expect it. I continued to finish throwing the remainder of the balls as that would be sufficient for a quick warm up and later if I got the word I would not have to rush. As I finished then other players started to come as I joined my team. I then got the word I would start the game.

My first pitch was a strike as that was a great indicator for me about how my day would go. I only had three strikeouts, one walk for five innings as I only gave up 4 hits as I picked up the win as my team had smoked the Cardinals 11-2. So my confidence had increased immediately in pitching. My bat was silent and nothing to brag about but that will come around soon, I hope. Next week we are playing the League Champs from last season and we usually have a rough time with this team and guess who is starting again next Sunday against the Twins, yep me on the mound!

Early preparation and training during the week has started and also checking the internet to check out the team from their past few games. I know they are a good team and a bit cocky so we shall see how I will do on Sunday. I look forward to the challenge and I hope I am victorious. The Long Island Braves, my traveling team has started communication for our yearly world series tournament in Phoenix, Arizona come fall 2010. That is a good baseball time for me to look forward to and work hard so I will be efficient there as well.

Sunday baseball continued as I kept marching on! I got the nod to start the game as, yes I was there at O Dark Thirty batting, stretching and shooting hoops. Our game was at Ferullo Field in Woburn, Ma and real nice field for once. We were playing against some arch rivals, The Twins. It happen to be the first team I played for in this league 10 years ago! How time flies. There were many great teammates there but also a lot of new players as well.

My first game in the league I played for the Twins. Yes, my very first game as I went 3 for 3 at bat and after beating out a bunt I had a heart attack on the field. I was hospitalized and did my rehab and fought to come back but things were different. The scare for the players was too much for them and also much for me. I still have my Twins shirt that the Doctor at the hospital had cut with scissors. Then a team from no-where, The Braves had signed a ball for me and the manager brought it to my house as a gift! I was touched.

My teammates were not so thoughtful and ignored me. I have been on many teams since then and always had a battle pitching and playing against them. On my resent team, The White Sox, we'll my white sox team has not beaten them since 2003! Today I said to myself, I am going to win this game; I went out to the mound and had the usual hecklers and I pitched like crazy. I hit my spots, threw exceptionally hard and went 7 innings allowing only 3 hits, I struck out 3 and 1 walk. I collected a valiant effort and won the game. That was very sweet.

One of my friends, Joe Girard from the 82nd airborne, came to watch my game and he enjoyed watching a game, which a fellow paratrooper (me) played in. I fortunately had a great game for him to witness. Between innings you had to see this; Joe had gone around and picked up trash that other people neglected to put in trash cans. It was more of a sample of the "baby boomers in action and making the difference in our current society. That was refreshing to see. We met for coffee after the game and besides talking about the game we caught up on Military retirement issues, the state of our country and upcoming events. All and all nice to have someone you know come to watch you play the game you love.

The next game, having no visitors but there were familiar friends on the opposing team. We were losing the game but caught up quickly with two outs, last of the ninth, two men on base I hit a long line drove to toe up the game and another teammate captured another hit as our rally continued and we went ahead in the game. Now it was up to me to close the game. I went out and produced a ground out and then shut them down with two k;s and we won the game as I collected a save.

Memorial Day weekend there were no games at all; so more rest but I was itchy to play. I continued my personal workouts and training as usual. I did however meet with Jimmy Lyons and Frank Kavolaskas for our usual hitting buckets of balls at the high school usually on Friday evenings. On a lazy holiday Sunday as I was waiting for my friend Jimmy to come to workout My wife's Grandson, Cole 8 years old came to the field with his Dad as I helped him with batting techniques as that was fun to help him and the feeling of helping a youngster improve his mechanics. Beyond that, I would find time of my own to train as well.

With my new fantastic batting "T", I would find a field no one was using and put cones as markers on the infield between short stop position and 2nd bas position and hit a bucket of balls a few times a week as my goal was to hit the balls off the T between the cones right up the middle of the field. This was great as I could get so much effective contact hitting and did not have to beg people to come to practice. Sometimes I would find a secluded ball field and have incredible privacy and very effective practice time.

The next Sunday had weather problems again! My usual time getting up is usually about 4;30 am on Sunday mornings as I shower, have a quick breakfast, feed the dogs and head to the high school ball field and get some swings off the T before the game. I am on the field at 6;00 am and train for a half hour then head to the game field and do more stretching and prepare for the game in a more serious manner.

At today's game rain was heading out way but before game time things were ok. We were home team and I had the start. There was a young ballplayer from the opposing team who passed away that week so tough for the other team to play without their friend. Prior to the game there was a moment of silence and a prayer for him.

I took the mound as its was muddy and conditions continually got worse; I got the first two outs quickly then of course a few ground ball errors then a score, unearned run. We came back and tied it up and I continued to pitch well as I struck out 3, no walks and allowed one hit. Then I after the lead off guy got on base in the 4th inning, I hit a nice line drive hit between short and third. Then a hit batter now bases loaded and on the verge of a real strong rally-the rain worsened and the umpires called the game. Just one more inning and we would have had the game count but now it's re-scheduled for late in the season.

My night league is moving right a long and I am doing well there. I closed out our first game in fashion as I was very strong with command. I have been strong everywhere I have pitched this year. I feel very confident and it doesn't matter who I pitch to my confidence is there.

This is a new season as we meet them for the first time. My team is the D-Rays and they are the Diamondbacks. We continued to once again beat this good team and I closed the game out pitching the last three innings with no walks, 4 strike outs and a shut out so it was sweet! This was one more fun night game to lock into my memory bank. Mike McNally gave me a game ball for pitching so well. I was throwing very hard and that felt great!

After my over 30 league and night league are over I will once again for the third year straight defend my batting excellence in the homerun/hitting contest. I will again be in the over 48 division and its not that I am better than anyone else it's a matter of performing exactly when you have to in this contest. We all face the same pitching and get the same amount of baseballs to hit. One must make each hit counts. It's like clutch hitting! The field is marked off, so many points at each distance and then of course the long ball. So I am defending champion once again as they will be gunning for me.

My fall 2010 plans are basically planned right now. My Over Thirty League is over before Sept but the playoffs carry till late Sept. Then I have the Ray Lammie classic at Long Island, New York for a weekend tournament, 24 September thru 26 September; I will be staying at Ray Voorhees home along with other players to participate in this tournament. The importance of this tournament is Ray Lammie. He was my baseball friend that I went to several tournaments with as we were on the same team and our wives had been a part of things as well as we went to dinner and had a nice friendship. Ray unfortunately died this past year from cancer and so many friends will be coming to this tournament for celebrating our friendship with him and the massive donations of his cancer cause foundation as all funds will be raised in his honor so a must participate for me.

Las Vegas over 50 baseball has been thought of since the last time I played out there, which was 2003. I played 4 straight years but have not been back till now. I will go with several other players I know from my over 30 league in Lowell, ma- so going with friends I am familiar with is always special. I will go out there 24 October and play every day till 30 October then off I go to the next tournament in Phoenix, Arizona for the World Series Tournament.

The one I have been waiting for once again, is phoenix World Series over 55 + division; Our team will stay at a 5 star resort. "The Legacy Golf Resort"

This is so much fun and so much baseball as we will play anywhere from 8 games to 11 games if we continue to win! Our team is great defensively and offensive as well and we do have our arsenal of pitchers and hitters to. This is by far the best fun group baseball team ever. We have five lawyers on the team. Yes, they are spoiled and that's why we are in a five star hotel! Otherwise we would be in a shelter, tent or campsite!

Then we have a variety of players, a Nurse, Car salesman, a chef, a clown for hire, and iron worker a Judge and real estate enthusiast! Oh yea; me retired Military and passionate ball player! All personalities are different just as all teams gathered but this team is special! We all go shopping together for our suites, and lunches. Then we go to the sports bars for dinners as well as we catch the World Series games and we share other time at the spa by the pool after the game downing a few beers. No one ever complains or gets mad at each other no matter what happens as we became a team with special chemistry!

This of course is yet still two months away as I am so excited planning so early. I have all things like air, hotels, tournament fees and all things under control and planned out right now in July! Yes early but necessary. My night league team is undefeated and dong great. My Sunday league team has a longer season and we are a .500 club team. I have been pitching great this year every place I have pitched in either league but my hitting has been spotty and not consistent.

I still maintain heavy duty presence practicing, working out at the gym and preparing mentally constantly but as I have said many times there is a lot of luck in sports and if the stars are lined up we are doing well. I have been hitting like crazy in practice but sometimes things change game time but the next bat may change things around as I am hoping so anyway.

Winding down to the Ray Lammie Tournament in just a few weeks now is so pleasant as I am with a good group of people and ballplayers to honor our Friend Ray Lammie. Today is September 11, 2010. It is sad to look back and remember our 9/11 tragedy as we were all taken by surprise and devastated by our attack in New York, and Washington. The war is still strangling our country as well as the Liberals and we ask when things will be normal again. My step daughter Shelly was at the World Trade Center and deeply scarred and only she knows the pure horror of being at the scene on that day. I am sure there will be more attacks as my Military mind tells me to be vigilant and stand tall.

Despite the world situation, mood of our country and the economy hay wire by the Liberals we must live and stay strong. My baseball gives me peace of mind and restores my passion and relieves all tensions brought on by people and news. My season has been sub-John DeCosta in my mind. I am still leading the league as a pitcher and in both leagues as well. My team on Sundays the over 30 league has been a bust in my opinion as definitely not as last seasons fight. We had players missing, dropped out and the rest had no heart and my lonesome on the mound had to deal with horrible defense, poor hitting and no heart from my team.

I started to lose confidence so I took up offers to play on a Boston team in the Boston Baseball Amateur League over 40 and played three games with them. Great group of guys and played against old rivals and for me I played well. My pitching was superb as I had an oo.ooo era after 3 games; I batted .444 and played well. I also got asked to play in the Leominster, Ma over 40 leagues as I played one game and pitched a 2 hitter and had five k;s but lost 3-2 but all confidence for me. I then had a few lessons at my connector batting cage with my instructor Adam Mc McCusker for a refresher and that went extremely well as my confidence has come to normal for me.

I recently played in an all star game and yes, nothing to brag about as our American side of the diamond had a poor showing. We were losing 18-1 and it's only the 5th inning and now they call John DeCosta to come and save the game. No chance but I thought I guess this is a trick or just a work out for me. I pitched well despite the game being boring and a lost cause. I had no walks and 3 k;s and worked on pitches, control and again confidence. I collected 3 hits as I hit the ball sharply, line drives they were as I like.

I had a brake in the action as I was writing my friend Bill Lee about buying one of his special baseball bats and as I was doing that and in conversation with him he got a contract to play for an Independent professional baseball league in Brockton, ma-yes my home town area. The Brockton Rocks. I told him I would cheer him on and be there. So he was the attraction and the park filled with capacity waiting for his showing. He came in a fancy new red car around the warning track and got out with a standing ovation by home plate and went to the mound and warmed up for the game.

Bill, started his game with his historical oofis pitch that drew a lot of wonders from the crowd by the player/batter from the Tornadoes hit a line drive up the middle. He pitched a great game after that with 3 k;s, no walks and won the game 7-2 after 5 2/3 innings pitched. As it turned out Bill Lee at age 63 is historical in the fact oldest professional pitcher to win a professional game. Gee, I am 3 weeks older than him and get no praise at all lol!

I get no respect! Just joking! I get a lot of attention and it's appreciated very much. My dream would be to play for one of these professional leagues and fly over the ball park in a helicopter, parachute in and land next to the mound, rip of my jump suit and start warming up and pitch the game! That would be my dream.

My white sox team is on their last two play off games as the season is basically over and going through the motions because they are out of contention and as soon as these last two games are done with I can concentrate on my tournament games and off season baseball training and consider what to do and where to play for 2011 baseball season.

Oh, I forgot to mention; I had played a total of 10 years in over thirty baseball in Lowell, Ma-! Many of those years have been very rewarding and a life time of wonderful memories. Yes, I did bounce around the league on various teams but I felt at each time I moved it was a learning experience. I spent the most time on the Red Sox team, 4 years and developed what I would think a life time of memories. At the time I moved I felt, gee we are a .500 club every year. Each year was exactly the same and our losses were by one or two runs. I felt I needed to make a change and have a re-birth in my baseball life and hopefully build on my skills, ability and confidence. That did happen each time and as a result I played beyond my expectations! I was now having much more fun.

Our last few games in the playoffs were pretty much brutal! I personally felt my team had no heart, no drive and couldn't walk without tripping and chewing gum at the same time! What ever happens is meant to be, I think! After a disastrous loss to the last place team I could not wait to get to my car and go home. I was in no mood to shake hands and lie that we had a good season because for me it was horrible. Time to move on!

I sat quietly in my home for a week or so. I played for a Boston team, The North Shore Thunder and pitched so well with an extreme low era and I hit the cover off the ball. In the three games I had a two hitter and a three hitter on the mound and batted .480.

I then played in a game in my old league, the Townsend Astro's as they neared the end of their season. Leominster over 40 League I pitched another three hitter but lost the game 4-3 but I was happy with my performance. My next opportunity came when there was the annual fall tournament or fall classic as its advertised. My name got around as I was looking for a team then I got a phone call from the Aubushon Hardware team in the over 40 league so I jumped on this opportunity to play another three games. I did not know a sole on this team which was very difficult at my age. I told them I could pitch but many say that. I asked the coach to give me a side session and see how I will do. Sure enough when the team pitching started got in trouble was called in to pitch and opened up some eyes as we played against the tournament strong contenders and I shut them down the last three innings of the game.

The next game, same thing the started got in trouble 3rd inning and I pitched the last 4 innings and pitched very well but little too late but I now had the respect of the team. I was getting my hits, getting on base, stealing bases and scoring runs so they were pleased with me. The last game was the best game in the tournament. It was the all-star team and many of the players I had played with 12 years ago. So, like an old home week as I was able to connect with many old teammates.

I did not pitch in this game although they were foolish to not put me in this game. I could have easily made the difference. It was a close, bite the nails type of game. I played 3rd base and made a bundle of plays and won the respect from both teams on that. I was snatching up balls, made two double plays, tagged a guy out and fielder numerous balls at the hot corner. It sure felt good to be back in rare form. I again was able to steal bases, get my hits in under pressure conditions and in the extra innings we lost because the pitcher got in trouble, loaded the bases and walked in the winning run.

Very sad but I kept my team in the game. I was very happy with my performance and my teammates want me to play next season with them. That is a great reward!

Getting away from OTB in Lowell was sad because of many good friends I had made during these years but leaving "metal bats" was a great reason to leave. I mean, all of the baseball tournaments are wooden bats. Wooden bats are real baseball to me so after playing a season that was not I as, I was so disappointed in my play and the statistics. I took all of the blame and felt that all of the training I d, the lessons, the off season training etc there had to be another reason. When I played three games in Boston,4 games in Leominster and did extremely well with the wood bat at the plate and my pitching being superb, I knew instantly that my league had provided very poor defense for me and meta bats provided very un- earned hits as they would have easily been ground out or little pop ups.

I then decided to pursue my teams for 2011 season so I know how to train and prepare me for next season. I will play for a new Boston over 48 + division a few nights a week. I am also slated to play in BABL over 38+ Division. So lots of baseball and that is the basics, then play offs then tournaments so now I am relaxed, content and know how to train for my next season.

The Ray Lammie Tournament with my New York friends was cancelled so I was disappointed I could not go there but I had my fall tournament in Leominster and that was fun and no traveling at all. That was the three games I spoke of with the Aubushon Team.

To bring you back to my early portion of the Eastside Kid, second chapter as I talk about my earliest mentor in baseball. I can clearly remember being 9 years old and watching little league baseball, on Brockton's eastside Downey Little League. There was a player name Herby Jones that I admired and watched him hit homeruns from both sides of the plate. He was also a dominating pitcher too. I remember saying to myself as I peeked over the chain linked fence watching Herby at bat. I would say to myself that I hope I can play like him when I grow up! Little did I know that I did grow into a mold of him in others eyes later in my baseball career?

We'll 53 years later I would contact Herby. Keep in mind that as a child I never spoke to him ever. We'll I contacted him through classmates website and we exchanged emails and developed a relationship for over a year or so. I sent him my book, signed and also with a baseball signed by me and our relationship continued. He then sent me a Red Sox shirt. Herby came back home for a Brockton High School re-union and when he arrived he stayed with his sister in Duxbury, Mass. I called and made arrangements to meet him at a local ball field in Brockton's eastside O'Donnell's I went early, brought bats, glove balls and walked around the infield as I awaited Herby's arrival. I had numerous memories while I was waiting as many things about the park had changed in many years.

Herby drove up and called his family to let them know he arrived safely. He got out of his car and we shook hands and hugged as that was our very first meeting in person in 53 years. I said to Herby, you know Brockton has changed and maybe we should go to a better park that is safer. Brockton had changed for both of us and not as we remembered and definitely not safe.

We went to Edgars Playground that had been developed into a nice ball park and we hopped the fence and gathered the equipment and started passing the ball. That was very much fun for both of us. He hadn't thrown a ball in years and for me this was like having breakfast, so normal.

When he was already stretching and mentally preparing him, I pitched him a bucket of baseballs. He started off skittish but soon got into the groove and started hitting the line drives he was accustomed to years ago. He took a break and then pitched balls to me. I hit my usual line drives. It was a beautiful sunny day and the temperature was about 74 and perfect for us. We finished up and then went to breakfast and chatted more about baseball and also of old memories in our early lives. Truly, a momentous day for both of us.

My Tournaments out west in Las Vegas and Phoenix are coming soon! Thinking baseball as always and my workouts is a regular scenario each week for me and our guys from the traveling team are still holding practice on Sundays until we go west. The Las Vegas tournament will be my last time playing with metal bats as I am soo happy. Its fun at times but not real baseball to me. Hopefully designator hitters, astro turf and metal bats will disappear forever!

Thinking baseball ,I saw some kids playing in their front yard a few times as I thought wow that is great. Then in darkness when I was leaving real early in the morning I decided to toss some baseballs onto their lawn. Kind of like an Easter hunt or we could call this the mysterious baseball appearance. I rolled down my window and had all of the baseballs I my front seat so I threw the balls onto their front lawn from the car and sped off and went to Boston to pick up Beth from her work. I felt pretty good about my little treat of baseballs to strangers!

My wife had a nurse friend, at her work; as her 4 kids were interested in baseball, I gave them a baseball soft toss machine as I never use it anyway and gave them a bucket of balls to go with it as well. Just another way of giving to the baseball sport as it made me feel good about my deed.

I have just returned from my baseball trip from Las Vegas and Phoenix World Series so I will share with you more baseball stories from the hot sun areas of our west coast baseball! I spent my first week playing for the Lowell Millers team from the Lowell, Ma- area not far from Boston. We had all played either together or on different teams, from the same league, Lowell over 30 baseball. So we all knew each other, familiar with each others capabilities, and thought we would do pretty well out there in Las Vegas over 50 baseball tournament. We played 5 games together and won our division championship.

Most of the team had stayed at a hotel called the Plaza, in the old historic portion of Real Old -Downtown Las Vegas; our hotel was not like the new-other end of Vegas like Bellagio, Caesars Palace or Venetian but that's what they had decided on, where to stay at. The first day was always difficult getting your room, unwinding etc but we all went to the batting cage not long after getting off the long flight but we dealt with it, as we acclimatized to the change and actually had fun hitting the ball at the batting cage preparing for the game the next morning.

Our hotel was situated next to the entrance of "Freemont Street Experience? This is a must see if you are out there. There is a large metal design on the ceiling high above on the street. It was round with little holes in it. It appeared to look like an erector set type look during the day but at night as the clock chimed hour by hour the show was on ,on the ceiling. Loud acoustical sound and the ceiling came alive with birds, butterflies, imagination and a series of jets flying down the street and a historical patriotic theme had ravished your attention high above after dark when a show would start on the hour while it was dark till very late or early am.. Everything in Las Vegas is a gimmick and this was yet anther.

This street was about one half mile or so long with exciting casinos, shows, performers etc very exciting. At the intersections a stage and singers and dancers perform to the Halloween themes of music as the people were wall to wall there on Freemont Street with vendors, auto car shows, girls trying to lure you into the strip clubs and free drinks offered to get you in. There were artists, people on stilts, go go dancers to take pictures with etc. Very exciting street. The only place for real relaxing was Starbucks for a latté!

I therefore only pitched 3 innings of baseball in this tournament as I assumed the closer position with our many pitchers.. I pitched very well for two games; the first game closing out the game with two ground balls and one strikeout as I felt pretty confident with my effort.

The last game I was unstoppable as well, with the same result; then a tough play at first as I dove to touch the base with a little race between (me the pitcher)and batter heading to first base. It was so close but not worth the argument. I later struck the next batter out as we completed the game and received another save. The middle game was a problem for our whole team as the field was astro turf, but had a terrible muddy mound and we got over confident and each of us had our worse game pitching, hitting, fielding and we should have all just stayed home. My pitching was terrible as well. So we ended the tournament with a win and championship so a good finish for the Lowell team. I then headed for Phoenix World Series.

I headed to the airport saying goodbye to Las Vegas as I was on a shuttle bus making way too many stops but I was early and relaxed after a week of baseball. I flew southwest to Las Vegas but now US Airways for this leg of the plan. My plane no soon got up and we were down in Phoenix. The weather quickly had changed and now some real heat to deal with.

Yes, my baggage is safe all baseball gear here so now it's a taxi to Legacy Golf Resort. All goes smooth and wouldn't you know I am in the same identical room as when I was here for last year's tournament. I got all moved in and waited for my roommate to come as well as meet the other ballplayers. The next day we had an organized practice at Tempe Diablo Complex and Field #4 for a few hours as the rest of the team floated in. We had pretty much the same squad as last year but 3 could not come and 3 new rookies were there with pretty deep shoes to fill. We had our managers speech from Fred Schwartz, we practiced hard and now going shopping for the week and preparing for tomorrows first game.

I was the starting pitcher and I would not disappoint! We played at Surprise Complex in Surprise, Arizona as I pitched a gem! I pitched 9 innings, 117 Pitches, 44 balls, 73 strikes, hit one batter with no walks and 6 strikeouts-a 3 hitter, as we won 17-3 against the Hollywood Stars. This team had tied us in last years tournament and prior to that had beaten our team, (I was not there then). So our first game went well for the team. It went downhill after that. We lost all remaining games. I pitched again but after we had a losing effort.

In the stadium game I started the game off and pitched another 4 innings, a gem again but no hitting and massive errors led to our demise. We would not gather any concentration at all. So the tournament ended early for us and our flights homeward bound were now planned. It was a long season with yet again adding more memories and more new friends but now it's as said many times "wait until next year".

Great to be home, with my wife, and dog's; then, I will share my stories and experiences with her as well. I found her some nice Martini glasses to bring a smile to her face so now it's unpacking as the dogs liked that. If I place a bat bag or clothing bag on a bed or pool table they get instantly sad but unloading makes them quite happy. They understand and sense so much more than people know or realize.

Now, its plans for off season training, once again. This time however I will be changing all teams. I played in one league for ten years. I am having a real tough time as Its harder to fool the batters again and again after everyone of them have faced me through the years. Therefore it's not as much fun. They have metal bats in this league and refuse to change over to wood. Most all of the leagues are now wood bat but this league has hung strong and stubbornly supporting the continuance of keeping the metal bats! Maybe because their batting averages are so high! Lol For me being a pitcher, I am so tired of that dreadful laser like line drives at me on the mound and at third base. So I am moving to three other wood bat leagues come spring 2011 season.

I have been recruited for some teams and leagues and took my notes and mentally thought out what would be best for me. So, after checking on their previous accomplishments of teams I thought how, I will help these teams and how the teams will help me as well. I wish to make every effort count.

I will play for the Cardinals over 40 team in the(BABL) Boston Amateur Baseball League, then I will play on a new team in the over 48 + Division league, and up in NH I will play for the Falcon's in the over 50 baseball league there. So lots up in the air but still a lot of baseball and that's not even talking about playoffs nor tournaments to attend.

I have a strong hint to my wife about a Wilson A2000 baseball glove as a hot request for my soon to come birthday. Unfortunately I'll be 64 ears old still playing the game and still trying to play my best. I seem to always be able to plan out 75 games each season so that will keep me happy. My major thought form day to day is, yes, "another day above ground" Could be worse as I would not be writing this at all.

I have my physical coming up as well as the nuclear stress test that tells all and a check with the surgeon about my arms wear and tear and more medical advice to with stand.

There's always something medical to deal with at my age but really most people have to deal with things of all sorts after age 40. I am doing very well with my body, physical status but it's the workings on the inside my body that is so troublesome.

The world news has crushed our American people as well as the economy bust for some time now. The professionals in sports do not seem to be attacked financially in any way but us peasant type people that love sports have a tough road ahead of us. Our economy has burst so to speak and it show in our baseball leagues and tournaments as many ballplayers have to bail out because of their commitment to their families and baseball has to be a 2nd choice which is very understood.

My wife and I are in the thought of downsizing and with hopes we can squeak out of this mess and insure our dreams as in her to have her own horse and ride in the back yard somewhere and me to find more happiness in a smaller more manageable home, pursue baseball and care for the animals. New Hampshire seems to offer the best quality of life for us as that will be a tentative plan for us. Moving and relocating is not fun at all regardless of the circumstances but something for the better to accomplish.

Facing the off season before me now and thinking about 2011 season and the many changes has good and bad challenges before me. Meeting new players is always hard. There are the jealousies, conflict of positioning on the new team, why you are there, and your addition in quality to the new team. It usually takes a few practices, a game or so, so they see your capabilities and worth and the adjustment is completed, usually. There are always the skeptics and fitting in to the new groups on the team as sometimes men are far worse than women in a sewing circle as far as behind the scenes envy, and team talk. Hopefully that will pass quickly.

For me personally all is taken seriously and I will always be Johnny Hustle whether its practice, a game or during my alone time training. I always spend quality time training on my own to better myself and maintain my mechanics as getting older is something that each of us deal with but maintaining a high competitive level is difficult from year to year. The younger guys are training as well. I am usually the old guy so my work load, preparation and challenges are much more, I think.

My wife is currently in the midst of purchasing her own horse as that was a dream of hers for some time now. She will continue to ride anyway and as I search for tournaments, she seeks opportunities for trail rides, twenty and thirty mile events or a beach ride during the winter and spring events and her continued lesson structure. Then there is more riding clothes, horse gear, protective gear and planning just like it is for me with baseball. I do understand that, go get the best equipment and best instruction and do it right the first time.

This just reminds me of my birthday gift which is on its way to me right now! Yes, a Wilson A2000 baseball glove. I have not purchased a real good glove in so long and felt this would be a great start of 2011 for me! No new bats as I have many bats I have a rack of 27 and two smaller racks that hold 7 bats in each plus my memorabilia bats. I also make bat racks for friends as a gift! This past summer and fall I had sanded, and repaired so many wood bats as I enjoyed that very much. I think I brought back 6 wood bats that were broken and trashed at tournaments and now are fixed and ready to go.

The old method of repairing wood bats from years ago was to use tape, nails, screws-wrap tight and wish and hope for the best results. The results were never positive in the long run. My new method is this! I separate the splintered brake, lift with a sharp tool and slide either gorilla glue, a wood epoxy, put in vice and let harden for 24 hours. Then I sand bat to perfection. It's not ready yet! I then drill 4 to 5 holes 3/8" through the bat in different angles and push strong glue in the holes and fit a wooden dowel through the hole. I let that harden for another 24 hours, then sand again and now the bat is ready for use. I have had very good luck with this process and you still have the option of taping if you choose.

Chapter Forty Six

Famous off Season

My future in baseball is unknown at present all I have is passion, desire and to train through the holidays, winter and be ready for 2011 season. I will re-peat my personal instruction join other leagues with batting cage team training and test the waters. I do have many of the teams organized and ready to go for spring but the real final plans will be finalized come February.

I like the off season as it feels so good to throw the ball hard and try new pitches and fix the minute problems with mechanics and see where you are. Most ballplayers are not ready nor train as I do and I am happy about that! I do excite the instructors as most of their students are high school, college or younger. They are amazed in my production and enthusiastic attitude and the way I do my homework and prep for the lessons. Sometimes during the lessons there is a crowd watching as they are next ready for either instruction or ready to take over the cage tunnel. They watch and regardless of their age they respect my ability for my age and that respect, feels quite good. I guess this goes way back for me as far as a crowd goes.

Way back in my early years as I talked about my Junior High School days I spoke of the basketball games. We'll, I'll repeat a little just to give you an understanding. I shot lights out in pre game warm ups on my basketball teams as people in the crowd would notice my ability. I of course was so dreadfully afraid of crowds that I always had my back to the crowd as best as I could manage. Then at half time once again I would put on a shooting show! Ok, this is what happened, When I was in the game I would miss every shot I took especially lay ups. So the show had meant nothing. When I went away to visitor games in tournaments or away from town I would shoot like crazy in the games. I guess that problem of mine was a home team fright.

Later in life I had over come that and now when there is a crowd at a baseball game the sky is the limit as I love to have a crowd now. Crowds in over 30 + games do not happen very often unless it's a championship game or at a MLB stadium game we are playing in. So when I am having a lesson at the batting cages or in any game I like the attention as I for sure do not wish to screw up at all. I have already experienced the humiliation years ago and now mentally I do know I have the confidence to beat defeat.

Today was very special as my wife Elizabeth had just purchased her first horse as it was such a long time dream for her. She purchased a Morgan Mare, pure black and about 14.1 hands and absolutely a delight and wonderful personality and well mannered eight year old horse. We named her "Chocolate Truffles" Yes, it is all hers so after spending half the morning freezing myself I was happy when we headed home. We have to board the horse at a local farm as The Contryman Farm, in Mason New Hampshire. Someday we will be able to move to a more manageable home with a small barn to house our animals.

I have a birthday coming up Sunday. Yes, a new age for me "64" I'll be glad to get past this hurdle and move on just like the holidays. Christmas just 3 weeks away! How time passes. I do not think I will be attending any tournaments this off season as usually I go to West Palm Beach or Wooded Bat Classic but with changing teams this new 2011 season I think I will concentrate on cage training, private instruction and stay in shape because again as every year I have to re-prove myself again and again on new teams so that is my focus.

It is now January 2011, I have my baseball all set for the coming season as about 117 days till opening day but who is counting! During these winter months I have 20 lessons with batting and pitching lined up with instructors at Connector Batting Cage in Lowell, Ma. My previous instructors have moved on to Coach and teach at local colleges so Besides Adam McCusker my batting coach I will have a minor leaguer coach Billy Maloney do me the honors as I am sure I will be fine . I will wait till the fall for future baseball tournaments and my summer will be filled with about 75 baseball games with the three leagues I will play in. I am excited to test my talents and attach new challenges this season and I hope you the reader will do the same. I am challenging you to go after your dream as well.

My heart problems, medical problems and age, are what they are, a devastating disease that is "progressive in nature" and all you can do is exercise, take medication, proper dieting and live your life the best you can. That is your only weapon of defense but it works! Baseball has filled my heart with such a wonderful feeling.

Last year I was able to provide my radio interview with a St Louis, Missouri Radio Station with Donna Linn the Host and Owner of that Radio Station in which had also changed may status and brought my story to life , available 24/7 world wide. With face book, classmates, baseball associates, the internet and this radio interview, my limited marketing experience has allowed me to reach out, to more friends to share my story and personal friendships and more. My new bonds with complete strangers has also surfaced in which has been another journey for me. I have been blessed by the emotions that have surface just from readers and new acquaintances learning about John F DeCosta. I found that so powerful and never sure about the feelings that have developed through this accomplishment I have endured.

I hope I have brought you back in time, to see for yourself that our early days, and memories has been rewarding to you as well. I definitely feel I am a better person for my efforts and inspired you the reader with my passion to enjoy the love I have for baseball, friendships, animals, family and life. The successes I have experienced through my lifetime have been totally unexpected although very honored for every little accomplishment. My Military experience in particular, U.S.Army Paratrooper and Special Forces Soldier and the many schools, training and experiences there have molded me with non stop drive to complete any dream I have had. Writing my story has not just been a personal matter or goal as it has indeed been a tool to learn about myself and answer many un-answered questions I had about my life. I believe everyone has a story; experiences happen for a reason much like a report card on our lives. The lives I have touched before writing my story and after will always be close to my heart.

My health has always been an issue and the older I get, the more challenging life becomes. My quality of life, playing baseball and my emotional attachments to family, friends, and my wife, I feel with all that I do, everywhere I shall go and the example I share. I have always been a giver in life as giving or lending a hand is another breath of fresh air for me to cherish.

If you can imagine, just for a moment; you're a kid 12 years old, or an adult and you are about to start a baseball game! You have your hat set just right on your head, with the hat curved on the bill. Your chewing bubble gum with the biggest smile as you smash your fist into your glove. The grass is freshly cut, there are pure white chalk lines down each foul line, the dirt is raked just right, you are at your most dominant position on the field and ready to play ball and the players are waiting for the sound…. The umpire says "play ball" but wait! I may be the one on the mound throwing a heater near your chin! Let's be careful out there and have fun. Your desire, love for the game, hard work, practice, teamwork and sportsmanship must be your state of mind!

I am "The Eastside Kid"
By John F DeCosta

EPILOG

Early in the fifties I was just starting baseball. I was in the Little League farm system at age seven, and played into the majors of Little League. My special wonderful years of the 1950s, the thrilling moments, with terrific friends, I will cherish forever. Being an eastside kid in Brockton, Massachusetts has had a very special bond for me and other real eastside kids. It's not that we were tough, I guess it was the true grit, the attitude, and the loyalty to the friends on your team, the neighborhoods, and the idea of belonging to each other. That was similar to what I experienced in the military. During the fifties I raised pigeons for a hobby, went fishing with my dog Ginger, and played a lot of baseball all day, everyday. Tumors were discovered in my wrist when I was twelve, and the surgeries that followed ended up destroying baseball for me after Little League. My dreams had ended too soon, and the loss of baseball from my life brought a sadness that stayed with me for quite some time.

Somehow I managed to get through the terrible teens and eventually found my way into the military, where I became a mature adult. I did, however, go in and out of the military, through several relationships and different employments, and I moved much too often. My stability was misdirected, but finally, after a decade or so, I was able to find love, and experience the military in a much more positive and meritorious manner. I am extremely proud and honored to be not only a paratrooper but a master paratrooper.

My life has been full and exciting, as I have found a variety of experiences and challenges that have been rewarding. I am especially proud of the person I have become. The most important women in my life are my mom, and my wife Elizabeth. While my mother was alive, she provided me with a strong sense of spirituality, wisdom and strength, as my wife does for me now. I also have been blessed with the gift of rediscovering baseball late in my life. To achieve the goals I have reached, playing baseball has allowed me to relive my childhood of eastside baseball, as I knew it.

Adult amateur baseball has brought me into Over 30 baseball, which allowed me the experience of playing on Doubleday Field in Cooperstown, New York, as well as more local games in Lowell, Massachusetts. It gave me the chance to play in the MSBL the Men's Senior Baseball League, in Boston. I've also had the opportunity to play in the stadiums in Orlando and Fort Myers, Florida, at the Phoenix World Series, and in Las Vegas' Over 50 baseball. And I continue to play in any sandlot I can find. Therefore I am rich with baseball memories, and working on more.

My mom would be so happy to know I have stopped smoking, that I am an avid reader, and am now writing stories of my own. My wife Elizabeth has inspired me with culture, reading, and has even helped me improve my manners. I really enjoyed the opportunities I have had helping youth, other baseball players, Veterans, Paratroopers, and loyal friends whenever I was able to. Being a giver in my life time has always rewarded me with great joy.

My family and the precious people in my life, as well as my baseball friends, have allowed me to be the best I can be. I never wanted anything unless I earned it on my own merits completely, and they all know this. These friends I speak of are a strong bond in my life. My dreams are to make a difference, to set the example, and to inspire others to enjoy this game of baseball. I could always look into my opponents' eyes and relay instant messaging, saying, "I and you are one," just as Sadaharu Oh once said. Now I understand and I believe his thoughts.

My love for this game has been rewarding. I even sleep with my baseball glove and bat and have them with me on the couch when watching Major League Baseball. Baseball is my heartbeat, my passion is for the game, and I am the Kid from The Eastside!

John F. DeCosta
Carp Diem

John F DeCosta
Personality Buzz:

1. What is my favorite choice of an automobile?

    Answer: 1966 Corvette Stingray Coupe

2. What would be my favorite type of snack?

    Answer: Two Combo Pizza-Cheese and Crackers

3. What are my favorite movies?

    Answer: The Rookie, Mickey Mantle and Roger Maris 61, The
    Babe Ruth Story, Lou Gehrig Story, The Dirty Dozen, All
    Clint Eastwood Movies

4. What is my favorite meal?

    Answer: Steak and Fries, Lasagna and Meatballs, Beef Stew

5. Who are my favorite sports athletes?

    Answer: Mickey Mantle, Bobby Orr, Sadaharu Oh, Babe Ruth, Joe
    DiMaggio, Nolan Ryan, Pedro Martinez, Derek Jeter, Tom
    Brady, Doug Fluttie and Larry Bird

6. What are my favorite teams?

    Answer: Yankee's, Red Sox, Patriots, Celtics, Bruins and Any team
    I am on!

7. What would be my favorite music to listen to?

    Answer: Country Weston, 50's and 60's music

8. Who are my favorite movie stars?

    Answer: Rachel Welch, Clint Eastwood

9. What would be my favorite dream field to play baseball on?

    Answer: Double Day Field-Cooperstown, New York

John F. Decosta

John F DeCosta is a new author who relates his writing to mainly baseball, basketball, and Military type subjects. The start of his writing career began with an article called; "Sports was a way of life for the Eastside Kids". This article appeared in the Brockton Enterprise Newspaper-Brockton, Massachusetts November 2004.

The opportunities seemed to continue to march on. A story about a WW11 Veteran, a POW, A Government Postal Worker and family man, this veteran's uncle was the first pitcher to pitch in Fenway Park for the Boston Red Sox-1912. The family of Buck O'Brien had asked John to do a life story about their father and uncle. Then another opportunity came several months later as Berge Avadanian personally requested to have his life story re- done for him. Berge was also a WW11 Veteran and Paratrooper who Jumped on D-Day -6 June 1944, and made four combat jumps into Sicily, Italy, Holland, and Normandy. This story was also written for the Avadanian family.

The writing continued once again, while I had assumed the position of Vice Chairman for the Lt General James M. Gavin Chapter of the 82nd Airborne Division .John had written an article published in the Monthly Newsletter for the chapter, lifting the sprits of camaraderie and brotherhood for all paratroopers. This story was also re- published in the National Magazine, the "Paraglide" The 82nd Airborne Divisions monthly magazine. The Brotherhood stories for paratroopers became very popular and again John provided a story about a given person, soldier, and paratrooper and one to emulate, Mr. Stephen Baptiste- from Onset, Massachusetts and this time this particular story was published in The American Airborne Associations Magazine distributed worldwide.

In 2007, 2008 the messenger newspaper for the Town of Townsend, Massachusetts John had written bi -weekly baseball articles for his column, called "The Baseball Corner" by John F DeCosta "The Eastside Kid". This averaged about 18 articles per year.

The most recent and memorable writing so far is the publication of "The Eastside kid", by John F DeCosta July 2007 with Trafford Publishing Company -Ontario, Canada This book can be found at www.trafford.com/07-0885 or www.amazon.com   This is a baseball story starting in the 1950's a passionate story with, pine tar, red dirt, and wood bats show baseball the way it was till present day baseball as an adult, sharing military experiences within the baseball story. In addition, there are more than 85 short stories unpublished.

The Eastside Kid

By John F DeCosta

I value the opinions of all my readers.
Replies can be sent to;
theeastsidekid@comcast.net - and or
www.trafford.com
Your feedback is appreciated.